DARK SIDES OF SPORT

Edited by
Jörg Krieger
Stephan Wassong

DARK SIDES OF SPORT

Edited by
Jörg Krieger
Stephan Wassong

COMMON GROUND RESEARCH NETWORKS 2019

First published in 2019
as part of the Sport & Society Book Imprint
http://doi.org/10.18848/978-1-86335-150-8/CGP (Full Book)

BISAC Codes: SPO058000, SPO066000, SPO019000

Common Ground Research Networks
2001 South First Street, Suite 202
University of Illinois Research Park
Champaign, IL
61820

Copyright © Jörg Krieger & Stephan Wassong 2019

All rights reserved. Apart from fair dealing for the purposes of study, research, criticism or review as permitted under the applicable copyright legislation, no part of this book may be reproduced by any process without written permission from the publisher.

Library of Congress Cataloging-in-Publication Data

Names: Krieger, Jörg, editor. | Wassong, Stephan, editor.
Title: Dark sides of sport / [editors] Jörg Krieger, Stephan Wassong.
Description: Champaign, IL : Common Ground Research Networks, 2019. | Includes bibliographical references and index.
Identifiers: LCCN 2019012820 (print) | LCCN 2019019061 (ebook) | ISBN 9781863351508 (pdf) | ISBN 9781863351485 (hardback : alk. paper) | ISBN 9781863351492 (pbk. : alk. paper)
Subjects: LCSH: Sports--Corrupt practices. | Sports and state.
Classification: LCC GV718 (ebook) | LCC GV718 .D27 2019 (print) | DDC 306.4/83--dc23
LC record available at https://lccn.loc.gov/2019012820

Cover Photo Credit: Sandra Bräutigam (German Sport University Cologne)

Table of Contents

Notes on Contributors ix

Introduction 1
    Jörg Krieger and Stephan Wassong

Chapter 1 5
Towards a Global Framework to Fight the Dark Side of Sport
    Jean-Loup Chappelet

Chapter 2 17
Sporting Power, Policy and Diplomacy: Catalysts and Gateways
    Gary Armstrong, James Rosbrook-Thompson, Mahfoud Amara and Iain Lindsay

Chapter 3 31
Secret Operations at the Simple Games: The Free Europe Committee, Cold War Tourism, and the 1964 Winter Olympics
    Toby C. Rider

Chapter 4 45
How Fears Changed the Games: Of Terror, Security and Costs
    Jörg Krieger

Chapter 5 61
The Human Rights Impacts of Olympic Games
    Daniela Heerdt

Chapter 6 77
Environment and Sustainability: Ecological Thought and the Olympic Games
    Alberto Aragón-Pérez

Chapter 7 93
The Russian Doping Scandal in the Context of Global Political Relations
    Thomas M. Hunt and Austin Duckworth

Chapter 8 107
Sex Testing in Sport
    Lindsay Parks Pieper

Chapter 9 121
Sexual Harassment in Elite Sport
    Terry Engelberg and Stephen Moston

Chapter 10 135
In the Dark: The Construction of Sport and its Coaching Rhetoric
    Susannah Stevens and Ian Culpan

Chapter 11 151
Sport and Global Culture Industry: the Olympic Games, Modernity, and Dialectic of Enlightenment
    Jung Woo Lee

Chapter 12 167
Racism in Elite Sport: A Re-examination of the Historical Case of South African Football
    Gustav Venter

Chapter 13 183
The Fortress and the Cave Dwellers: A Story from Bosnian-Herzegovinian Football
    Gary Armstrong and Massimiliano Maidano

Chapter 14 196
Sport for Development and Peace (SDP): The Shadow from Within
    Cora Burnett

Notes on Contributors

Mahfoud Amara is the Director of the Sport Science Program at the College of Arts and Sciences, Qatar University. He has joined Qatar University in fall 2018 and is Associate Professor in Sport Social Sciences and Management. He has published a number of papers and chapters on sport business, culture, and politics in Arab and Muslim contexts. He undertook research for a range of national and international bodies and he was an invited speaker to a number of national and international conferences, workshops and symposia for his work on sport in the Middle East and North African region and sport and multiculturalism debates in Europe.

Alberto Aragón-Pérez has a Ph.D. of the Autonomous University of Barcelona (as research member of its Olympic Studies Center). He has a M.A. on Ancient History and another M.A. on Olympic Education and Management. He has been Archive Officer of the Olympic Studies Center Juan Antonia Samaranch in Barcelona for the last five years. His research interests are environmental issues within sport and the history of contemporaneous Olympic Movement. Since 2017 he has been a Member of the Commission of Sustainability, Cooperation and Integration of the Spanish Olympic Committee.

Gary Armstrong is Senior Lecturer in Criminology at City, University of London and Visiting Professor in the School of International Politics at the University of Warsaw. He holds a Ph.D. in Social Anthropology from the University College, London and has published extensively on issues pertinent to sport for three decades.

Cora Burnett is Professor at the University of Johannesburg, South Africa, and also the Director of the UJ Olympic Studies Centre. She holds two doctorates – one in physical education and one in anthropology, as well as two masters (cum laude) of which one is in Olympic Studies. She is the Vice-President of the Sociology of Sport Association and has published 135 peer-reviewed research articles and chapters, as well as co-authored *Sport in Society: Issues and Controversies* with Jay Coakley in 2014.

Jean-Loup Chappelet, Ph.D., is an Emeritus Professor of public management at the Swiss Graduate School of Public Administration (IDHEAP) of the University of Lausanne. He was IDHEAP Dean from 2003 to 2011. In 1995, at IDHEAP, he launched the first sport management course in Switzerland which is still held every fall. He was Guest Professor at the University of Lyon (France), the University of Louvain-la-Neuve (Belgium), Seoul National University (South Korea) and Tsukuba University (Japan).

Ian Culpan is Emeritus Professor in the School of Health Sciences, University of Canterbury, New Zealand. He established and is currently a Co-Director of the New

Zealand Centre for Olympic Studies. He has strong research interests in physical education teacher education, well-being, curriculum development, pedagogy, the socio-cultural aspects of sport and Olympic/Olympism education. He has a high international profile, led and directed many national initiatives and has published and presented his work nationally and internationally.

Austin Duckworth, Ph.D., recently received his Ph.D. in Physical Culture and Sport Studies from the University of Texas at Austin, United States. His research interest concerns the manner in which mega-sporting events fit within broader international relations between states.

Estella (Terry) Engelberg is an Adjunct Associate Professor in the College of Business Law and Governance at James Cook University, Townsville, Australia. Her areas of research expertise are doping in sport, sexual harassment, and organizational commitment. She has authored more than 70 journal articles, book chapters, commissioned reports and books.

Daniela Heerdt is a Ph.D. researcher at Tilburg Law School in the Netherlands, conducting research on responsibilities for human rights violations that occur in the context of mega-sporting events. She also works as a Research Officer at the Centre for Sport and Human Rights, where she supports the remedy workstream. Before starting her Ph.D. research, she worked as a lecturer and junior researcher at Utrecht and Tilburg University and taught classes on international law and business and human rights in South Africa and Zimbabwe.

Thomas M. Hunt, J.D., Ph.D., is an Associate Professor in the Department of Kinesiology and Health Education at the University of Texas at Austin, United States, where he also holds an appointment as Assistant Director for Academic Affairs at the H.J. Lutcher Stark Center for Physical Culture and Sports.

Jörg Krieger is an Assistant Professor in Sport and Social Science at Aarhus University, Denmark. He has a Ph.D. from the Institute of Sport History and the Olympic Studies Centre of the German Sport University Cologne. He is the author of *Dope Hunters: The Influence of Scientists on the Global Fight Against Doping in Sport, 1967-1992*. Since 2019, he is Chair of Common Ground's Sport and Society Research Network.

Jung Woo Lee is the Programme Director of the M.Sc. Sport Policy, Management and International Development, and Lecturer in Sport and Leisure Policy at the University of Edinburgh, United Kingdom. He received a Ph.D. in the sociology of sport from Loughborough University, United Kingdom. He is the editor of Sport in Society Asia Pacific Special Issue in S*port in Society*. He is also an editorial board member of *Journal of Global Sport Management*. His research interests include sport and social identity, sport and Inter-Korean relations, sport mega-event studies and globalization of sport.

Iain Lindsay is CEO of Trusted Sport Foundation CIC - an international organization that promotes and enables enhanced transparency, integrity and safeguarding within sport. He holds a Ph.D. in sport science / sociology and has published on a broad range of sport related themes.

Massimiliano Maidano is a Ph.D. candidate in political sociology at City University of London, United Kingdom. He holds a M.Res. in Social Anthropology from Brunel University, United Kingdom and a B.A. in International Relations from the American University of Rome, Italy. His research interests gravitate around foreign politics, sport, hooliganism, identity, nationalism with a focus on the Balkans, Central and Eastern Europe. He has conducted extensive research on Croatian football supporters and Bosnian-Herzegovina football as part of his Ph.D. research.

Stephen Moston is an Associate Professor and Head of Course in Forensic Psychology at CQUniversity, Townsville, Australia. His research focuses on the use of interviews with witnesses and suspects in investigations across a wide range of offences, from regulatory breaches such as doping in sport, the investigation of sexual harassment, and criminal offences.

Lindsay Parks Pieper is an Associate Professor of Sport Management at the University of Lynchburg, United States. She received her M.A. degree in Women's History (2010) and a Ph.D. in Sport Humanities (2013) from Ohio State. Her book *Sex Testing: Gender Policing in Women's Sport* explores the history of gender verification in the Olympics.

Toby C. Rider is an Associate Professor of Kinesiology at California State University, Fullerton, United States. He is the author of *Cold War Games: Propaganda, the Olympics, and U.S. Foreign Policy* (University of Illinois Press, 2016) and co-editor of *Defending the American Way of Life: Sport, Culture, and the Cold War* (University of Arkansas Press, 2018). In addition to this, Toby is the Co-Director of the Center for Sociocultural Sport and Olympic Research.

James Rosbrook-Thompson is Senior Lecturer in Sociology at Anglia Ruskin University in Cambridge, United Kingdom, and Assistant Editor of the journal *Urbanities*. He holds a Ph.D. in sociology from the London School of Economics and Political Science (LSE) and has published extensively in the areas of urban sociology and the sociology of sport. His most recent book (co-authored with Gary Armstrong), *Mixed-Occupancy Housing in London: A Living Tapestry*, was published by Palgrave Macmillan in 2018.

Susannah Stevens, Ph.D., is the Manager of the Child Well-being Research Institute at the University of Canterbury, New Zealand and the Co-Director of the New Zealand Centre of Olympic Studies. She is an academic advisor to national organizations including Physical Education New Zealand and Sport New Zealand;

and is contracted both nationally and internationally for her expertise in child well-being, physical education, movement pleasure, physical activity and sport, and the unique amalgamation of sociological, philosophical and pedagogical theory within her work.

Gustav Venter is Head of the Centre for Sport Leadership at Stellenbosch University, South Africa. He holds a Ph.D. in history from the same institution, and his primary research focus is directed at the historical intersection between sport, politics and race in the South African context. He also has a particular interest in how historical forces continue to shape contemporary issues in South African sport.

Stephan Wassong is Full Professor at the German Sport University Cologne, where he is Head of the Institute of Sport History and Director of the Olympic Studies Centre. He is the Executive Director of the international degree programme M.A. Olympic Studies and Member of the IOC´s Olympic Education Commission. In 2018, he was elected President of the International Pierre de Coubertin Committee.

Introduction

Jörg Krieger and Stephan Wassong

International sport is currently going through a challenging and defining period. Wide-ranging doping revelations including those of sporting stars like Lance Armstrong and those from leading sporting nations such as Russia and Kenya have tarnished the image of sport considerably in recent years. And the accusations do not stop. At the start of 2019, former Austrian cross-country skier Johannes Dürr revealed his sophisticated doping practices and blamed German and Austrian officials of providing him with forbidden performance-enhancing substances and procedures. His allegations led the exposure of a blood doping network based in Erfurt, Germany. However, doping is by far not the only dark side that sport currently has to tackle. 2017 and 2018 saw a court trial in the United States against former national gymnastics team doctor Larry Nassar that resulted in his lifelong imprisonment. For several decades, Nassar had molested hundreds of young female athletes. Revelations in other countries followed promptly. In Austria, former Olympic skier Nicola Werdenigg went public with rape allegations against teammates that occurred in the 1970s. Werdenigg highlighted that her case was not an isolated incident. Similarly, in South Korea, short trackers publicly accused former Korean national coach Cho Jae-beom of sexual assault.

The dark sides of sport cannot only be witnessed on and around the sporting field. Various corruption cases involving leading officials have erupted the highest circles of international sport in this decade. There appears almost no bidding procedure for a mega-sporting event that was not in the public spotlight for corruption allegations in the past years. The negative reputation of the international sport system paired with the growing gigantism of the global sporting events subsequently led to a rejection of bidding city populations in Europe to stage Olympic Games. Recently, negative local public votes in Canada (for the Winter Olympic Games in 2026), Germany (Winter Olympic Games in 2022 and Summer Olympic Games 2024), Poland (Winter Olympic Games in 2022) and Switzerland (Winter Olympic Games in 2022 and 2026) forced bidding committees to withdraw their bids. Moreover, the rising costs for staging the Summer Olympic Games reduce the pool of potential host cities to global mega cities such as Tokyo, Paris and Los Angeles.

This is not to say that international sport did not go through comparable challenging phases prior in the past. In fact, ever since the origins of the modern sport at the end of the 19th century, the international sport movement has faced phases of tests and reforms. The founder of the modern Olympic Games, French Baron Pierre de Coubertin, already struggled to keep his Olympic Movement alive at the beginning of the 20th century. The Olympic Games in 1900 (Paris) and 1904 (St. Louis) became a side show of the world fairs with very little recognition for the Olympic Games and its educational intentions. Only after the successful Olympic Games in London in 1908 and in Stockholm 1912, the Olympic Movement began to receive international recognition (Molzberger 2012).

International sport also had to overcome influences through fascist and racist political regimes that misused sport to propagate their causes. This was particularly evident in the 1930s, when Hitler's Germany and Mussolini's Italy began to understand the immense symbolic power of sport and misused global sport events such as the 1936 Olympic Games in Berlin and the 1934 Football World Cup in Italy for their causes. At the same time, these much publicized sporting events might be considered victories for the ideas of international sport (Young 2004).

With the entrance of the Soviet Union into the Olympic Movement after the Second World War, the Olympic Games developed into "Cold War Games" that culminated in two major Olympic boycotts in 1980 and 1984 (Torres and Dyreson 2005). Simultaneously, the International Olympic Committee (IOC) faced challenges to find potential host cities for the Summer Olympic Games against the background of the financial disaster of the 1976 Montreal Olympic Games.

In the last decade of the 20th century and into the new millennium, negative effects of professionalism and the commercialization have resulted in the strengthened appearance of challenging issues. The unsuccessful fight against doping has caught a lot of public attention, latest since the positive doping test of Canadian sprinter Ben Johnson following his win in the 100m race at the 1988 Seoul Olympic Games. Even the foundation of the World Anti-Doping Agency (WADA), triggered by the Tour de France scandal in 1998, did not result in a significant improvement of the global anti-doping fight. The end of the 1990s also saw the biggest Olympic bribery scandal when it was revealed that IOC members had accepted bribes in exchange for their votes for Salt Lake City as the host city of the 2002 Winter Olympic Games (Dichter and Kidd 2012). This "Salt Lake City Scandal" led to a reform in the structure and organization of the IOC (MacAloon 2011), but the modifications only had a limited effect. The IOC brought about additional recommendations for reforms in its *Olympic Agenda 2020* (IOC, 2014), mainly targeting decision-making processes within the organization. However, as outlined above, the *Agenda* did not stop international sport further slipping into a challenging phase. The dark sides of sport remain omnipresent.

In light of the longevity of the dark sides of sport, is it not surprising that academics have explored the challenges for international sport from various perspectives. Historical, sociological, political, cultural, legal, economic and interdisciplinary investigations into the complex challenges of sport exist. Without question, those publications have enriched the sport studies literature and contributed to a better understanding of the internal and external threats for sport. However, the majority of the studies focuses on individual topics with a strong emphasis on doping, amateurism and politics. Consequently, we identified a gap in existing academic literature that tackles various dark sides of sport in one book and this is precisely what we attempt in this edited collection. We aim to provide an insightful overview on sports' contemporary challenges that allows for the identification of similarities and differences.

We have invited leading international scholars in their research fields to provide their insights to our collection and all of them have accepted our invitation. Academics from five different continents have contributed. Such geographical diversity allows for a broad variety of cultural perspectives and a comparison of approaches. All scholars deal with a specific threat to sport. Whilst the focus is on the Olympic Movement due to its global relevance and economic impact, other negative phenomena such as violence in football, challenges within the sport-for-development sector and a general critique on empowerment are equally explored in the book. The chapters differ significantly as a large variety of methods, informed by sport history, sport sociology and sport politics, are employed.

We hope that this edited collection can develop into a valuable contribution to the academic literature on international sport. Even though the provision of solutions goes beyond the scope of this edited collection, the socio-historical focus of our book contributes to a better understanding of present political and economic actions because it explains the preconditions for the main stakeholders' decision-making. We argue that individuals in sport organizations must appreciate the interests, dependencies and objectives that have established the present sport system.

REFERENCES

Dichter, Heather, and Bruce Kidd. 2012. *Olympic Reform Ten Years Later*. London: Routledge.

International Olympic Committee. 2014. *Olympic Agenda 2020—20+20 Recommendations*. Lausanne: International Olympic Committee.

MacAloon, John J. 2011. "Scandal and Governance: Inside and Outside the IOC 2000 Commission." *Sport in Society* 14(3): 292-308.

Molzberger, Ansgar. 2012. *Die Olympischen Spiele 1912 in Stockholm. Zwischen Patriotismus und Internationalität*. St. Augustin: Academia Verlag.

Torres, Cesar R., and Mark Dyreson. 2005. "The Cold War Games." In *Global Olympics: Historical and Sociological Studies of the Modern Games*, edited by Kevin Young and Kevin B. Wamsley, 59–82. Amsterdam and Oxford: Elsevier.

Young, Christopher. 2004. "A Victory for the Olympic Idea. Berlin 1936 in its Sporting and Socio-Cultural Contexts." *Stadion* 32: 147-172.

Dark Sides of Sport

CHAPTER 1

Towards a Global Framework to Fight the Dark Side of Sport

Jean-Loup Chappelet

Corruption in business has probably always existed, but it first became a major issue in the management of organizations in the 1970s, following revelations that American civil and military aircraft manufacturer Lockheed had bribed politicians in several countries, most notably Germany, Italy, and Japan. As similar scandals broke in other countries, governments around the world, under pressure from the United States, began cracking down on "private corruption" involving corporations (through bribes and retro-commissions, for instance). [1] At the same time, intergovernmental organizations such as the Council of Europe, OECD (Organization for Economic Cooperation and Development), and United Nations drew up international conventions against corruption, whose recommendations have been incorporated into the national laws of the numerous countries that have ratified them. These intergovernmental organizations also put in place mechanisms to monitor (private) corruption, such as GRECO (Group of States against Corruption), a very effective body set up by the Council of Europe. In Switzerland, home to many of the world's largest sport organizations, ratification of these international conventions was followed by new legislation to combat private corruption that went much further than the country's existing laws, under which money laundering, dishonest management, and filing false documents were already criminal offences. The new measures were first introduced as part of a 2005 bill on unfair competition and then incorporated into the country's criminal code in 2015 so that they could be investigated by the police on their own (without a complaint being filed by a direct party to the case).

Corruption in sport has probably always existed, too. Even the ancient Olympic Games was not immune, as attested by the statues and mini-temples dedicated to Zeus, called Zanes, that were erected beside the alley into the stadium at Olympia using money from fines imposed on cheats.

Most historians agree that modern (today's) sport was born in 18th- and 19th-century England with the industrial revolution. The first modern sports, such as horse racing, running, boxing and football, evolved out of traditional and rural games in pre-

---

[1] Public corruption, that is, corruption by and of public officials, especially in relation to elections, has been illegal for a long time in most countries, and is not dealt with in this report as sport organizations' officials are not public officials.

industrial Britain. Competitions involving these activities, the forerunners of contemporary sports events, became extremely popular with the newly emerging working classes, who saw them as a source of amusement away from their daily toil. For participants, competitions were a way of earning money, as athletes were generally paid and could win prizes (usually cash). Spectators could also make (and lose) money through betting, which was an essential part of sport and leisure for many people. Bets were placed with and paid off by bookmakers, a new profession that grew up around competitions. The possibility of making money tempted some bettors to try and guarantee they would win by rigging competitions (match-fixing).

One of the earliest types of competition was foot racing (running and walking, then called "pedestrianism"), which began around 1820. Pedestrianism was very popular in the British Isles, attracting large numbers of spectators, many of whom bet on the outcome. As contemporary lithographs show (See for instance the figures in Guy-Ryan, 2016), it was not unknown for spectators to attack racers (pedestrians) if they thought they had cheated to allow other bettors to win. Pedestrianism even found its way into Britain's public schools, with Rugby School, for example, holding what it called "crick run" races as early as 1837.

Sports such as wrestling, running and cricket developed quickly in England, partly because of the betting associated with them. In fact, the main reason for establishing fixed rules for cricket in the middle of the 18th century was to avoid arguments between bettors (Munting 1996). Laws governing gambling and betting were first introduced in Great Britain in the 19th century, through the 1845 Gaming Act and the 1853 Betting Act. The tight restrictions these laws placed on commercial gambling, which were aimed specifically at the lower echelons of society encouraged the development of underground betting (Brooks and Lavorgna 2018, 79-80).

The rigging of running races (run by so-called "pedestrians") in England (for betting purposes) in the 18th and 19th centuries is one of the reasons why Olympic sport was founded on the dogma of amateurism—gentlemen athletes did not want their competitions to be sullied by links to money (through betting or prize/appearance money).

The issue of corruption in sport has once again come into the spotlight in these early decades of the 21st century, largely as the result of scandals within FIFA (Fédération Internationale de Football Association), in 2015, and the IAAF (International Association of Athletics Federations), six months later. The later scandal was linked to doping fraud involving many athletes. Sport had, of course, been hit by other scandals prior to the FIFA and IAAF affairs. Most notably this was the case with the "Salt Lake City bid scandal", which rocked the IOC (International Olympic Committee) in 1999, and the fallout from ISL (International sport and Leisure)'s bankruptcy, which affected several international federations in 2001. The IOC quickly dealt with the Salt Lake scandal by expelling six members (four others resigned or had died) who had accepted cash and/or excessive gifts from the Salt Lake City bid committee prior to the election of the host city for the 2002 Winter Olympics. Another ten IOC members were reprimanded for their improper behavior. In the ISL bankruptcy, a long investigation by police from the Zug canton (where ISL was based in Switzerland) showed that around 15 senior officials within football and other sports had accepted bribes from ISL during the 1990s. However, none of the protagonists faced serious charges, as corporate bribery was not then illegal in Switzerland (it was even corporate-tax deductible). Nevertheless, FIFA's president when the bribes were paid (João Havelange) resigned from the IOC when the scandal documents became public in 2011. More recently, three IOC members have been accused of corruption (ticket touting, construction kickbacks, bribes for votes) in relation to the Rio 2016 Olympic Games.

Despite the numerous conferences on corruption in sport that have been held since the beginning of the 21st century, the academic literature contains very few papers on sports corruption in general, as most research has focused on a specific type of misconduct (doping, match-fixing, harassment, poor governance, etc.) (for an overview see: Chantelat 2001; Maenning 2005; Brooks, Aleem and Button 2013;Transparency International 2016; Kihl 2018; Kihl, Skinner and Engelberg 2018). Hence, this chapter provides a global overview of a problem that is often examined from a single perspective, such as doping, bad governance, conflicts of interest or vote rigging in the attribution of sporting events. It is important to have a comprehensive picture of corruption in sport that encompasses all the different scourges that exist, because all these scourges are interrelated and tarnish the sport's fundamental values of integrity. In fact, sports corruption can be considered the antithesis of sporting integrity. This overview paves the way for a new, comprehensive approach to promoting the true spirit of sport and combatting what can be referred to, paraphrasing former US president Bill Clinton, as the "dark side of sport" (Chappelet 2009).[2]

CORRUPTION ON OR OFF THE FIELD OF PLAY, INDIVIDUAL OR ORGANIZATIONAL CORRUPTION

For corruption to occur there must be at least one corrupt party, a cheat who attempts to achieve some sort of personal gain (financial or other) by seeking to obtain an unfair advantage that will enable him or her to accomplish, or not, an act within his or her sphere of responsibility. *On* the field of play, cheating may be carried out by athletes (even if it is others who encourage them to cheat), referees, coaches, the athlete's direct entourage, or even bettors and spectators.

Corruption can also take place *off* the field, for example, by people with managerial responsibilities, such as club executives, national or international federation officials, sports contract negotiators, voting members for the attribution of a sports event (Cassani and May 2017), event organizers, or administrators, etc. The corruptor may be a broker or intermediary/agent involved in negotiating agreements involving sport organizations (e.g., sponsorship, broadcasting, or construction contracts), sports event bid committees or organizing committees, sports event executives or managers, sports bettors, or betting operators, etc.

---

[2] Clinton is credited with coining the term "dark side of globalization" during a speech to the United Nations (Chappelet 2009).

Sometimes, corruption is not always just down to individuals ("bad apples"); entire organizations may be imbued with a "culture of corruption" ("bad barrels").

FOUR FACETS

It is possible to distinguish four separate though interlinked, facets to sports corruption, with each facet corresponding to one of the main types of cheating affecting sport at the beginning of the 21st century.

First, doping is an attack on the integrity of sport, as it deprives clean athletes of the elation of winning, even if they are later placed ahead after the original winner is disqualified due to a failed drugs test. Athletes who dope are not only guilty of breaking the rules of their sport, they are attempting to obtain personal gain, either directly or indirectly, as a result of their undeserved victories (cheating to win). In most cases of doping, only the athletes involved are punished (usually via sporting sanctions, although sports doping is a criminal offence in a few countries such as Germany and Italy), even if the athlete's entourage often bears some, if not a large part, of the responsibility for this form of cheating and therefore could deserves more severe punishment than the athlete (providing performance enhancing substances to athletes is a criminal offence in many countries but is not well monitored). Doping affects all sports and all levels of sport, with even weekend athletes taking a huge variety of substances and supplements, forbidden or not, in the hope of boosting their performances. Using such substances/supplements can become an addiction and therefore, given the numbers of people involved, a public health problem. Doping and supplement misuse/addiction undermine the health benefits of sport.

Absence of fair play (or foul play) can be seen as the second facet of sports corruption. Originally coined by Shakespeare and adopted by sportsmen at the end of the 19th century, fair play is a relatively vague concept that can be defined as respecting both the letter and the spirit of the rules. Thus, an absence of fair play opens the way for behaviors, illegal or not, such as hooliganism, violence on the field of play, manipulations, tanking, unfair competition, and abuse and harassment of all types (sexual, racist, etc.). Viewed from this perspective, match-fixing (cheating in order to lose) can be categorized as demonstrating an absence of fair play. Match-fixing (manipulating the final result) and spot-fixing (manipulating a specific aspect of a game) have grown in conjunction with the growth in sports betting, especially since the arrival of online betting at the turn of the century. Any sports event can be rigged, even if football, tennis, and cricket are the sports most affected (Pielke 2016). Not playing fair and not respecting a sport's written and unwritten rules undermines the benefits of sport for education.

These first two facets of sports corruption mostly concern athletes on the field of play, who either want to win at any price or to lose (in order to win in a different way), and their entourages. They do not directly affect the organization of competitions, unlike the third and fourth facets of sports corruption, which involve competition organizers, their managers, and their organizational cultures.

A lack of ethics among some sport organization officials is at the heart of the sports corruption problem. Unethical officials have accepted a wide range of inducements, in cash or in kind, in return for supporting a host candidate's bid, awarding a contract, or supporting a potential appointee. This lack of ethics has also led some sport officials to turn a blind eye to certain cases of doping, athlete trafficking, discrimination, vote rigging, recurring abuse, or match-fixing, hence the overlap between this facet and the two previous facets. But these unethical behaviors occur mostly when the organizations involved tolerate them or do not have adequate monitoring procedures or an adequate system of governance, including rules on conflicts of interest, control mechanisms, and checks and balances.[3] Under Swiss law (article 102 of the criminal code), if a case of corruption cannot be attributed to one or more individuals, the organization concerned can be prosecuted for mismanagement (in which case, the organization is criminally responsible). Ethical shortcomings and poor governance by sport officials and organizations undermine the beneficial effects of sport for economic development.

Finally, the unsustainable management of a sports event, or even a sport (such as motor sports or snow sports on totally artificial runs), can be considered a problem of corruption. It can lead to badly designed sport facilities and gigantism, which makes hosting sports events too expensive or un-respectful of the environment, or to the building of "white elephants", that is, facilities that are too big (or unsuitable) for use after the event by current and future generations (Paramio Salcines, Babiak and Walters 2013; Bayle, Chappelet, François and Maltese 2011). Unfortunately, in many countries construction projects, whether or not they are sport-related, are synonymous with corruption due to the number, complexity, and lack of transparency of the contracts they involve. Rules governing the award of contracts for sustainable construction projects (procurement rules)[4] can reduce this problem. At the same time, standards imposing decent working conditions, such as those drawn up by the International Labor Organization (ILO), should be met. Lack of sustainability of sport or in the running of sport undermine the beneficial effects of sport for sustainable development (balanced in the three spheres of economic, social and environmental development).[5]

---

[3] An independent report published in December 2018 by law firm Ropes & Gray claimed the USOC (United States Olympic Committee) and USA Gymnastics (the US national governing body for this sport as recognised by USOC) had facilitated Nassar's abuse of hundreds of athletes and had failed to act when the allegations against the disgraced team doctor emerged. Nassar is currently serving up to 175 years in prison, having been found guilty of sexually abusing dozens of American gymnasts. US Senators have called on the Federal Bureau of Investigation (FBI) to investigate both USOC and USA Gymnastics following the report, which stated Nassar "acted within an ecosystem that facilitated his criminal acts".
[4] Such as those drawn up by the OECD.
[5] In December 2018, the Tokyo 2020 Olympic Organising Committee and the United Nations (UN) have signed a letter of intent aimed at promoting the contribution of sport to sustainable development, more specifically, work together to achieve the UN's Sustainable Development Goals (SDGs).

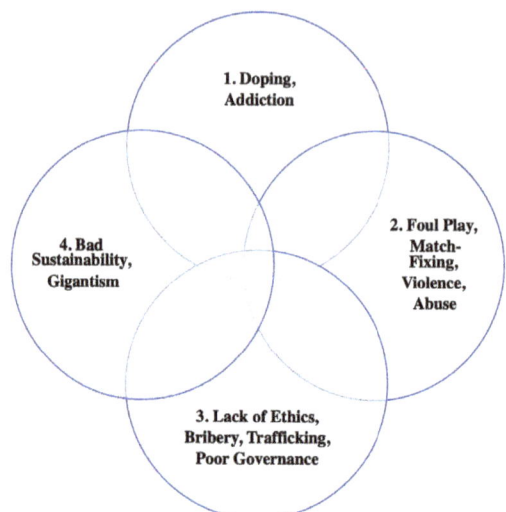

Figure 1: "The four overlapping facets of sports corruption."
Source: Author

Figure 1 summarizes these four overlapping facets of sports corruption or the dark side of sport, which make sport unsafe and is capable of obscuring its bright side (health, education, economic development, social, and environmental development, etc.).

HOW CAN SPORTS CORRUPTION BE FOUGHT?

The fight against sports corruption is slowly but surely taking shape through a variety of public and private measures, and national and international legal frameworks, in addition to educational programme which are run in many countries (see footnote 12).

In the case of doping, numerous national laws and international conventions to combat doping have been introduced since the 1970s and 1980s, and a World Anti-Doping Agency (WADA) was created in 1999 by the Olympic Movement and national governments. WADA regulates this sector via a (private) world anti-doping code and an international anti-doping (public) convention, drawn up by UNESCO in 2005, which has now been ratified by most of the world's governments, i.e. made law in their countries (WADA 2018). The countries which have ratified the UNESCO anti-doping convention must create a NADO (National Anti-Doping Organization) to fight the scourge within their territory and according to the World Anti-Doping Code.

In contrast to the fight against doping, which is a combined public-private undertaking, regulating fair play has traditionally been left in the hands of sport organizations (IFs and NFs –International and National sport Federations), through their sporting rules, aided by decisions by referees, sport officials and, sometimes, jurisprudence passed down by the Court of Arbitration for Sport (CAS). In 2015 the Council of Europe approved a convention (treaty under public law) against match-fixing that is open to non-member states and is undergoing ratification. In addition, a

Council of Europe convention, drawn up in 1985 and revised in 2016, provides for "an Integrated Safety, Security and Service Approach at Football Matches and Other Sports Events" and regulates the violent behaviors of spectators.

Ethical failings by sports executives are increasingly being addressed through general national legislation against corruption and lack of ethics that can also be applied to sport (e.g., France's "Sapin 2 Act") and by the international treaties drawn up by the United Nations, OECD, and Council of Europe mentioned in the introduction. The American, Austrian, Brazilian, French, Norwegian, and Swiss[6] prosecutors are working on the FIFA, IAAF, IBU (International Biathlon Union), and Rio 2016 cases, as well as on other sports "scandals". Like in the corporate sector, sport organizations are adopting increasingly stringent principles of governance; however, compliance with these principles must be monitored by independent bodies to ensure governance continues to improve over time. The recently ASOIF (Association of Summer Olympic International Federations) created GSMU (Governance Support and Monitoring Unit) is such a body (ASOIF 2018). The IOC and NOCs (National Olympic Committees) have a special responsibility of being ethical organizations according the Olympic Charter (rule 2).

As yet, there are no national or international laws pertaining to the sustainability of sports events and sports in general, even though most countries and sport organizations recognize the importance of sustainability to life in society. Alongside countries, it is up to sport organizations to show they are accountable in this respect (Gauthier 2015). Many event organizers are following the ISO (International Organization for Standardization) 20121 standards of sustainability for sporting events established at the time of the 2012 London Olympic Games. Also of note are the recommendations relating to sports event sustainability made by the UNESCO conference of sports ministers in 2013 and by the OECD in 2016, as well as the United Nations' Guiding Principles for Businesses and Human Rights (2011) and IUCN (International Union for Conservation of Nature) Sport and Biodiversity guide endorsed by the IOC in 2018. The IOC Sustainability Strategy for the Olympic Movement published in 2017 should also be taken into consideration. OCOGs (Organizing Committees of the Olympic Games) are particularly responsible to fight the lack of sustainability at this arguably largest sport event in the world.

In summary, the task of fighting the four facets of the dark side of sport is mainly entrusted to WADA and NADOs (doping), IFs and NFs (fool play), IOC and NOCs (ethics) and OCOGs and other event organizers (lack of sustainability), in partnership of governments and intergovernmental organizations.

Focusing on the four abovementioned facets of the fight against sports corruption generates an integrated approach to promoting the healthy and positive side of sport, an approach that is elegantly and memorably encapsulated in the acronym SAFE for a Sustainable, Anti-doping, Fair play, Ethical sport (see figure 2).

---

[6] Since 2015, 25 cases related to FIFA are under investigation by the Attorney General of Switzerland.

Figure 2: "The four overlapping facets of SAFE sport for sports integrity."
Source: Author

In fact, several countries have already embraced the SAFE approach to sport or some of its underlying principles (see next section). These four facets are often overlapping because sometimes a case involving one of the facets will also involve others. For instance, the 2015 IAAF scandal involved bribes (facet 2 "lack of ethics or foul-play") related to doping sanctions (facet 1 "doping"). Gigantism (facet 4 "bad sustainability") can be caused by poor governance of procurements and lead to corruption (facet 3 "lack of ethics"). One of the three reasons to fight doping (facet 1 "doping") in the UNESCO convention against doping is that it goes against the "spirit of sport" and is unfair to opponents (facet 2 "foul-play").

EXISTING PROGRAMMES INSPIRED BY THE SAFE SPORT CONCEPT

To the author's knowledge, there is no comprehensive programme covering all four facets of sports integrity summarized by the SAFE sport acronym, although this acronym has been used recently by several organizations in relation with sports integrity issues. A short review gives food for thought to put in place programmes to fight the dark side of sport in the future.

In the USA, following the Nassar case,[7] a non-profit organization was created under the name Center for SafeSport. It concentrates on the fight against bullying, harassment, hazing, physical abuse, emotional abuse, sexual misconduct, and other abuse in sport, i.e. on the fight against the second facet (clockwise) of the global

---

[7] This case involves a former medical doctor for the US Gymnastics Federation who sexually abused hundreds of gymnasts training for competitions, and who was sentenced to a life in prison in 2018. Following this scandal, the leadership of the federation was totally replaced and the US Gymnastics federation might lose its accreditation with the United States Olympic Committee, allowing it to represent its sport at the Olympics.

framework presented above (figure 1). It is supported by the USOC (United States Olympic Committee), the USPC (United States Paralympic Committee), NBC Sports Group, the NBA (National Basketball Association), WNBA (Women National Basketball Association), ESPN (a TV cable network) and private individual donors (US Center for SafeSport 2019).

In 2017 a UK charity, the NSPCC (National Society for the Prevention of Cruelty to Children), created a programme called Safeguarding in sport. Safeguarding refers to the process of protecting children (and adults) to provide safe and effective care, particularly in a sports setting. This includes all procedures designed to prevent harm to a child. Again, this programme concentrates on the fight against the second facet of the global framework presented above (figure 1) (CPSU 2019).

In other countries, programmes which aim at fighting some of the scourges of today's sport have been launched recently. For instance, in the Netherlands, there is a programme called VeilingSportKlimaat (which could be translated by "Safe sport environment"). cf. www.veiligsportklimaat.nl . In Switzerland, the programme Cool and Clean has been in existence for more than ten years to fight the addiction to alcohol, tobacco and drugs among young club members through specific courses organized in sports clubs throughout the country (Swiss Olympic 2019).

In Japan, the "Be the Real Champion Games Education" package was created in 2017 by a joint effort of the Japan Anti-Doping Agency and Japan Sports Agency to promote the values and integrity of sport (see www.playtrue2020-sp4t.jp/edu_package/about). It wishes to expand "the infinite possibility of sport for the future of sport and society." It promotes fair play in all its aspects (to sport, to him/herself, to other athletes, to other persons on the field, in daily life, etc.) Anti-doping education plays an important part in this programme. WADA proposes also many educational programmes and tools to fight doping.

Sport organizations have also started similar programmes. For example, the IOC set a SAFE Sport booth at the Olympic village of the Youth Olympic Games (YOG) in Buenos Aires 2018 following its launching in February 2018 of guidelines and a toolkit to safeguard athletes from harassment and abuse in sport (IOC 2019). Similar booths were organized at the Winter YOG in Innsbruck 2012 and in Lillehammer 2016.

SSI (Safe Sport International) was created several years ago but began to be well known only recently. It focuses on non-accidental harms, that is those perpetrated knowingly and deliberately, that undermine both the mental and physical health of the athlete and the integrity of sport (again the second facet of the framework). Sadly, there is plenty of evidence that such violence happens in sport. SSI feels that the time is right for a coordinated international effort to prevent and respond to this violence as part of the global effort to uphold and protect the sporting values. SSI will collaborate to develop and support the implementation of international frameworks for safe sport, developing safeguards for adult athletes and managing the transition from child to adult sport. SSI is supported by several sports organizations including the International Paralympic Committee, and brings together the thought, policy and practice leaders in sport through collaboration, such as the women in sport networks, the IOC and many others. Cf. www.safesportinternational.com

In 2014 and 2015, the EU (European Union) and the Council of Europe supported a joint project called "Pro Safe Sport" (PSS) (Council of Europe 2019a). It was aimed at promoting a safe and healthy environment for young athletes. PSS was followed in 2017 by a new joint initiative: Pro Safe Sport Plus (PSS+) (Ibid.) focusing on sexual violence against children in sport. The expression Safe sport, understood mainly as a key word for the protection of athletes, is now a pillar of the sport policy of the Council of Europe (Council of Europe 2019b).

Conclusion

There is no need to go back to Antiquity to see massive changes in sport today, as modern sport has evolved almost beyond recognition since the late 19th century, when its foundations were built on a strict ethos of amateurism. The abandonment of this ethos in the 1970s and 1980s in response to the increased commodification of sport is one of these main changes. Although modern sport is governed mostly by private, non-profit associations, it received enthusiastic support from the public authorities throughout the 20th century, often via physical education at school and subsidies for local sport clubs and national governing bodies. Today, the sports sector is an economic, social, and environmental phenomenon of great importance. In the fight for integrity, against the dark side of sport, against sports corruption, in the widest sense of the term, sport organizations are starting to work intelligently with the public authorities, which are showing greater readiness to legislate in this area, even criminalizing certain offences, especially when the underworld (mafia) is involved. The IAAF, which created an independent Athletics Integrity Board (AIB) in 2017, is a prominent example of how some sport federations are responding to the problem of corruption in all its forms. As the board's chairman has stated, the AIB is intended to do much more than deal with cases of doping; its objective is to drive all cheats out of athletics. In 2018, the IOC has also launched an International Partnerships Against Corruption in Sport (IPACS), uniting the sport movement with intergovernmental organizations including OECD, UNODC (United Nations Office on Drugs and Crime) and the Council of Europe, as well as the UK Government. IPACS currently concentrates on three topics: corruption in sports procurements, awarding of sports events, governance of sports organizations. These topics relate to facets 2 and 3 of figure 1).

Nevertheless, sport today often lacks credibility and legitimacy with both politicians and the general public. It is known to be beneficial for health, education, economic development, and social integration, etc., but a seemingly never-ending stream of scandals, eagerly reported by the media, is undermining sport's acknowledged benefits to such an extent that, as for globalization, it is now possible to talk about a dark side of sport, about unsafe sport.

The ethos of amateurism has been abandoned in the 1970-1980s, but it has not been replaced. Today, it is essential to promote an approach that can be used to fight corruption while reminding us of sport's positive objectives. SAFE sport provides such an approach.

REFERENCES

Association of Summer Olympic International Federations (ASOIF). 2018. "Governance Task Force." Accessed December 1, 2018. http://www.asoif.com/governance-task-force.

Bayle, Emmanuel, Jean-Loup Chappelet, Aurélien François, and Lionel Maltese. 2011. *Sport et RSE. Vers un management responsable?* Louvain-La-Neuve: DeBoeck.

Brooks, Graham, Azeem Aleem, and Mark Button. 2013. *Fraud, Corruption and Sport.* London: Palgrave MacMillan.

Brooks, Graham, and Anita Lavorgna. 2018. "Lost Eden: the Corruption of Sport." In *Corruption in Sport, Causes, Consequences and Reform*, edited by Lisa A. Kihl, 79-90. London: Routledge.

Cassani, Ursula, and Philomene May. 2017. "La corruption dans l'attribution de compétitions sportives: de l'ancien au nouveau droit [suisse]," In *Le droit en question, Mélanges en l'honneur de la Professeure Margareta Baddeley*, edited by Audrey Leuba, Marie-Laure Papaux van Delden, and Foex Bénédict, 351-378. Geneva: Schulthess.

Chantelat, Pascal. 2001. La corruption dans le sport." *Le Débat* 114: 125-139.

Chappelet, Jean-Loup. 2009. "A Glocal Vision for Sport (and Sport Management)". *European Sport Management Quarterly* 9(4): 483-485.

Child Protection in Sport Unit (CPSU). 2019. "Child Abuse in a Sports Setting." Accessed February, 2019. https://thecpsu.org.uk/help-advice/introduction-to-safeguarding/child-abuse-in-a-sports-setting.

Council of Europe. 2019a. "Pro Safe Sport." Accessed February 1, 2019. https://pjp-eu.coe.int/en/web/pss/home.

———. 2019b. "Safe Sport." Accessed February 1, 2019. https://www.coe.int/en/web/sport/safe-sport.

Gauthier, Ryan. 2015. "The IOC's Accountability for Harmful Consequences of the Olympic Games: A Multimethod International Legal Analysis." PhD diss., Erasmus University, Amsterdam.

Guy-Ryan, Jessie. 2016. "The Hot 19th Century Sport That Launched Modern Athletic Betting? Competitive Walking." Accessed January 11, 2019. https://www.atlasobscura.com/articles/the-hot-19th-century-sport-that-launched-modern-sports-betting-competitive-walking.

International Olympic Committee (IOC). 2019. "Safe Sport." Accessed February, 2019. www.olympic.org/athlete365/library/safe-sport

Kihl, Lisa, James Skinner, and Terry Engelberg. 2017. "Corruption in Sport: Understanding the Complexity of Corruption." *European Sport Management Quarterly* 17(1): 1-5.

Kihl, Lisa, ed. 2018. *Corruption in Sport: Causes, Consequences, and Reform*. London: Routledge.

Maenning, Wolfgang. 2005. Corruption in International Sports and Sport Management." *European Sport Management Quarterly* 5(2): 187-225.

Munting, Roger. 1996. *An Economic and Social History of Gambling in Britain and the USA*. Manchester: Manchester University Press.

Paramio Salcines, Juan-Luis, Kathy Babiak and Geoff Walters. 2013. *Routledge Handbook of Sport and Corporate Social Responsbility*. London: Routledge.

Pielke, Roger J. 2016. *The Edge: The War against Cheating and Corruption in Sport*. Santa Fe: Roaring Forties Press.

Swiss Olympic. 2019. "Cool & Clean." Accessed February, 2019. http://www.coolandclean.ch/fr.

Transparency International. 2016. *Global Corruption Report: Sport*. Transparency International.

US Center for SafeSport. 2019. "About." Accessed February, 2019. http://www.safesport.org.

World Anti-Doping Agency (WADA). 2018. "Home". http://www.wada-ama.org.

Wenn, Stephen R., Robert K. Barney, and Stephen R. Martyn. 2011. *Tarnished Rings, the International Olympic Committee and the Salt Lake City Bid Scandal*. New York: Syracuse University Press.

Dark Sides of Sport

CHAPTER 2

Sporting Power, Policy and Diplomacy: Catalysts and Gateways

Gary Armstrong, James Rosbrook-Thompson, Mahfoud Amara and Iain Lindsay

Sport clearly has the potential to unite people and has done so throughout history. The longevity of sporting practice is remarkable and illustrates its ability to overcome most fall-outs. Sport and games outlive political philosophies and accommodate political transformations. At the same time, we need to note how new ideas and political regimes can burden sport; politicians have often recognized the significance of sport in their non-sporting ambitions. This potential has a long history. The stretch of time between AD 394—when the Olympic Games were suppressed by the Roman Emperor Theodosius I—and 1896—when the first modern Olympic Games were held in Athens—saw nation-states come into being. Since then, the spirit of Olympism has been frequently undermined and flagrantly violated by the forces of nationalism. The pursuit of being the sporting best is at times commendable but can also be dismissive of other peoples and philosophies. Strengthening bonds of the in-group might depend on the denigration and humiliation of the out-group. Those who see sport as holding diplomatic possibilities must do their best to ensure that the celebrations of the victors preserve the dignity of the also-rans.

TACTICS AND PRINCIPLES: REFLECTIONS ON 'SPORTS DIPLOMACY'

If politics is the art of the possible, then diplomacy involves convincing others (normally the representatives of states or certainly those with access to power) that one possibility is more desirable than another. Practitioners of diplomacy have characterized this process of persuasion in more or less cynical ways. While the US Government's one-time Foreign Secretary Henry Kissinger defined diplomacy as the art of restraining power, its essence was perhaps best encapsulated by the Italian diplomat Daniele Varè, who described it as the art of letting the other party have things your way (Black 2010). Academic experts, not a group given to axiomatic neatness, have found diplomacy more difficult to define. As American political scientist Paul Sharp has argued:

> the distinguishing characteristics of diplomatic service (if there are any) remain unspecified except for a general sense that they lie outside what is

> regarded as the normal range of human interactions. In the absence of this specification, therefore, diplomacy acquires the character of a magic balm-like "political will" which, when called for and applied to a problem in sufficient quantities, will in some mysterious way get things moving and make things right. (Sharp 2009)

He also broadens the scope of diplomacy, contending that diplomatic action is possible wherever human beings live in different groups. More specifically, then, if we follow Sharp we should pay attention to contrasts between inter- and intra-group dynamics and the kinds of concepts and perspectives adopted by those charged with managing inter-group relations and disputes.

In the absence of a universal definition of sports diplomacy we might develop Sharp's characterization to include the use of sport by inter-group actors to bring about desired ends. Though on the face of it this may seem somewhat vague, a generous definition is needed if it is to encompass the myriad cases discussed in this paper. A definition of this kind is also useful as it does not assume or specify whether an outcome is just or morally acceptable. As Sharp points out, the term 'diplomacy' has a talismanic quality, and talismans can be used for good or ill. We would therefore be forgiven for deferring questions about morality while examining the actions of (official and unofficial) diplomatic practitioners operating at the nexus between politics and sport. This does not rule out the possibility of identifying successful or unsuccessful instances of sports diplomacy. A policy, scheme or agreement can, of course, be effective and still be ethically dubious.

This is not the only reason for sport being a curious choice as a vehicle for diplomacy. As well as being inherently competitive and adversarial, most team sports are invasion games and are thus acts of symbolic warfare. The vocabulary of the average sports pundit bears this out. Talk of 'strategy' and 'tactics', 'outflanking', 'smashing' and 'destroying', etc. has clear martial connotations. The use of sport as mental and physical preparation for military combat is also worthy of mention. Whether or not the Duke of Wellington genuinely attributed success at Waterloo to the playing fields of Eton, we can agree with sports historian J. A. Mangan (2004: 14) that:

> In history war has served sport and sport has served war. To concentrate on one without the other is to be guilty of an incomplete entry in an incomplete ledger—the association is that strong. Military activities have become community recreations, and community recreations have become military activities. The one has reinforced the other.

Despite these antagonistic and martial potentialities, sport has long been used to further diplomatic ends. In what follows we examine the role of sports diplomacy in the capacity of gateway and/or catalyst in the case of the Olympic Games, apartheid South Africa, Northern Ireland and Catalonia and the Middle East/Arab World. We should begin, however, by briefly outlining what we mean when we talk about gateways and catalysts, respectively.

UNDERSTANDING SPORTS DIPLOMACY: GATEWAYS AND CATALYSTS

Gateways are fundamentally about raising awareness in the context of a particular cause or desired outcome. The kind of openings they provide can, for example, afford international exposure to causes which had hitherto only resonated domestically. They can also open up alternative perspectives, bringing new identities and affinities into focus. Catalysts, on the other hand, are about accelerating the realization of a particular diplomatic objective. These are the events, partnerships, agreements, visits, etc. which oil the wheels of the diplomatic process and thereby promote an outcome desired by one or other interested party. Of course, it is possible for a moment or event—the hosting of a sporting mega-event, for example—to be both gateway and catalyst. However, we hope that the distinction will be of analytical worth in distinguishing between the characteristics of a phenomenon in terms of awareness and acceleration, and in doing so give a comprehensive account of its diplomatic potential. In many ways the Ancient Olympics exemplified the role of sports diplomacy as gateway and catalyst. The ancient Games sought to both refine and solidify notions of Greekness among a dispersed Hellenic population. Those living in places such as modern-day Egypt and Syria could renew their allegiance to an identity which had civic, ethnic, religious and aesthetic dimensions (among others); while strengthening the ties which bound Greeks together this, of course, tended to sharpen the distinction between Greeks and non-Greeks, i.e. the rest of the world's known population. The catalytic elements of the ancient Games were also important. The Games presented the Hellenic elite with an opportunity to gather at Olympia and discuss current affairs and forge diplomatic ties (Swaddling 1999).

While harking back to ancient Olympia, and inspired by recent archaeological finds, the founder of the modern Olympic Movement, Pierre de Coubertin, set out to forge an identity rooted in the values of Olympism (MacAloon 2013). However, as we will see, the history of the modern Games has demonstrated that the event is as likely to provide a forum for national chauvinism as international unity. As Aaron Beacom, an expert on the Olympic Movement, has argued, "The modern Olympic Movement, developed on the basis of an interpretation of the past, aimed at creating an ideology which would shape the evolution of international sport. The reality was ongoing tension between internationalist aspiration and nationalist pride" (Beacom 2012, 27).

Faster, Higher, Stronger: The Olympic Games

The much-lauded Olympic 'Family' doesn't have the option of retreating into domesticity. De Coubertin determined that—unlike their ancient equivalent—the modern Games would be a moveable feast. The Ancient Games brought together athletes from all corners of the Hellenic (and later Roman) world, an emblem of unity as much as competition. The modern Olympics have become a crucible of international competition, where nations struggle to assert their prowess, their dominance, or their very existence via athletic performance and Olympic-related displays.

Sport's attempts to be inclusive see it accommodate many dubious characters and regimes. German sports administrator and former middle-distance runner Carl Diem was instrumental in lobbying the IOC to grant the 1936 Olympic Games to Berlin (Krüger and Murray 2003). His efforts were rewarded when he was named Secretary General of the Organizing Committee. Within two years of the Games being awarded to Berlin in 1931, Adolf Hitler had swept to power in Germany. As a diplomatic gateway, the Games would be an opportunity for Germany to showcase the virtues of Nazism and its valorization of physical fitness, youthfulness and order. They also promised to demonstrate the superiority of the Aryan race. However, the image that Hitler wanted to portray to the world was one which would have to be carefully stage-managed. The Nazi regime's contempt for those who were not 'fit' in biological terms would have to be tempered and in many cases disguised altogether. Diplomatically, 'Jews not wanted' signs were taken down from key tourist attractions, while those travelling to Berlin from other nations were not subject to the regime's anti-homosexual laws. In the 'clean up' of the city which took place in the lead up to the Games, Hitler authorized the Chief of Berlin's police force to round up all gypsies and detain them in a camp for the duration of the Games. The event went ahead as planned. The President of the US Olympic Committee, Avery Brundage, had—perhaps diplomatically—seen nothing untoward on his pre-Games visit to Germany in 1934.

Some sporting politics arise out of inactivity. In the 1980s the Olympic Games became the forum for perhaps the most famous expression of soft power in the history of sport, with both the 1980 and 1984 Games becoming catalysts in the context of Cold War geopolitics (Mertin 2007). More specifically, the United States and the USSR would use the Olympics to both consolidate and promote the victory of their ideology on the international stage. In December 1979 Soviet forces invaded Afghanistan to prop up a Marxist government whose path to office had been cleared by Soviet authorities. Within a month President Jimmy Carter had declared that the US would be forced to boycott the Moscow Olympics (scheduled to take place in summer 1980) if Soviet forces did not leave Afghanistan. The Soviets did not heed Carter's warning, and the United States set about organizing the boycott. Allies were contacted and pressured into following the USA's lead.

Its efforts proved to be successful. A total of 65 nations refused the invitation to take part, with Japan, West Germany, China, the Philippines, Argentina and Canada among the nations boycotting. Rather than face the prospect of not competing at all, athletes from boycotting nations were invited to compete in the National Boycott Games which took place in Philadelphia.

The succeeding Games prompted a sporting retaliation. With the 1984 Summer Olympics due to take place in Los Angeles, the Soviet Union vowed to boycott the Games and set about lobbying its allies to do the same. While not enjoying the same level of success as their American adversaries, Soviet representatives did manage to sway fourteen of their allies, including East Germany, Czechoslovakia, Hungary and Bulgaria, to not turn up. As in 1980, boycotting athletes were invited to attend an alternative event, 'the Friendship Games', hosted in venues across the Soviet Union. However, not all people excluded from elite sporting venues had an alternative arena to perform in. In some instances, state-sponsored segregation of peoples was vehemently defended and alternative visions refused.

Forbidden Congress: Apartheid South Africa

The apartheid policies of South Africa (in place between 1948 and 1990) were based on so-called racial distinctions between blacks, whites, coloreds and Indians. The ordering of movement predicated on these distinctions had huge implications for South African sport and, indeed, the nation's international profile. In the vast majority of cases, inter-racial sport in the domestic context was not permissible. Spectators were also subject to segregation along racial lines. Only white athletes could participate in organized sport; non-whites were effectively barred from representing South Africa. International governing bodies recognized South Africa's national sports associations despite their organized competitions according to the principles of racial segregation. The segregationist South African Olympic Games Association (SAOGA) was a full member of the IOC, and in cricket the all-white national team of South Africa was received by Australia, New Zealand and England. Concomitantly no fixtures or exchanges were organized by the South Africans with the national teams of India, Pakistan or the West Indies (Booth 1998).

The pressure for change saw a combination of representation, statute citing and diplomatic fudging. The challenge mounted against the status enjoyed by South Africa's all-white sporting bodies within the international sports community gained traction in the mid-1950s. Having tried unsuccessfully to lobby national sports organizations about their plight, non-white South African sportsmen sought a gateway to international forums whereby their situation could be brought to the attention of a global audience. In 1955 the non-racial South African Soccer Federation (SASF) approached FIFA in order to underline that its membership was more than double the size of the all-white Football Association of South Africa (FASA) (Alegi 2010). It took six years for FIFA to heed SASF's calls, eventually suspending FASA in 1961. Unsurprisingly, the suspension caused outrage among FASA's officials and sympathizers who contested the decision, pointing out to FIFA President, Englishman Stanley Rous, that the way competitive soccer was organized in South Africa accorded with national law, and that any overhaul of its regulatory structures which aimed at integration of the 'races' would therefore be illegal. This put Rous in an awkward position. Many of the men who represented FASA he counted as friends. Rous decided to send a two-man delegation (comprising himself and James McGuire, who was President of the United States Soccer Federation between 1952 and 1954, and again between 1971 and 1974) to South Africa in order to find out what was happening 'on the ground'. A report he co-authored recommended that FASA be reinstated, largely on the grounds that FIFA rules did not insist upon multiracial football. This chimed with Rous' steadfast insistence that politics and sport should remain separate spheres. The racialist body duly resumed full membership of FIFA in 1963. This decision provoked ire not only among members of SASF and other South Africans who championed the cause of anti-Apartheid, but the Afro-Asian member-nations of FIFA who together comprised an increasingly powerful voting bloc. Diplomatic efforts had to be ramped up and intensified.

Happenstance and serendipity can play an understated role in diplomacy. In 1964, FIFA's Congress took place in Tokyo. It was a busy year for the Japanese capital, which also hosted the 1964 Summer Olympics. And what at first sight appeared to be relatively minor coincidence would act as a major catalyst for the cause of anti-apartheid sport. Many representatives of African and Asian member associations did not attend the meetings of international federations, in many instances the cost of international flights proved prohibitive. But levels of attendance improved when meetings were staged during major international sporting events. This meant that many more representatives from African-Asian member-nations were present at the FIFA Congress that year than may ordinarily have been the case (Corrigall 1971). They thus constituted a vociferous voice and an influential bloc of votes when it came to discussing and deciding on the future of South African representation within FIFA. The Congress determined that FASA's suspension should be re-imposed with immediate effect. However, it wasn't until 1991 that a new non-racial South African governing body for football, the South African Football Association (SAFA), was founded, with South Africa resuming membership of FIFA in 1992. Rous was eventually buffeted by the political winds he tried so hard to ignore, losing the FIFA presidency to the Brazilian schemer (and former Olympian) Joao Havelange in 1974.

The Puck of the Irish? Sport and Sectarianism in Northern Ireland

In the context of the sectarian dynamics of Northern Ireland, sporting institutions have expressed both nationalist and loyalist sentiments as well as having hopes for peace pinned on them as vehicles for the expression of apolitical, non-sectarian values (Coyle 1999). Founded in 1891 by a group of local cricketers who decided to turn their talents to the 'beautiful game', Belfast Celtic Football Club was an important catalyst in the context of nationalist-loyalist relations. Named after the Glasgow-based Celtic FC, and sharing the same dual sporting and social mission—priding itself on charity work and a non-sectarian player recruitment policy—it played its home matches at Celtic Park in the predominantly Catholic area of West Belfast. Celtic enjoyed their first league success in 1900, clinching the title with a victory over Belfast archrivals Linfield FC, a club which identified strongly with Protestantism and an overt political loyalty to the British monarchy. Amid the political turmoil of the Irish War of Independence (1919-1921), Belfast Celtic was forced to withdraw from the Irish League when sectarian conflict manifested itself on the terraces. The club left the league as champions.

Sporting diplomacy can fall on deaf ears. Sometime the forces of fission are greater than sporting attempts at fusion. Re-joining the league in 1924, the 'Mighty Belfast Celtic' as it was affectionately dubbed by fans, won four consecutive league titles and produced many players that would go on to win international caps. By the late 1940s, however, politically charged violence once again engulfed Ireland's football stadia. Like many local derbies, the annual showdown between Belfast Celtic and Linfield FC traditionally took place on Boxing Day. On the December 26, 1948,

Celtic entered the final stage of the match enjoying a one-goal lead. However, Linfield scored an equalizing goal in the final minute, a goal which triggered a pitch invasion by Linfield supporters, who took advantage of somewhat lax security arrangements in attacking a number of Celtic players. Among the most seriously injured was Celtic striker Jimmy Jones, who suffered a broken leg. The incident once again prompted the club to withdraw from the Irish League, citing the seeming inability of police and stewards to protect its players (Coyle 1999). Belfast Celtic would not take part in a competitive fixture again. Though once a promising accelerant for the promotion of cross-sectarian competition, the club ultimately foundered on the politico-religious loyalties it sought to channel and perhaps mitigate. Today the shopping center built on the site of Belfast's Celtic Park bears a plaque which reminds visitors of the sporting entity which used to call it home.

Sometimes sporting diplomacy can seek solace in new conversations and, in doing so, forge new diplomatic gateways. In 2000, a sporting organization was founded in Belfast by Canadian entrepreneur Bob Zeller, who ventured that non-sectarian, apolitical sport could be good for business. For this ambition to have any chance of being realized, a sport had to be chosen that was free from political and religious baggage. The sport was Ice Hockey. The Belfast Giants is a member of the UK's Elite Ice Hockey League, with home games played at Belfast's Odyssey Arena. The founders of the club were eager that it did not express affinity with any demographic defined in terms of faith or political ideology. The club's neutrality would be signaled by the banning of replica football jerseys (which could be illustrative of someone's loyalties along sectarian lines). Furthermore, fans were prohibited from bringing national flags into the playing venue while the United Kingdom national anthem, which can be heard prior to games at other stadia throughout the Elite League, is not aired in the Odyssey Arena. As the club motto has it, "In the land of the Giants, everyone is equal", and most commentators agree that the attempt to cultivate a non-sectarian fan-base has been relatively successful (Devine et al. 2007); the Giants are the second most supported club in the Elite League, regularly attracting more than 4,700 fans.

In other European cities and around other sporting contexts flags, anthems and proclamations were articulated in a spirit of *concord*.

Crowns and Pyramids: Catalonia and the 1992 Olympic Games

Much like their ancient equivalent, the modern Olympic Games have in numerous cases been used as both gateway and catalyst in relation to one or other political objective. The 1992 Barcelona Olympics were no exception, with the organizers and the wider Catalan community seeing the Games as an opportunity to showcase their submerged identity to the world as a global 'coming out' party which underlined the distinction between Catalans and the Castilian Spanish. This possibility made the latter profoundly anxious as to the possible post-Olympic repercussions (Moragas Spá et al. 1995).

The Catalans have long sought independence from the central Spanish state. Though statutes of Autonomy have granted more power to the region, the objective of absolute independence has remained elusive (though it may now be coming into focus). Emerging towards the end of the nineteenth century and vivified by events such as the Spanish Civil War (1936-39), Catalan nationalism has found expression in literature, philosophy and art. Until the mid-1970s these expressions risked the censure of state authorities, with the Catalan language and Catalan symbolism being suppressed by the Fascist regime of General Franco (1939-1975).

It was in the context of this post-Francoist ongoing struggle for greater Catalan autonomy that the Games were awarded to Barcelona in 1986. As with the awarding of other Olympiads, an initial bout of celebration gave way to tense and emotionally charged discussions about how best to communicate a distinctive brand of (sub-state) nationalism to global audiences. As a gateway, how could the event heighten awareness of the Catalan cause? As a catalyst, how could expressions of Catalan culture promote the ultimate objective of Catalan independence?

A more technical set of questions concerned the exact geo-political locus of the Games. To what extent would this be the city of Barcelona versus the region of Catalonia? And what of the wider Spanish state? The fact that the Games had never been awarded to Madrid was, of course, not lost on the organizers; as well as making the event even more of a milestone achievement for Catalans, it also reinforced the self-perception of unique aesthetic and intellectual genius. However, it also brought with it considerable pressure; everything needed to be planned with precision and executed with panache.

As well as the usual investment in infrastructure, the symbolism of the event was carefully stage-managed. It was ensured that Catalan gained approved status as an official Olympic language, that the Catalan flag would appear alongside the flag of the central Spanish state, and that the mascot of the Games would be Cobi, a Catalan sheepdog rendered in cubist style. As well as underlining a distinctive (and by no means subordinate) set of cultural sensibilities, these gestures also seemed to subtly acknowledge the restrictions and persecutions of the Franco regime. The opening ceremony was also important as it allowed the organizers to draw from a wider and more elaborate repertoire of Catalan socio-cultural life. Of the three-hour ceremony, nearly half was devoted to performances which showcased elements of Catalan music, art and folk traditions (specifically the segments of the "Sardana", a traditional Catalan circle dance, and "Els Castellers" or human pyramids" (Moragas Spá et al. 1995, 94). Though the catalytic potential of the Games may not have been fully realized—most broadcasters did not narrate the ceremony as a conflict between Catalonia and central Spain (Moragas Spá 1995)—the event certainly succeeded in providing a gateway to an international audience. If the current stalemate over Catalan independence is resolved, the role of sport and, more specifically, the 1992 Barcelona Olympics, should not be overlooked.

Ice Cold Diplomacy: The 2014 Sochi Winter Olympics

The Sochi Winter Olympics of February 2014 were mired in controversy, becoming a gateway for widespread condemnation of the country's anti-gay laws, its human rights record more generally, and its relationship to Chechnya (as well as Circassia). As a result, boycotts and political protests by athletes, fans and heads of state threatened to derail the Games.

One cause for protest was a law (passed in 2013) which criminalized support for 'non-traditional' relationships. The law, as well as the physical abuse of LGBT protestors by Russian police, prompted widespread condemnation. President Obama warned Russia that if it wanted to observe the Olympic spirit, then "every judgment should be made on the track, or in the swimming pool, or on the balance beam, and people's sexual orientation shouldn't have anything to do with it" (The Week 2013). Russian Premier Putin, meanwhile, attempted to deflect criticism by insisting that gay supporters and athletes would feel at ease in Russia (Wharton and Loiko 2013).

Another element of the controversy surrounding the Games related to Chechnya, a federal republic of Russia which has struggled for independence since the dissolution of the USSR in 1991. Since then, the Chechens have fought two wars against the Russian Federation (1994-1996 and 1999-2000) and become embroiled in a sustained period of armed insurgency (2000-2009). As early as 2012 the Russian authorities claimed to have foiled a Chechen rebel plot to attack the Games. In December 2013, two suicide bombings in as many days heightened fears that Chechen separatists would use the Games as a forum for terror, an attack which followed a call by Chechen militant leader Dokka Umarov for "maximum force" to be used in scuppering the Games.

Although the event wasn't ultimately subject to a concerted boycott or a politically-motivated attack, it did provide a platform for expressions of defiance vis-à-vis Russia's stance on human rights and Chechnya. In many ways the figurehead of the Games was Dutch speed-skater Ireen Wüst, who is openly gay. She won more medals than any other athlete and joked about cuddling up to Vladimir Putin while she received his congratulations. The Russian authorities tried to head off any serious disruption by creating a protest park—situated half an hour from Sochi. However, journalists reported that the permission of three different government departments was required in order to protest there (Springer and Radia 2014)

Though many questioned the moral validity of the Winter Olympics being held in Sochi, at the very least the Games brought the issue of gay rights to the fore and highlighted the cause of Chechen independence (the death of Umarov in March 2013 perhaps underlined how urgent a threat he and his collaborators posed). Only time will tell whether the event acted as both gateway and catalyst in the case of these fraught dimensions of Russian (geo)politics.

Sport and Diplomacy in the Arab World

Sport—itself the legacy of colonial presence and European influence in the Arab region, and for some a product of European "cultural invasion"—has been incorporated in nation-building projects across the Arab world to varying degrees. It was first put to work in raising awareness of nationalist struggle against colonial presence in occupied Arab lands. The formation of the Algerian National Team in exile (in Tunisia) and its subsequent tour of the world, particularly visits to the Eastern Bloc, served to promote the Algerian cause for independence from France. It many senses it was an act of sporting diplomacy par excellence. A joint boycott of the 1956 Olympic Games by Egypt, Iraq and Lebanon, in protest against the tripartite military intervention of Israel, France and Britain in Egypt, is another high-profile example.

Top professional Algerian football players in the French league, the likes of Mekhloufi and Zitouni who were selected to play in the 1958 FIFA World Cup in Sweden for the French national team, were ordered by the Algerian National Liberation Front to leave France in a clandestine manner and abandon their material privileges to join the Algerian revolution. The discovery of the news in metropolitan France was a catalyst in the political debate around "events in Algeria" (Algeria was divided into three provinces) which up until 1958 were hardly mentioned in the French media. This was despite the increasing mobilization of French troops; by January 1, 1957 the French had 308,000 soldiers in Algeria to suppress the rebellion against French interest and to protect European settlers and the supporters of 'French Algeria'. From 1958 till 1962, Équipe FLN team played somewhere between 50 and 100 exhibition matches. In terms of symbolic impact, "winning somewhere around three quarters of its matches and playing an attractive game, the real victory came before each game, as the Algerian anthem was played and flag displayed per the conditions of their appearance" (Ross 2014).

The National Team model was reproduced by the Palestinian movement for independence. Its national football team is formed by Palestinians from the occupied territory, the West Bank, and the diaspora; refugee camps in the Middle East and Palestinian community in Latin America (Legrand 2014). The Palestinian Football Association, although founded in 1928, was not recognized by FIFA until 1998. Palestine has been recognized as a member of the Olympic Council of Asia (OCA) since 1986, and the International Olympic Committee (IOC) since 1995. The recognition of the Palestinian sport movement could be perceived as an important diplomatic step toward the full recognition of independent Palestine by the international community.

We cannot mention Palestine and the Olympic movement without discussing the 1972 Munich Olympic Games and the taking hostage of Israeli athletes in the Olympic Village by members of Black September—an event which brought the Arab-Israeli conflict into the international sporting arena. It remains one of the zones of tension between the Arab World and the Olympic Movement, characterized by the boycott of Israeli athletes in the Olympics, restricted mobility of Palestinian athletes from and to occupied territories, and Arab resistance towards the affiliation of Israel in the International Committee of the Mediterranean Games.

Sport in the Arab world has long been employed as a diplomatic tool to promote the consolidation of nation-state building and unity around a regime's ideology (one-party, monarchy, and military-states) and usually around the figure of the nation's father (leader or Zaim in Arabic); Bourguiba, Benbella, Boumedienne, Abd-Nasser, Sadam, Gaddafi, Kings Hussain, Faisal, and Hassan II, to name a few. To this end, the notion of diversity (cultural and religious) was supressed in the name of unity against external threats led by the so-called "imperialist forces" and the enemy of Arab Ummah (the all-Arab Nation). The denial of plurality and the portrayal of minority demands for political and cultural rights often integral to the demands of sporting participants, has partly fuelled the current conflicts in the region (Amara 2012).

During the Cold War era the Arab world was divided between Eastern and Western blocs, despite an effort to serve South-South and Arab interests. The presence of Arab states in these blocs and politico-economic alliances (e.g. Third-worldism, Pan-African unity) has also impacted on the sporting domain as symbolized by the boycott of the Olympic Games: Arab Sub-Saharan countries boycotted the 1972 Games to denounce the apartheid regime in South Africa; Egypt, Sudan, Mauritania, Bahrain, Morocco, Somalia, Tunisia and the UAE followed the boycott movement of the 1980 Moscow Games led by the US against USSR invasion of Afghanistan; while, interestingly, socialist Libya was the only Arab country to join the boycott of the 1984 Los Angeles Games.

Despite regional tensions bound up with politico-ideological and/or ethno-nationalist differences, there have been a number of attempts to use sport to claim a form of post-national unity in the name of an Arab and Muslim common identity and shared destiny. At least this is the way it has been expressed at state level. The aim has been to increase visibility in the region without necessarily entering into conflict with international sports federations and the International Olympic Committee. The Pan-Arab Games were established by the League of Arab Nations in 1953 as means of expressing cultural unity between Arab peoples across nation-state boundaries (Henry et al. 2003). In 2005 the first Islamic Solidarity Games, initiated by the Islamic Council, were held in the Kingdom of Saudi Arabia. The objectives of the Games were:

- To strengthen Islamic solidarity among youth in member states and promote Islamic identity in the fields of sports;
- To promote cooperation among member states on matters of common interest in all fields of sport activities;
- To preserve sporting principles and to promote the Olympic sports movement in the Muslim world;
- To make youth in member states aware of the objectives of the Islamic Council.

It is worth noting in relation to the region's sporting and political climate that in 2009 the Islamic Solidarity Games, which were supposed to take place in Iran, were cancelled. The decision was influenced by Saudi Arabia, where the Federation of Islamic Solidarity Games is located, and supported by other Arab countries. The cancellation followed the Iranian Organizing Committee's decision to use the contested term "the Persian Gulf" to refer to the sea separating Iran and the Arabian Peninsula. The Games were also threatened by military conflict in the region. As a consequence, the Islamic Solidarity Games of 2013 were moved from Syria to Indonesia.

Today, countries in the Gulf Cooperation Council are actively engaged in an international sport strategy to increase their economic, commercial and political influence. The decision to bid for and organize international sports events, as well as make direct investments in the international sport industry, has been taken with the aim of showcasing the Council's model of modernization and political stability. In branding their investment as beneficial to the development of sport, and serving the universal values of sport, these countries are promoting themselves politically as willing interlocutors in the struggle for conflict resolution and peace building and against extremism. Of course, the increasing visibility of Arab investors in sport, represented by wealthy individuals or state investment authorities, has not been welcomed by everybody. The acceptance of investment from wealthy Middle Eastern funds has been the subject of parliamentary debate, as in the case of Qatari investment in French sport. The Qatari president of PSG, Nasser Al-Khelaifi, has been accused by far-right movements in France of using sport "to propagate Islamist ideology" and advance its political agenda, particularly among French Muslims.

In times of upheaval in the Arab world, sport (and football in particular) has become a space for the expression of ultra-nationalist sentiments and popular chauvinism. In some cases, football is the direct cause of conflict between Arab countries, as was evidenced in the tension between Egypt and Algeria over the qualification to the 2010 FIFA World Cup in South Africa. Each country was claiming political and historical legitimacy, and promoting ethnic arguments around which should be considered truly "Arab". This identity based conflict played out within the football arena as both purported to be the true manifestation of and representative for Arabs in the international football arena. In this instance football brought to the surface the crisis of meanings around the Pan-Arab ideology, which is torn today between the 'sacredness' of Arab unity and the 'profane' of single Arab state (and regime) 'self-interests'. What was initially a football match between the two national teams became the cause of a quasi-diplomatic incident between the two nation-states, both members of the Arab Council (Amara 2012).

CONCLUSION

Nation-state building models based on the denial or the manipulation of political and cultural rights remain in modern society. These can be clearly observed in the Arab region, where football stadia have become tangible embodiments of unrest. The events that occurred in recent years in football stadia in Egypt and the death of hundreds of football fans stands as a reminder of the fragility of national cohesion and social contract in Arab societies. The manipulation of sport for strengthening political legitimacy of Arab regimes did not prevent the toppling of long-standing rulers such as Mubarek in Egypt, Ben-Ali in Tunisia, and Gaddafi in Libya. That being said, the use of sport within the Arab world, particularly within countries in the GCC, is an important vehicle in re-shaping the regional vision previously reduced to the insulting and simplistic paradigms of 'Oil and Terrorism'. Countries such as Qatar and the UAE are exemplars of such stratagems and are becoming influential actors in the global sport arena and are rapidly becoming key global hubs for sport-related investment and development.

Other issues can be observed by considering the United States whose sporting manifestations of soft power have suffered from inconsistencies within and between its other cultural forms, its political values and its foreign policies. Now, during a period when both Jintao and Putin have made the bolstering of soft power a key priority, China and Russia seem to be foundering on the same rocks. An event such as the 2008 Beijing Olympic Games could have been a triumph for Chinese soft power. However, not long after the visiting athletes and global media had returned home, China resumed its crackdown on human rights activists (Nye 2013). The parallels with the 2014 Winter Olympics in Sochi are obvious.

Some of the other stories told here should perhaps lead us to be skeptical about the power of sport to bridge various social divisions. The realities of sport in Northern Ireland demonstrate how ethno-religious conflict can be reflected in the organization and tenor of competitive sport, while the attempts of the UN and its various agencies to harness the power of sport to further the ends of 'development and peace' have produced a mixed set of outcomes. The actions of disenfranchised non-white athletes in Apartheid South Africa—together with those who identified with their cause—prove that sport can indeed be used as a powerful gateway and catalyst, with gains made in sport foreshadowing wider social and political changes.

Misconceptions, oversights and missed opportunities for good governance that become abundantly clear through hindsight speak to the lack of rigorous studies about sport and politics. As has been emphasized by the examples taken from the Arab regions the absence of specialized research centers that act as knowledge repositories is telling. The sporting fixture is always the kernel of something bigger and 'political'. We must deepen our understanding of the manner in which sport is utilized to maximize strategic impact in both public and private contexts. This will involve analysis at the level of both theory and practice; the ideologies that sport 'works' in accordance with the tools that build the bridges of understanding need to be disseminated. The realization of this ambition would necessitate the participation and input of variously: athletes, coaches, institutional power-brokers and those tasked with the governance of sport. Those who patronize, sponsor and broadcast sport must also be involved. Finally, we need remember that fans and followers sustain sport; how sport is followed and the potential that various fandoms carry should be integral to the future of an impactful and useable knowledge economy.

REFERENCES

Alegi, Peter. 2010. *Laduma: Soccer, Politics and Society in South Africa, from its Origins to 2010*. KwaZulu-Natal, SA: University of KwaZulu-Natal Press.

Amara, Mahfoud. 2011. 'Football, the new battlefield of business in Algeria: Djezzy and Nedjma…RANA MĀK YA AL-KHDRA'. *The Journal of North African Studies* 16 (3): 343–360.

Amara, Mahfoud. 2012. *Sport, Politics and Society in the Arab World*. London: Palgrave Macmillan.

Beacom, Aaron. 2012. *International Diplomacy and the Olympic Movement: The New Mediators*. Basingstoke, UK: Palgrave Macmillan.

Black, Jeremy. 2011. *A History of Diplomacy*. London: Reaktion Books.

Booth, Douglas. 1998. *The Race Game: Sport and Politics in South Africa*. London: Routledge.

Corrigall, Mary. 1971. 'International Boycott of Apartheid Sport'. Paper prepared for the United Nations Unit on Apartheid. (http://www.sahistory.org.za/articles/international-boycott-apartheid-sport-mary-corrigall).

Coyle, Padraig. 1999. *Paradise Lost And Found: The Story of Belfast Celtic*. Edinburgh: Mainstream Publishing.
Devine, Adrian, Connor, Robert and Devine, Frances. 2007. 'The War Is Over So Let the Games Begin.' In P. M. Burns and M. Novelli (eds.) *Tourism and Politics: Global Frameworks and Local Realities*. Oxford: Elsevier.
FIFA. 2014. 'FIFA World Cup™ in Brazil to promote peace and fight all forms of discrimination'. www.fifa.com/worldcup/news/y=2014/m=6/news=fifa-world-cuptm-in-brazil-to-promote-peace-and-fight-all-forms-of-dis-2-2368962.html.
Henry, Ian P., Amara, Mahfoud and Al-Tauqi, Mansour. 2003. 'Sport, Arab nationalism and the Pan-Arab Games'. International Review for the Sociology of Sport, 38(3): 295–310.
Krüger, Arnd and Murray, William J. 2003. *The Nazi Olympics: Sport, Politics and Appeasement in the 1930s*. Chicago, IL: University of Illinois Press.
Legrand, Christine. 2014. 'Chile's Gaza sympathisers rally behind Palestinian football colours'. *The Guardian*, December 4.
MacAloon, John J. 2013. *This Great Symbol: Pierre de Coubertin and the Origins of the Modern Olympic Games*. London: Routledge.
Mangan, J. A. 2004. *Militarism, Sport, Europe: A War Without Weapons*. London: Routledge.
Mertin, Evelyn. 2007. 'The Soviet Union and the Olympic Games of 1980 and 1984: Explaining the Boycotts to their own People'. In S. Wagg and D.L. Andrews (eds.) *East Plays West: Sport and the Cold War*. London: Routledge.
Moragas Spá, Miguel de, Rivenburgh, Nancy K. and Larson, James F. 1995. *Television in the Olympics*. London: John Libbey and Co.
Nye, Joseph. 2013. 'What China and Russia Don't Get About Soft Power'. *Foreign Policy*, April 29.
Ross, Tony. 2014. 'The other French team': Soccer and independence in Algeria. Retrieved from https://www.washingtonpost.com/news/monkey-cage/wp/2014/06/06/the-other-french-team-soccer-and-independence-in-algeria/ (accessed 7 June 2014).
Sharp, Paul. 2009. *Diplomatic Theory of International Relations*. Cambridge and New York: Cambridge University Press.
Springer, Andrew and Roda, Kirit. 2014. 'Openly Gay Medallist 'Cuddles' With Putin'. *ABC News*, February 10.
Swaddling, Judith. 1999. *The Ancient Olympic Games*. Austin, TX: University of Texas Press.
The Week. 2013. 'Sochi Olympics: will Russia's anti-gay law disrupt Games?' December 10.
Wharton, David and Loiko, Sergei. L. 2013. "2014 Winter Olympics: Where things stand 100 days before Sochi Games". *LA Times*, October 29.

CHAPTER 3

Secret Operations at the Simple Games: The Free Europe Committee, Cold War Tourism, and the 1964 Winter Olympics

Toby C. Rider

"In Principle," wrote Pierre de Coubertin in 1910, "the ideal sports spectator is a sportsman on holiday, taking a break in his own exercise routine to follow the exploits of a more skillful or better trained friend" (Müller 2000, 267). Coubertin certainly had a selective opinion when it came to the subject of crowds. He disliked overly large gatherings. He loathed boisterous behavior. He preferred that onlookers were discerning connoisseurs of movement. Nevertheless, a central function of his modern Olympic creation, one of its primary philosophical aims, was to bring people from different countries together so that they might better appreciate and understand other cultures through the mutual consumption of athletic competition. As the Olympics grew in size and stature during the first half of the twentieth century, hosting cities welcomed athletes as well as visitors from an increasingly diverse range of nations. The Games became a globalized spectacle, even if Coubertin might not have approved of everyone who visited and watched (Keys 2006).

Without question, too, this massive influx of tourists gave governments and politicians a further reason to take note of the festival. A host city could give its host state a political boost, just as Germany aimed to do in 1936. Organizing an Olympic Games, and wooing those who attend it, is a matter of national prestige. In many ways, the Olympics present an unrivalled opportunity to communicate, on a person-to-person level, with a large and diverse range of people for a two-week period. If one has a message to promote, an Olympic festival is an ideal place to promote it. In the Cold War era, when international affairs were dominated by two ideological messages—communism and liberal democracy—platforms such as the Olympic Games were especially significant. The droves of tourists who travelled to Olympic cities were targets for national and ideological exploitation, subjects that could possibly be influenced or swayed by political propaganda (Rider and Llewellyn 2015).

Throughout the Cold War, American and Soviet government officials did this frequently and strategically. They used Olympic cities to distribute judiciously chosen magazines, pamphlets, and books; to show ideologically driven movies; to organize cultural exhibitions and stage various forms of entertainment; and, in the case of the United States, to help Eastern European athletes to defect to the "free world" (Rider

2016). For the student of Cold War history, these activities are no surprise. They are symbolic of the "total" nature of the Cold War conflict. In the absence of a full-scale military confrontation between the Soviet Union and America, both superpowers focused instead on gaining a preponderance of power through the mobilization and exploitation of ideas and culture. As Tony Shaw has remarked, "virtually everything, from sport to ballet to comic books and space travel, assumed political significance and hence potentially could be deployed as a weapon both to shape opinion at home and to subvert societies abroad" (Shaw 2001, 59). Olympic cities, and their gamut of tourists, were an obvious transmission belt to connect with a large amount of people quickly, efficiently, and perhaps even effectively.

This chapter, then, seeks to further our understanding of the battle for the hearts and minds of Olympic tourists by examining how and why a U.S. funded front group, known as the Free Europe Committee (FEC), organized covert operations at the 1964 Innsbruck Winter Games. The Free Europe Committee, just one of a plethora of clandestine state-private initiatives directed by the intelligence community in Washington, was supplied with millions of government dollars to secretly support Eastern European exiles in a range of propaganda activities which, the exiles hoped, would lead to the collapse of Soviet control in Eastern Europe. The FEC looked upon the Olympic festival in Innsbruck, attended by thousands of tourists from the Iron Curtain countries, as an ideal venue to make "contact" with the "captive peoples" of the Soviet bloc. For the duration of the Winter Games, the FEC organized and staffed an information center in Innsbruck, an initiative inspired by America's long term goal of undermining communist rule in Eastern Europe through a gradual process of cultural infiltration (Hixson 1997). Staff at the center actively sought out Iron Curtain tourists at the Olympics, invited them to peruse and read a range of carefully selected literature, and encouraged them to meet and speak with fellow countrymen in exile.

The historical scholarship on government-led actions such as this is growing year upon year. Over the past decade, in particular, scholars have revealed that throughout the Cold War era the U.S. government, from Presidents Truman to Reagan, regarded the Games as important to national prestige and the conduct of foreign policy (see for instance Dichter 2018; Sarantakes 2009; Sarantakes 2011; and Rider 2016). In the case of the Lyndon B. Johnson administration (1963-68), the most comprehensive work has been done by Thomas M. Hunt. His research, based upon newly declassified documents, confirms that the Johnson White House viewed the Summer Olympics of 1964 (Tokyo) and 1968 (Mexico City) as a strategic Cold War issue. Aside from federal debates over funding the American Olympic team, Hunt explains that government actions included a live satellite broadcast of the Tokyo Games and an elaborate cultural exhibit at the following festival in Mexico (Hunt 2018). Hunt's seminal work, though, does not investigate the 1964 Winter Games in Innsbruck. As such, this chapter builds upon his ground breaking research. Moreover, it further illustrates the "dark side" of the U.S. government's sporting Cold War.

THE FREE EUROPE COMMITTEE AND THE SECRET COLD WAR

The Cold War emerged over a decade before the Innsbruck Games began. By the end of the 1940s, the Soviet Union had consolidated its hold on much of Eastern Europe. Western observers worried that Soviet influence might spread even further. They feared, in often apocalyptic ways, a world engulfed by communism. Like other Western powers, the United States took steps to counter Soviet expansionism. The Free Europe Committee, or the National Committee for a Free Europe as it was originally known, was a product of the U.S. government's covert "political warfare" strategy to "roll back" communism in Eastern Europe. American officials argued that only through political warfare, the "employment of all means at a nation's command, short of war, to achieve its national objectives," could the United States effectively challenge the Soviet Union without resorting to a nuclear attack (Corke 2006, 108). In 1948, this realization was quickly made policy when the government created the machinery for covert operations and placed it under the umbrella of the Central Intelligence Agency (CIA). Armed with a massive budget and a cast of World War Two intelligence veterans, the U.S. embarked upon a wide scope of clandestine operations in a global assault on communism (Miscamble 1992).

This worldwide crusade was further driven and galvanized by the co-option of private actors to the cause. American policymakers determined that foreign audiences would be far more responsive to the message of U.S. propaganda if it appeared that the message had not come from official government sources. As a result, they launched an unprecedented peace time commitment to support U.S. foreign policy objectives by working with and through private groups or, in more extreme examples, creating "private" organizations from scratch (Lucas 1999; Wilford 2008).

The Free Europe Committee fit into the latter category of this "state-private network." In postwar America, there resided many Eastern European exiles who had fled either the Nazi invasion or the subsequent Soviet presence in their respective countries. Covert operators in Washington recognized that the exiles possessed the necessary lines of contact to breach the Iron Curtain, and spread propaganda that might disrupt and encourage revolt against Soviet communist ideology. More still, the State Department reasoned that if they controlled the exiles in an unofficial capacity, the U.S. government could not be held accountable. And so in response to Soviet foreign policy and in light of the potential of the exiled community, the American intelligence community formed the Free Europe Committee in 1949. The organization's first press release stated that the FEC would aid the exiles in their "stand against communism" and, of course, made no mention of where the organization's funding came from. To anyone in the public that might be interested, the Committee simply appeared to be a private philanthropic group led by prominent American citizens. In reality, however, the Free Europe Committee secretly received millions of CIA dollars to fund Soviet bloc émigrés in an astounding breadth of activities. The most famous branch of the organization's propaganda machine, Radio Free Europe, started to broadcast in 1950, but the Committee also poured money into research centers, publications, "freedom" rallies, a Free Europe University in Exile, and a plethora of other exiled groups and individuals living in the West (Kádár-Lynn 2013; Johnson 2010; Mickelson 1983).

Within a year of its formation, the FEC began to support refugee athletes from Eastern Europe. The rationale for doing so was fairly straightforward. Many Iron Curtain countries were obsessed with sports and treated their athletes as heroes. Likewise, the Communist regimes placed a premium on elite sport because they believed victories in international competitions were powerful propaganda for the socialist way of life. But when Eastern European athletes defected, they became potent propaganda for the West. The FEC helped to magnify the stories of refugee athletes who condemned communism and helped them to continue their sporting careers. In essence, then, the FEC tried to turn sport from a strength of the Soviet bloc to a fallible weakness (Rider 2013c).

As part of this strategy, the Free Europe Committee arranged operations at the Olympic Games in the 1950s, but the manner of the operations changed over time and reflected, in many ways, the U.S. government's evolving policy toward the Soviet bloc. During the 1956 Summer Games in Melbourne, for instance, the Free Europe Committee encouraged and facilitated the defection of Hungarian and Romanian athletes (Rider 2013b). Yet the government's support for this sort of aggressive psychological warfare begun to dwindle in the post-Stalin era, when it became increasingly clear that cracking Soviet control in Eastern Europe was highly unlikely without a full scale military intervention. The reluctance of the U.S. president, Dwight D. Eisenhower, to go so far was highlighted in the clearest possible way in 1956, when the U.S. stood by and watched Soviet tanks quell the Hungarian Revolution (Tudda 2005).

Historian Walter Hixson notes that as Eisenhower's first term as president came to a close, "U.S. Cold War planners began to emphasize a gradualist approach" in their discussions on Eastern Europe. This policy was further articulated in 1955, when National Security Council directive 5505/1 stipulated that American strategy toward the satellites should "stress evolutionary rather than revolutionary change" by penetrating the region with ideas and culture (Hixson 1997, 101). Shortly thereafter, and as a result of this policy, the United States plunged into all manner of cultural contacts with countries in the Soviet bloc and, a little later, signed a cultural exchange agreement with the Soviet Union. Included in the effort to break down the "isolation of the captive peoples from the West" were sports tours and exchanges which allowed for American athletes to travel to and compete in Eastern Europe (Hixson 1997, 110; Rider and Witherspoon 2018).

Shattered by the failure of the Hungarian Revolution, the Free Europe Committee followed the pattern of change in Washington and gradually shifted away, to some degree, from the policy of "liberation" (Puddington 2000). FEC officials accepted, nonetheless, that the United States would not go as far as to tolerate the "status quo" in Eastern Europe, and concentrated instead on the "loosening of ties between the satellite states and the USSR by...maintaining the captive peoples sense of identity with the West." This process of "stimulating a gradual evolutionary change of a liberalizing nature" would become an "interim goal on the way" to the satellites achieving "national independence on democratic foundations." Although the FEC acknowledged that liberation would not come from American military action, the "residue" of the policy remained, as the organization continued to press towards ending Soviet hegemony. By embracing the approach of using cultural infiltration, the FEC noted that "East-West contacts"—including person to person interactions or the exchange of literature—were "extremely valuable" in the effort to advance liberalizing tendencies in the Soviet bloc (Free Europe Committee 1960; Free Europe Committee 1959a). A "broadening" of the FEC contacts program was therefore promoted with the view that "personal encounters" could possibly "achieve political objectives by...non-political means." In the spirit of this strategy, encouraging defections was not viewed as a productive exercise, for it might threaten the plan of "inducing cooperation" on the part of communist regimes (Free Europe Committee 1959).

THE STRATEGIC VALUE OF INNSBRUCK

Ever since the establishment of communist rule across Eastern Europe, sports provided an opportunity for Soviet bloc citizens to travel beyond the Iron Curtain. In particular, elite athletes regarded travel to the West as one of the major perks of the job, regularly getting to see and experience an outside world that was largely sealed off to their fellow countrymen. They may have been accompanied and monitored by state security agents, but they were still able to speak with Western athletes and sample Western culture (Rider and Witherspoon 2018). Yet before long, even the average Soviet bloc citizen could do the same. In the late 1950s and 1960s the communist tourism industry started to expand (Light 2013; Hall 1991). In addition to excursions within and between the satellite nations and the Soviet Union, state controlled travel agencies organized group trips to the West and to sporting events such as the Olympic Games. For instance, thousands of Eastern European tourists, sent in multiple groups, attended the 1960 Summer Olympics in Rome. This fact that did not escape the FEC, which capitalized on the moment by organizing a large scale contact program for the festival (Rider 2016).

By virtue of their location, the 1964 Winter Games were well suited for a similar program. First and foremost, Innsbruck had proximity in its favour. The frontiers of Austria bordered with Czechoslovakia, Hungary and Yugoslavia, and tourism between the states had already been increasing. Second, Austria's capitalist economy was growing from strength to strength. Its imperious mountain ranges, one of its most profitable commodities, attracted a mass of tourists for summer trips and winter skiing. Austria thus presented an "enviable image" to people in Eastern Europe (Farnsworth 1964, 58; Adams 2004). Third, the country had become home to waves of refugees fleeing from communism. The CIA sponsored dozens of East European émigré groups in cities such as Vienna and Salzburg, giving the FEC a pool of motivated people and resources to operate in Innsbruck (Kádár-Lynn 2013). When all these factors combined, Innsbruck presented a far better option for a contact program than the Summer Games in Tokyo later that year (Free Europe Committee 1964f).

By the end of 1963, the Free Europe Committee had located space in Innsbruck to establish a "hospitality center" for the duration of the Winter Games. In theory, it would be open to anyone, be they local or not. But strategically, the head of the FEC's West European Operations Division, Mucio Delgado, placed a "heavy emphasis" on contacting and communicating with Eastern European tourists (Free Europe Committee 1963; Free Europe Committee 1963a). Leading members of the FEC stressed that press coverage of the Games would be extensive, so the organization's "men on the scene" should guard against "untoward incidents" that could be "embarrassing to us." Contact operations had to be done discreetly if they were to done effectively. Careless and aggressive propagandizing with an anti-communist theme could easily be highlighted by socialist countries as an affront to the Olympic spirit. Such work might also dissuade Eastern European tourists from visiting the center, something they would already have do with great caution (Free Europe Committee 1964).

To run the center, the FEC added a further layer of clandestine cover. Although covertly funded through the CIA, Soviet bloc regimes recognized that it was a subversive organization committed to anti-communist outcomes. FEC strategists understood that the East-West contacts program would work more effectively if it were done through other private groups already committed to similar goals (Reisch 2013). To lead the Innsbruck operation, the FEC hired Kazimierz Knap, a well-connected and multi-lingual Polish exile based in Vienna. Knap found a willing Jesuit College in Innsbruck that "wished to engage in similar activities" as the FEC "but had neither the experience nor the personnel to do so." The group provided Knap with free rooms in its youth center—"right in the middle of Innsbruck"—thus hiding the FEC's direct association with the entire project. Knap and his two staff members were given use of an office, a meeting room with a radio and television, and a well-stocked library. A small kitchen also provided visitors with free tea, coffee, wine, soup (provided by the company, *Knorr*), and cheap sandwiches (Free Europe Committee 1963a; Free Europe Committee 1964e).

POLITICS, NATIONALISM, AND THE INNSBRUCK WINTER GAMES

The *IX Olympische Winterspiele* opened on January 29. The organizers of the event proudly labeled the enterprise, the "Simple Games," to capture their economic frugality. "No mad Olympic whirl, no sensationalism, no astronomical construction budget, no gigantic prices, nor publicity at all costs shall warp or mar the great festival of sport," explained the Innsbruck press manager, Bertl Neumann (1962, 50). The austerity, it appears, did not keep people away. Nearly a million spectators flocked to the competitions. For twelve days the historic streets of Innsbruck, bedecked with flags and the Olympic colors, bustled with tourists and athletes enjoying the sights and sounds of the winter carnival ("Memories of Innsbruck" 1964). Among the throng of visitors strolled members of the International Olympic Committee who, "during their intervals of leisure," took pleasure in experiencing "the well-known Tyrolean gaiety." The whole city, noted one observer, was "en fete" ("The Session of the International Olympic Committee at Innsbruck" 1964, 59).

On the eve of the Games, Avery Brundage, the president of the IOC, warned his colleagues about the rising tide of Cold War politics and state intervention associated with the Olympics. "[T]oday governments in many countries attempt to use sport in general, and the Olympic Movement in particular, for personal and partisan ends," he complained. "Let us, with the aid of public opinion, strive to convince government's that sport, like the fine arts, transcends politics" ("Speech by President Avery Brundage" 1964, 60). Brundage had been moaning about this issue for much of his life. At one point he even suggested abolishing national representation at the Games altogether, but garnered no substantial support from the rest of the IOC's members (Guttmann 1984). Given his perspective, Brundage would doubtless have approved of the way, Paul Aste, an Austrian athlete, delivered the Olympic oath on behalf of all the participants at the opening ceremonies. "For the glory of the sports and the honor of our countries," the oath previously read. Aste replaced "countries" with "teams," a symbolic gesture to obviate the nationalism associated with the Games ("Revised oath drops appeal to nationalism" 1964, 32).

It mattered not. The Innsbruck Winter Games, typical of the Cold War era, were surrounded in politics. In America, political leaders uttered customary complaints about the prospects of their national Olympic team and predicated another defeat to the Soviet Union in the overall medal count. The Soviets had "won" in 1956 and 1960. Most Americans expected the same again in 1964 (Hunt 2018). The outspoken senator, Hubert H. Humphrey, issued a dire warning. He complained that organizational strife and insufficient funds severely undermined America's preparations for the Winter and Summer Games, leaving the Soviet Union as favourites to dominate at both festivals. "We may be the laughing stock not only of the Nation, but also of the world, in respect to athletic sports competition," he argued. All the while, the Soviets were pouring resources into sports as "part of a global Red strategy to raise the profile of Moscow's prestige in the eyes of millions of sports enthusiasts" (Congressional Record 1962).

Nicholas Rodis, the special assistant for athletic programs in the U.S. State Department, put pen to paper on the very same issue. After speaking with sports authorities in America, he requested to be sent to Innsbruck to observe the Games so that the government might gain a "better understanding of the problems" the U.S. encountered during the festival. "Our diminishing prestige in Olympic competitions make it imperative that the President, Attorney General and the Secretary of State get a first-hand report on these matter," Rodis intoned (Rodis 1963).

Humphrey and Rodis were not saying anything new. The issue of how to support U.S. athletes at the Olympics had been a dilemma for American politicians ever since the Soviet Union competed at the Games for the first time in 1952. Leading strategists in the White House knew that the Olympics had a significant symbolic value, but they also backed away from promoting Federal intervention. While state-sponsored sport was a feature of the Soviet model—and common throughout the rest of the world—America's Olympic effort had traditionally been organized and funded by the private sphere. Thus, copying the communist model was not the American way and also smacked of outright hypocrisy. Not until 1978 did the government finally reform the nation's Olympic structure by handing the United States Olympic Committee the lucrative commercial rights to the five ring Olympic symbol in America (Hunt 2007; and Cooke and Barney 2018). Until then, the U.S. attempted to exploit the Games for Cold War advantage in secret ways, including the work of the Free Europe Committee.

The Innsbruck Contact Program

The FEC's "hospitality center" opened on the same day as the Winter Games. In order to advertise the facility, Knap arranged for the distribution of thousands of leaflets, hidden within Catholic publications, to local hotels hosting Eastern European tourists. The leaflet, a simple production, stated that the center was staffed by Eastern Europeans and aimed to assist tourists in the Austrian city. When FEC officials realised that this promotional campaign was insufficient, they instructed Knap to personally visit the relevant hotels and to also attend the range of concurrent sporting events. He and his staff even mingled in the crowds for the opening ceremonies. Athletes were especially hard to locate and speak to. Most were busy with competition, monitored by state security, and housed in the Olympic village some distance from the city. Still, the FEC's more proactive strategy paid dividends, as "groups and individuals began to come immediately and repeatedly to the Center" (Free Europe Committee 1964e).

While many visitors stopped by to eat, drink, or watch television, Knap and his staff emphasized the material contained in the center's makeshift library. After all, the FEC stressed the importance of literature to its overall approach to Eastern Europe. Indeed, the organization's book and literature program had grown to a monumental size since its inception in the mid-1950s. Millions of publications, produced on either side of the Iron Curtain, were directly mailed to East Europeans or distributed through various outlets across Europe. The target audience was as broad as the literature chosen. In the course of time, FEC strategists came to realize that while polemical or banned works might strike a chord with the Eastern European intelligentsia, they were less appealing to the average person (Reisch 2013). As such, the literature program despatched items that ranged from *Vogue* magazine and medical dictionaries, to more controversial publications such as Dr. Zhivago and Milovan Đilas', *The New Class*. This stream of "cultural materials," the FEC reasoned, would "res-establish as much as possible the normal flow of ideas, not only between the United States and Eastern Europe, but between Western and Eastern Europe" (Free Europe Committee 1959; Free Europe Committee 1960). One CIA officer involved in the program called it a "secret Marshall Plan for the mind" (Matthews 2003, 409).

The FEC center in Innsbruck was ideal for a literature operation. Tourists could stroll into the facility and read, publications could be taken away by individuals and even transported back home, or addresses could be gleaned and publications sent directly to people who wanted them. The reading room contained approximately five hundred books as well as a plethora of journals, magazines, and newspapers, in German, Hungarian, Polish, Czechoslovakian, Rumanian, Croatian and English languages. A considerable body of this material, approximately 400 books, was donated or loaned by refugee writers representing PEN-in-Exile. Knap estimated that 50-100 people a day entered the library, the majority of whom were Olympic tourists and athletes from Eastern European states. He reported that 1,500 publications were taken home by visitors, and noted that tourists were particularly interested in the literature produced by Eastern European exiles. Of course, not everyone approved of the library's holdings. Some tourists, loyal to the Communist Party, complained about the literature on the persecution of the Polish church (Free Europe Committee 1964e; Free Europe Committee 1964a).

In tandem with the reading room, Knap and his staff organized and engaged in person-to-person contacts with Eastern European tourists and athletes. Again, this was an important component of the FEC's overarching contact strategy. The FEC underscored the value of Soviet bloc travellers interacting and speaking with both Westerners and emigres from Eastern Europe. In the case of the latter, past experience had proven that Eastern European tourists had "showed themselves eager to engage in shop talk and talk of common acquaintances and to enjoy the relaxation of speaking their native tongue with a compatriot of foreign land" (Free Europe Committee 1959). In order to facilitate more of these interactions, the FEC helped organisations and groups to arrange hundreds of initiatives involving the participation of Soviet bloc citizens. Between 1962 and 1965, for instance, the FEC helped to sponsor 180 international conferences, the majority of which were in Western Europe (Reisch 2013).

In many ways, Eastern European tourists in Innsbruck did not need help in this regard. They could meet a diverse range of people simply by watching competitions and navigating the city. In between events, athletes from the Soviet bloc often spent time talking with rivals from the West. Soviet and American athletes regularly exchanged gifts; sometimes they drank vodka. In this sense, international sporting events such as the Olympics facilitated cultural transfer without the need for secret assistance (Keys 2007; Keys 2011; "U.S. Team Goes to Soviet Party," 1964).

The FEC charged Knap and his staff to get candid information on life and political opinions behind the Iron Curtain, and to specifically connect tourists with countrymen living in the West. He and his staff organized numerous meetings and diligently logged the content of the conversations and debates they listened to. The available documents do not mention the names of those interviewed—many refused to provide a name anyway. Some tourists were very cautious and reticent to speak, fearing repercussions upon returning home. Other interviewees, however, were more open, speaking about topics ranging from the communist sports system to standards of medical care in Eastern Europe. Knap found players from the Polish ice-hockey team to be very "sociable." He also observed that many of the interviewees focused on "material" problems at home and the contrast in Austria. They described their admiration for the standard of living in Austria, the possibilities for social advancement, the "abundance of food," and interest in the fashion and style of Austrians. Some Czechoslovakian tourists explained that they were buying shoes, nylon stockings, dresses and gold to take home. An Austrian newspaper even reported that one Polish athlete was caught trying to smuggle 147 pairs of stockings back to Poland (Free Europe Committee 1964b; Free Europe Committee 1964c; Free Europe Committee 1964e).

In addition to the contacts cultivated through the center, the FEC helped Hungarian émigré students living in Innsbruck to invite ten Hungarian students from behind the Iron Curtain to live at their house for the duration of the Olympics. Aside from plying their guests with an array of literature, the hosts attempted to provide the young Hungarians with an enjoyable experience of watching the Winter Games and invited other tourists from the satellite countries to join them. "This concentrated contact with 'Westerners' who spoke their own language," assessed the FEC, "made it possible for the visitors to take back to Hungary a far more thorough knowledge of the West than they could have acquired had they spent their time in Austria among friends from home" (Free Europe Committee 1964e; Free Europe Committee 1964a; Free Europe Committee 1963a).

One thing that most certainly resonated in the Soviet bloc were defections. Since the first Cold War Olympics in 1948, the event had provided athletes and tourists from the Soviet bloc with the chance to defect. One of the most famous mass defections occurred after the 1956 Summer Olympics in Melbourne, when dozens of Hungarians refused to return home. The FEC even helped 34 Hungarians to settle in America. After this episode, communist regimes kept a closer eye on their athletes, but could not completely prevent further departures (Rider 2016; Rider 2013a).

Unsurprisingly, then, a common question asked by dozens of visitors to the center regarded the delicate subject of seeking asylum in Austria. Although the FEC had a strict policy of not encouraging defections, especially after the failure of the Hungarian revolution, the center's staff willingly explained what individuals might expect when seeking asylum, and the complications of being a refugee. Knap predicted that several tourists would stay in Austria. Eventually, this news broke in the Western media, along with the story that an East German tobogganist, Ute Gähler, had defected to West Germany. The press reported that she was making the 25-mile journey from Innsbruck to the West German border ("E. German Girl Defects From Olympic Team" 1964). A week after the Games ended, American diplomats in Austria claimed that 29 Eastern Europeans who attended the Games asked for asylum (U.S. Department of State 1964).

Conclusion

Although Paul Aste's Olympic oath had attempted to quell the political and nationalistic aspects of the Innsbruck Games, it could never eradicate them. Throughout the festival, Americans still nervously noted the mounting number of Soviet medals. During the Games, journalist Sid Ziff of the *Los Angeles Times* declared, "never have Uncle Sam's athletes received such a drubbing as they are getting in the winter Olympics at Innsbruck" (1964, B1). By the end of the Games, the "drubbing" was complete. Nicholas Rodis, who had convinced the State Department to send him to Austria, watched the American performance and lamented that "when we send a team to compete in events like the Olympics it must have a chance to win" ("Brighter Days Ahead for U.S.," 1964, B1).

While America may have lost the athletic propaganda war by some distance, it was more competitive in the fight for the hearts and minds of Olympic tourists. For two weeks, the FEC's operatives in Innsbruck undertook a small but successful cultural program, finding and communicating with hundreds of Eastern European visitors to the Austrian city. Through literature and meetings, they were able to convey flashes of Western culture and, in so doing, reinforce the Cold War objectives and policies of the U.S. government. In the aftermath of the Games, the FEC happily concluded that its hospitality center had "obviously achieved its aims" (Free Europe Committee 1964e). Officers of the organization expressed praise for the "tangible benefits derived" from the project, and assessed that the center was a "source of fruitful East-West contacts" (Free Europe Committee 1964d).

It is hard, if not impossible, to say with any certainty what impact the FEC's center and the work of its staff had in Eastern Europe. How exactly did the literature distributed influence the opinion of those who read it or took it home? To what extent did the meetings and conversations between Soviet bloc citizens and exiles create change in the communist system? No one can say for sure. Yet it is possible to speculate, as some historians have, that Western cultural infiltration played an extremely important role in undermining the communist regimes of the Soviet bloc and contributed to their gradual disintegration. Sporting competitions such as the Olympic Games, notes historian Barbara Keys, should be considered as part and parcel of this process, because they also exposed athletes (and tourists) to alternative ways of living. In essence, the Olympics "opened up a 'back door' to subtle but arguably significant openings to global culture" that challenged the "closed nature of the Soviet system" (Keys 2007, 133).

Although the FEC clearly appreciated the value of the East-West contacts it had funded and arranged at Olympic host cities, the strategy of exploiting the festival in this regard ceased after Innsbruck. FEC planners determined that the 1964 Tokyo Summer Games would be too costly for such a program and did not present the same type of opportunity with regard to the potential volume of Eastern European tourists. The absence of operations in 1968, though not clear in the available records, can most likely be explained by the structural changes in the FEC throughout the 1960s. The organization gradually poured more and more resources into its most visible propaganda arm, Radio Free Europe, while cropping and downsizing its other émigré operations. Then, at the end of the decade, investigative journalists exposed the CIA's state-private network and revealed that the Free Europe Committee was one of the notable recipients of covert government funds. Although the exact amount of government money funnelled to the FEC during its two decades of work is not entirely clear, the figure is believed to be well in excess of $300 million (Kádár-Lynn 2013). Of the various exile initiatives directed by the FEC, only Radio Free Europe survived the subsequent government investigation. The broadcaster became an officially financed arm of the government and continued to broadcast the Olympics for the remainder of the Cold War, much to the frustration of the Soviet bloc (Rider 2015).

Yet aside from the secrets and the intrigue, all of which are so synonymous with the period, the story of the Free Europe Committee's contacts program further illuminates the "total" scope of the Cold War. The protracted ideological stalemate permeated all aspects of the Olympic festival in Innsbruck, from the symbolic combat of the athletes, to the hustle and bustle of tourists wandering the streets of the hosting city. Reaching the population of the Soviet bloc, a controlled society, was always one the greatest challenges for those employed by the Free Europe Committee, but the Olympics provided often unique opportunities for exiles to walk side by side with their "imprisoned" countrymen and often beyond the eyes of chaperones or secret police. For this reason, the Games were an ideal space for trying to communicate ideas, ideas that the Free Europe Committee hoped would be taken back behind the Iron Curtain.

REFERENCES

"Brighter Days Ahead for U.S." *Los Angeles Times*, February, 11. 1964, B1.

Adams, Carly. 2004. "Innsbruck 1964." In *Encyclopedia of the Modern Olympic Movement*, edited by John E. Findling and Kimberly D. Pelle, 345-50. Westport, Connecticut: Greenwood Press.

Congressional Record. 1962. September 25, 1962, Bureau of Educational and Cultural Affairs Historical Collection, Box 92, File 12, University of Arkansas, Fayetteville, Arkansas.

Cooke, Nevada and Barney, Robert. 2018. "Preserving 'the American Way'": Gerald R. Ford, the President's Commission on Olympic Sports, and the Fight Against State-Funded Sport in America." In *Defending the American Way of Life: Sport, Culture, and the Cold War*, edited by Toby C. Rider and Kevin B. Witherspoon, 67-82. Fayetteville: University of Arkansas Press.

Corke, Sarah-Jane. 2006. "George Kennan and the Inauguration of Political Warfare." *The Journal of Conflict Studies* 26, no.1: 101-119.

Dichter, Heather. 2018. "Sport Is Not So Separate From Politics: Diplomatic Manipulation of Germany's Postwar Return to the Olympic Movement." In *Defending the American Way of Life: Sport, Culture, and the Cold War*, edited by Toby C. Rider and Kevin B. Witherspoon, 173-87. Fayetteville: University of Arkansas Press.

"E. German Girl Defects From Olympic Team." *The Washington Post and Times Herald*, February, 10, 1964, A8.

Farnsworth, Clyde A. "Austria bulging with affluence." *New York Times*, January, 10, 1964, 58.

Free Europe Committee. 1959. "Free Europe Committee and East-West Contacts." June 10, 1959, C.D. Jackson: Papers, 1931-67, Series II Time INC. File, 1933-64, Subseries A. Alphabetical File, 1933-64, Box 53, (2) "Free Europe Committee, 1959," Dwight D. Eisenhower Presidential Library, Abilene, Kansas.

———. 1959a. "Plan of FEOP Operation in Europe." December 1959, RFE/RL INC. Corporate Records, Box 197, (7) "Free Europe Organizations and Publications," Hoover Institution Archives, Stanford University, California.

———. 1960. "Evaluation of Current FEC Mission." February, 18, 1960, C.D. Jackson: Papers, 1931-67, Series II Time INC. File, 1933-64, Subseries A. Alphabetical File, 1933-64, Box 53, (2) "Free Europe Committee, 1960," Dwight D. Eisenhower Presidential Library, Abilene, Kansas.

———. 1963. "Letter from Mucio Delgado to John Richardson." November 13, 1963, RFE/RL INC. Corporate Records, Box 245, (6) "Olympic Games General, 1963-64," Hoover Institution Archives, Stanford University, California.

———. 1963a. "Letter from John Leich to Mucio Delgado." November 15, 1963, RFE/RL INC. Corporate Records, Box 245, (6) "Olympic Games General, 1963-64," Hoover Institution Archives, Stanford University, California.

———. 1964. "Letter from Gordon Davis to John Page." January 14, 1964, RFE/RL INC. Corporate Records, Box 245, (6) "Olympic Games General, 1963-64," Hoover Institution Archives, Stanford University, California.

———. 1964a. "WEOD Working Document Report—Olympic Program and Pen-In-Exile." February 7, 1964, RFE/RL INC. Corporate Records, Box 245, (6) "Olympic Games General, 1963-64," Hoover Institution Archives, Stanford University, California.

———. 1964b. "Innsbruck Olympic 1964, Part II." April 2, 1964, RFE/RL INC. Corporate Records, Box 245, (6) "Olympic Games General, 1963-64," Hoover Institution Archives, Stanford University, California.

———. 1964c. "Innsbruck Olympic 1964, Part III." April 2, 1964, RFE/RL INC. Corporate Records, Box 245, (6) "Olympic Games General, 1963-64," Hoover Institution Archives, Stanford University, California.

———. 1964d. "WEOD Information Report—Innsbruck Olympics, 1964." April 14, 1964, RFE/RL INC. Corporate Records, Box 245, (6) "Olympic Games General, 1963-64," Hoover Institution Archives, Stanford University, California.

———. 1964e. "WEOD Nugget Report—Innsbruck Winter Olympics, 1964." May 8, 1964, RFE/RL INC. Corporate Records, Box 245, (6) "Olympic Games General, 1963-64," Hoover Institution Archives, Stanford University, California.

———. 1964f. "Letter from Smith to Richardson." September, 28, 1964, RFE/RL INC. Corporate Records, Box 245, (6) "Olympic Games General, 1963-64," Hoover Institution Archives, Stanford University, California.

Guttmann, Allen. 2015. *The Games Must Go On: Avery Brundage And The Olympic Movement.* New York: Columbia University Press.

Hall, Derek R. 1991. *Tourism and Economic Development in Eastern Europe and the Soviet Union.* London: Belhaven Press.

Hixon, Walter L. 1997. *Parting the Curtain: Propaganda, Culture, and the Cold War, 1945-1961.* New York: St. Martin's Press.

Hunt, Thomas M. 2007. "Countering the Soviet Threat in the Olympic Medals Race." *International Journal of the History of Sport* 24, no. 6: 796-818.

———. 2018. "Sport and American Foreign Policy During the 1960s." In *Defending the American Way of Life: Sport, Culture, and the Cold War*, edited by Toby C. Rider and Kevin B. Witherspoon, 189-203. Fayetteville: University of Arkansas Press.

Johnson, A. Ross. 2010. *Radio Free Europe and Radio Liberty: The CIA Years and Beyond.* Stanford, California: Stanford University Press.

Kádár-Lynn, Katalin. 2013. "At War While at Peace: United States Cold War Policy and the National Committee for a Free Europe, Inc." In *The Inauguration of Organized Political Warfare: Cold War Organizations Sponsored by the National Committee for a Free Europe/Free Europe Committee*, edited by Katalin Kádár-Lynn, 7-70. California: Helena History Press.

Keys, Barbara. 2006. *Globalizing Sport: National Rivalry and International Community in the 1930s.* Cambridge, Massachusetts: Harvard University Press.

———. 2007. "The Soviet Union, Cultural Exchange and the 1956 Melbourne Olympic Games." In *Sport zwischen Ost und West*, edited by Malz, Rohdewald, and Wiederkehr, 131-45. Osnabrück: Fibre.

———. 2011. "The 1960 Rome Summer Olympics: Birth of a New World?" In *Myths and Milestones in the History of Sport*, edited by Stephen Wagg, 287-303. London: Palgrave Macmillan.

Light, Duncan. 2013. "'A Medium of Revolutionary Propaganda': the State and Tourism Policy in the Romanian People's Republic, 1947-1965." *Journal of Tourism History* 5, no. 2: 185-200.

Lucas, Scott. 1999. *Freedom's War: The American Crusade Against the Soviet Union.* New York, New York: New York University Press.

Matthews, John P. C. 2003. "The West's Secret Marshall Plan for the Mind." *International Journal of Intelligence and Counterintelligence* 16, no. 3: 409-27.

"Memories of Innsbruck." *Olympic Review* (May, 1964), 72

Mickelson, Sig. 1983. *America's Other Voice: The Story of Radio Free Europe and Radio Liberty.* New York: Praeger Publishers.

Miscamble, Wilson D. 1992. *George F. Kennan and the Making of American Foreign Policy, 1947-1950.* Princeton, New Jersey: Princeton University Press.

Müller, Norbert, editor. 2000. *Pierre de Coubertin 1863-1937: Olympism: Selected Writings.* Lausanne: International Olympic Committee.

Puddington, Arch. 2000. *Broadcasting Freedom: The Cold War Triumph of Radio Free Europe and Radio Liberty*. Lexington, Kentucky: The University of Kentucky Press.
Reisch, Alfred A. 2013. *Hot books in the Cold War: the CIA-funded secret book distribution program behind the Iron Curtain*. New York: Central European University Press.
"Revised oath drops appeal to nationalism." *New York Times*, January, 30, 1964, 32.
Rider, Toby C. 2013a. "Eastern Europe's Unwanted: Exiled Athletes and the Olympic Games, 1948-1964." *Journal of Sport History* 40, no. 3: 435-453.
———. 2013b. "The Cold War Activities of the Hungarian National Sports Federation." In *The Inauguration of Organized Political Warfare: Cold War Organizations Sponsored by the National Committee for a Free Europe/Free Europe Committee*, edited by Katalin Kádár Lynn, 515-546. Saint Helena, CA: Helena History Press.
———. 2013c. "Political Warfare in Helsinki: American Covert Strategy and the Union of Free Eastern European Sportsmen." *International Journal of the History of Sport* 30, no.13: 1493-1507.
Rider, Toby C. and Llewellyn, Matthew P. 2015. "The Five Rings and the 'Imagined Community': Nationalism and the Modern Olympic Games." *SAIS Review of International Affairs* 35, no. 2: 21-32.
Rider, Toby C. 2015. "Filling the Information Gap: Radio Free Europe-Radio Liberty and the Politics of Accreditation at the 1984 Los Angeles Olympic Games." *International Journal of the History of Sport* 32, no. 1: 37-52.
———. 2016. *Cold War Games: Propaganda, the Olympics, and U.S. Foreign Policy*. Urbana: The University of Illinois Press.
Rider, Toby C. and Witherspoon, Kevin B. 2018. "Making Contact With the Captive Peoples, The Eisenhower Administration, Cultural Infiltration, and Sports Tours to Eastern Europe." *Journal of Sport History* 45, no. 3: 297-312.
Rodis, Nicholas. 1963. "Letter to Donald Cook." November 19, 1963, Bureau of Educational and Cultural Affairs Historical Collection, Box 90, File 9, University of Arkansas, Fayetteville, Arkansas.
Sarantakes, Nicholas Evan. 2009. "Moscow Versus Los Angeles: the Nixon White House Wages Cold War in the Olympic Selection Process." *Cold War History* 9, no.1: 135-157.
———. 2011. *Dropping the Torch: Jimmy Carter, the Olympic Boycott, and the Cold War*. New York, New York: Cambridge University Press.
Shaw, Tony. 2001. "The Politics of Cold War Culture." *Journal of Cold War Studies* 3, no. 3 (Fall): 59.
"Speech by President Avery Brundage." *Olympic Review* (May, 1964), 60-62.
"The Session of the International Olympic Committee at Innsbruck." *Olympic Review* (May, 1964), 59.
Tudda, Chris. 2005. "'Reenacting the Story of Tantalus': Eisenhower, Dulles, and the Failed Rhetoric of Liberation." *Journal of Cold War Studies* 7, no. 4 (Fall): 3-35.
U.S. Department of State. 1964. "Austrian Matters." February, 20, 1964, Record Group 59, Central Foreign Policy Files, 1964-66, Box 19AA, National Archives, College Park, Maryland.
"U.S. Team Goes to Soviet Party." *The Washington Post and Times Herald*, February, 8, 1964, B4.
Wilford, Hugh. 2008. *The Mighty Wurlitzer: How the CIA Played America*. Cambridge, Massachusetts: Harvard University Press.
Ziff, Sid. "Red peril is real." *Los Angeles Times*, February, 3, 1964, B1.

Chapter 4

How Fears Changed the Games: Of Terror, Security and Costs

Jörg Krieger

Introduction

Constant threats and attacks on sport events have made sport´s stakeholders conscious about terrorism as a dark side of sport. In November 2015, the international football friendly match between France and Germany in the *Stade de France* in St. Denis, Paris, was scene to the first explosions during terror attacks that later erupted the entire city of Paris. As a result of such incidents, security and counter-terrorism strategies have been implemented as core concepts in the organization of mega sport events (Giulianotti and Klauser 2012). In some cases, preventive measures have led to successful operations ahead of sport events. For example, ahead of the 2016 Rio Olympic Games, Brazilian police arrested twelve people suspected of planning terrorist acts during the time of the Olympics (Yan, Jones and Darlington 2016). Nevertheless, fears of terror remain a constant feature in the preparation and staging phases and lead to major challenges for event organizers and governing bodies of sport alike.

The Olympic Games as the world´s biggest sporting event are perhaps most of all affected by such developments and in the last decades security costs have risen exponentially. This development has led to the emergence of a new fear amongst the populations of potential host cities. In recent years, various negative referenda have resulted in cancellations of Olympic bids. In Germany, local citizens have rejected two bids, for the 2022 Winter Olympic Games (in Munich) and the 2024 Summer Olympic Games (in Hamburg). An omnipresent argument by those campaigning against the Olympics was that of high costs, caused mainly by rising security budgets.

Against this background, this chapter details the development of Olympic security from the terror attack at the 1972 Munich Olympic Games to rising security costs at the Olympic Games in the 21st century. It highlights the emergence of safety fears amongst various Olympic stakeholders, with a specific focus on the International Olympic Committee (IOC) and the local organizing committees. I argue that those fears resulted in the IOC becoming increasingly anxious about security and the requirement for Olympic hosts to compile sophisticated security packages in cooperation with national and international authorities. This development and the resulting financial gigantism of the Olympic Games has led local residents to reject the possibility of hosting the event, as has been witnessed on a regular basis in current bidding processes for Olympic Games.

TERMINOLOGY

It is important to distinguish between the terms "terror" and "terrorism" when exploring security aspects of sporting events. Terror defines a policy of repression, for example by totalitarian regimes. In contrast, terrorism describes a tool by non-state actors/groups to fight a state or another group. David Andrews, Jamie Schulz and Michael Silk (2010) argue that this differentiation is necessary when exploring the political history of the Olympic Games as there have been multiple incidents of "terrorist" acts by the Olympic state against the entire—or parts—of the host populace. The political regimes ahead of the 1968 Mexico City Olympic Games and the 1988 Seoul Olympic Games violently crushed (Mexico) and suppressed (South Korea) student protests (Spaaij 2016). Others claim that the operations by the authoritarian Chinese state ahead, during and after the 2008 Beijing Olympic Games can be characterized as terrorist acts (Andrews, Schulz and Silk 2010).

This chapter uses the term "terrorism" not as terrorism by the state or terrorism that is supported by states, but terrorism exercised by groups that do not have any governmental power (Pfahl-Traughber 2016). This does not mean that the other forms of terrorism or alternative security threats to sporting events are not equally important to explore. However, the adopted perspective that investigates the safety concerns within the Olympic Movement requires a focus on potential external terrorist threats. The rationale for this is due to that such incidents caused the wide-ranging debates inside the IOC that eventually led to coordinated security operations at the Games. The resultant security measures aimed to protect the values of the Olympic Movement through the pre-identification of sources of threats that have effective means to threaten those said values.

These considerations also explain the starting point for the elaborations in this chapter that begin with the terror attacks during the 1972 Munich Olympic Games: the Munich attacks were the first "terrorist" threat to the Olympic Movement. Moreover, the tragic events in 1972 led the IOC to give the task to secure the Olympic Games to the Organizing Committees (Duckworth and Hunt 2016)—alongside wide-ranging implications and cost increases for potential host cities due to the need for security operations.

FEARS OF TERROR: THE MUNICH TERROR ATTACK AND ITS IMMEDIATE CONSEQUENCES

On September 6, 1972, the terror attack by the Palestinian terror organization *Black September* that kidnapped Israeli athletes inside the Olympic village shocked the world of sport and the watching audience. The attack ended with the death of eleven Israeli hostages, five kidnappers and one German police officer (Schiller and Young 2010). Whilst German state officials and the security service had received hints about a potential attack prior to the Olympic Games, the attack was unexpected for the main stakeholders in the Olympic Movement and destroyed the illusion of the Olympic Games as a peaceful global sporting event (Krüger 1997). That said, it is no coincidence that the Olympic Games became target for a terrorist attack. Shortly after the attack, the Palestinian National Liberation Movement *El Fatah* claimed that sport was the "religion of the Western world" and therefore the terrorists used the most popular event of this religion to receive the world's attention (Guttmann 2002). This strategy proved successful in Munich—over 900 million television viewers witnessed the attacks and the rescue attempts by the German police force, provoking fears about terrorism worldwide.

One might have expected that the IOC would have launched a detailed investigation into the attack from Munich. However, this was not the case. Whilst the attack resulted in the individual members of the IOC becoming aware, in the worst of circumstances, about terror threats on the Olympic Games, the discussions in the IOC Executive Board during and after the terror attack reveal that the leading IOC members were mainly concerned with practical questions of scheduling and "selling the Olympic spirit" (Duckworth and Hunt 2016). After the Games and the take-over of the IOC presidency through Lord Michael Morris Killanin in 1973, an increased awareness about the need for security measures emerged, although the internal IOC discussions mainly focused on protection for IOC members rather than the athletes. Moreover, as had already been the case during the Munich Games when the IOC members thought that the attack was a national political matter, the IOC tasked the Organizing Committees with securing the Olympic Games.

For the Games of the subsequent Olympiad in Innsbruck (winter) and Montreal (summer), the events in Munich had organizational and financial consequences linked to aspects of security. In Austria and in Canada, armed forces secured the Games leading to the new public perception of the Olympic Games as a high security area. Thus, those Games in 1976 mark the beginning of military forces becoming highly involved in the organization of the Games. Moreover, in Montreal a high wire fence surrounded the Olympic Village and the identities of all people entering the Olympic Village were checked. The Organizing Committee concluded in its *Official Report* that "Olympism survived" inside of the Olympic Village (Organizing Committee of the 1976 Montreal Olympic Games 1978, p. 279), implying that the increased security efforts did not have a negative influence on the athletes' experiences. This evaluation was acknowledged by the IOC, which felt confirmed in its belief that the Organizing Committees could deal independently with security.

Today, the 1976 Montreal Olympic Games are considered to be the first Olympics with a visible security operation (Clément 2017). Against the backdrop of the Munich terror attacks, the IOC did not only accept the changing image of the Olympic Games, it also encouraged the Organizing Committees to install security measures. That said, security was not at the forefront of the IOC's concerns despite the incidents from Munich. Rather, the selling of the Olympic spirit to a global audience remained its main consideration (Duckworth and Hunt 2016). The fear over the Olympic Games losing attractiveness appeared stronger than concerns about safety.

SECURITY AND POLITICS (1976-1988)

The time period between the 1980 and the 1988 Olympic Games is characterized as the period of politicization of the Olympic Movement (Gutmann 2000). The two big politically-motivated boycotts in 1980 (Moscow) and 1984 (Los Angeles) as well as the political tensions on the Korean peninsula ahead of the 1988 Seoul Olympic Games fall into this decade. Such political dimensions obviously impacted the security of the respective Olympic Games and elevated the extent of the security operations to a new level. Hence, it was less terror attacks but rather the Olympic Games' apparent symbolic significance for global politics that increased security measures.

At the Olympic Games

The Soviet invasion into Afghanistan in December 1979 caused the first major political Olympic boycott that took place for the 1980 Moscow Olympic Games (Torres and Dyreson 2005). The boycott was led by the United States and meant that the Soviet's biggest political rivals and potentially many American Olympic tourists remained absent from the Games. Nevertheless, the preparatory security operations focused on the separation of Soviet citizens from foreigners. This was in stark contrast to the security measures in 1976 because Soviet and foreign intelligence did not anticipate any significant danger from terrorist attacks. Thus, fears focused more so on politics rather than terrorism.

That said, an IOC meeting during the Moscow Games proved to be a watershed moment in Olympic security. At the 1980 IOC Session, a key figure in IOC security aspects appeared when Ashwini Kumar from India was elected as IOC member. Kumar had been a long-serving member of India´s police force and encouraged IOC President Juan Antonio Samaranch to invest more resources into security. In 1983, he was appointed IOC Security Delegate (IOC, 1983). Kumar resurfaced the IOC's interest in the subject and brought the topic of security back into the internal agenda. He was concerned that the IOC headquarters and the IOC President could become a target of a terror attack and recommended personal security for leading IOC officials. Moreover, Kumar, together with IOC President Samaranch´s attention to potential terror threats, shifted the responsibility of security operations from the Organizing Committees to the national governments of hosting Olympic events.

As a result of Kumar´s appointment, the IOC began to adopt the role of the liaison between the different stakeholders involved (Duckworth and Hunt 2016). Such talks took place for the first time ahead of the 1984 Los Angeles Olympic Games when Kumar presented several reports and a list of potential international and national terror threats, composing mainly of domestic terror groups. Consequently, security in Los Angeles differed considerably from the Moscow Games through the involvement of a major intergovernmental security system. Already at the 1981 IOC Session, the organizers reported that "there was a complete programme to ensure the safety of athletes attending the Games with [an] all governmental security organization, at state, city, county and federal level" (IOC 1981b, p. 8). Described by Robert Lindsey of the *New York Times* as the "largest and most expensive ever imposed on a peacetime enterprise in the United States", it cost the Organizing Committee, the federal and the national governments more than $150 million to secure the Games. The central part of the Olympic security system was a sophisticated accreditation system with identity cards that were handed out to more than 20,000 people. As in 1976 and 1980, the security mechanisms proved effective - no major incidents occurred at the 1984 Games. Nevertheless, the Soviet Union appeared not convinced about the security in place in Los Angeles and eventually boycotted the Games. It stated fears about the lack of safety for its citizens, both participants and spectators, as the official reason.

Whilst research has mostly focused on the boycotts of the 1980 and 1984 Olympics, the third Olympic Games of the decade, held in Seoul, South Korea, in 1988, posed the biggest security threats to the Games due to the geo-political situation on the Korean peninsula. The IOC anticipated issues with North Korea, aware that the country "had the capability of turning the Games into a bloodbath" (Radchenko 2011). After awarding the Games to South Korea in 1981, the North Korean government approached the IOC at various times with threats to boycott and sabotage the 1988 Olympic Games if three requirements were not met: 1) the joint organization of the Olympic Games; 2) an equal split of staging the events between the two countries; 3) a change of the official name to "Korea Pyongyang Seoul Olympic Games" (Ibid.). Kumar advised Samaranch to enter talks with the North Koreans and be prepared to hand some events to the North in order to avoid disturbances. Several talks took place between 1985 and 1988, in which the IOC offered North Korea the staging of up to three Olympic events. However, the North Korean officials remained stubborn, constantly demanding more events and recognition. Once the discussions did not make any progress in the months prior to the Games, Pyongyang reacted violently. In September 1986, agents instructed by the North Korean government triggered a bomb explosion at Gimpo International Airport a week before the 1986 Asian Games in Seoul (Lee 2010). Later, North Korea supported political protests in South Korea and on November 29, 1987, North Korean agents bombed a *Korean Air* flight, killing 155 people. The attacks did not only target South Korean civilians. IOC President Samaranch received threatening letters such as those from the "Mundungsan Death-Defying Corps", making violent statements on potential disruptions of the Olympic Games. In response to global concerns about security in Seoul, governmental agencies responded. For example, the United States Congress' Committee on Foreign Affairs sent a delegation to Seoul to investigate the security operations (Fascell 1988).

Due to anticipated violence from North Korea but also other sources such as the Japanese Red Army (JRA) and the LPO, a total of 112,009 personnel including trained volunteers was deployed to secure the Olympic Games (Kumar 1988). The security planning began already during the bidding phase, led by the National Security Planning Agency (NSPA). Another political measure included that of contacting the Soviet Union to instruct North Korea to refrain from terrorist acts (Cho 2009). The South Korean security authorities also closely cooperated with foreign intelligence organizations to exchange information on possible terrorist threats. Eventually, the 1988 Seoul Olympic Games did not experience any major security threats during the staging of the event. Hence, Kumar summarizes rightly:

The Republic of Korea was a daring choice for staging the Olympic Games in 1988, given western concerns about the ability of Korea to provide the requisite degree and standard of security at the Games. These concerns, however, ignored the security skills being honed in Korea (Kumar 1988).

Clearly, staging Olympic Games from the 1980s onwards demanded political maneuvering as much as heavy financial investments into security.

A Permanent Olympic Site?

Academic literature to-date has typically posited the idea of a permanent Olympic site as a counter-measure to host nations misusing the Olympic Games for political reasons, although the topic is equally pertinent to discourse on safety concerns. This suggestion by Greek politicians and sport officials foresaw hosting the Olympic Games in the same location on a regular basis, mainly to circumvent the political controversies surrounding the Olympic Games in 1980s and to reduce the costs for the organizers.

The initial suggestion by Greek Prime Minister Constantine Karamanlis following the conclusion of the 1976 Montreal Olympic Games was rejected by the IOC Session in 1977 (Albanidis, Barney and Choutas 2007). However, following the discussions in the United States on a potential boycott of the 1980 Olympic Games, the proposal reappeared on the agenda of the IOC. The idea found support from various politicians such as US President Jimmy Carter, Australian Prime Minister Malcolm Fraser, West-German Foreign Minister Hans-Dietrich Genscher and the *European Council* (Ibid.). Despite such political backing, the IOC postponed detailed discussions again until the Olympic Congress in Baden-Baden in 1981. There, the IOC under its then new President Samaranch debated the topic "The Future of the Olympic Games" (IOC 1981a). Prior to that, Samaranch had already sent queries on the topic to IOC members, the NOCs and the IFs; with the responses presenting only limited support for the idea of a permanent site. Eventually, the IOC put the idea on the shelf once again. The proposal reemerged briefly after the 1984 Los Angeles Olympic Games and again the IOC informed the Greek government that it would study the proposal in detail. However, whilst the media continue to occasionally pick up the topic of a permanent Olympic site ahead of Olympic Games, the IOC has thus far never dealt in detail with the idea again (Albanidis, Barney & Choutas, 2007).

From International to Domestic Terror

As previously outlined, whereas domestic terror attacks had already been considered a threat at the 1984 and 1988 Olympics, the issue only continued to demand greater attention from security operators at the two Summer Olympic Games in the next decade.

The Catalan city of Barcelona became the IOC-chosen city to host the first Summer Olympic Games in Western Europe following the 1972 Munich Olympic Games. Kumar identified two specific challenges for security preparations already in

1989. First, he considered the difficult political and administrative relationship between Barcelona and Madrid an issue that required the IOC's attention. Second, he perceived the Basque separatist organization *Euzkadi Ta Askatasuna* (ETA) and the Catalan organization *Terra Lliure* (Kumar 1989; IOC 1991) the main terror threats. Attacks by ETA then disrupted the preparations for the Olympic Games continuously and killed a total of 50 people in 1991. ETA also claimed responsibility for an arson attack on a hotel close to the Olympic Village two months ahead of the Games (Spaaij 2016). Whilst a significant part of the security preparations focused on the protection of the Olympic events and facilities during Games time, the Spanish authorities also took severe measures against ETA in the months leading up to the Olympic Games. Eventually, those activities led the security forces to no longer feel resigned to potential ETA disruptions during the Olympic Games (Riding 1992). In total, the fears of domestic terror threats led to the deployment of 12,000 national policemen, 3,000 local police officers and an additional 10,000 military personnel for the 1992 Olympic Games. The official costs for security operations accumulated to approximately $210 million (IOC 1992). Athletes from the United States and from Israel received special security inside the Olympic Village and during transportation from the Spanish authorities due to requests from the respective governments (Riding 1992).

At the 1996 Atlanta Olympic Games, the local Organizing Committee and the IOC had to realize that the global popularity of the Olympic Games and the growing public attention to the event was still an effective platform for terror threats, despite massively increased security efforts. The US-American Eric Rudolph abused the attention for a political protest when he triggered two explosions in Atlanta's Centennial Park that killed two and injured more than 100 people. Rudolph's action was motivated by his rejection of the US-American politics regarding abortion. The pipe bomb could have been more devastating had it not been spotted prior to the explosion, allowing for authorities to have already started evacuating members of the public (Samaranch 1996). Despite the fatality of the incident, the IOC quickly informed the public that the park was not part of an Olympic venue and outside the security area of the Organizing Committee.

Whilst the 1996 Olympic Games will partly be remembered for the terror incident, the security operations continued the trend of increasing efforts and rising costs. The federal government alone contributed $101 million to a total of around $200 million official safety- and security-related projects. In February 1996, a few months ahead of the event, Kumar heavily praised the employed Olympic security systems:

> To sum up the aspects of Olympic Security that I reviewed [sic] bore signs of sound planning and meticulous attention to details. Sound organizational plans have been laid and cooperation sought from all and sundry to the mobilization of manpower, incentive training and assembling this state of the arts technologies to support security (Kumar 1996, p. 5).

Without question, Kumar's findings give an insight into the expectations of the IOC but also the realities of Olympic security by the second half of the 1990s. Sophisticated, military-like operations that involved authorities of all governmental levels had replaced the simplistic efforts by the Organizing Committees with little state support. The rapidly evolving gigantism that led to an increased global exposure, but also a rise of spectator numbers at the Olympic events themselves, required large security operations. Fears had expanded to worries of domestic violence, individual attackers and terrorist attacks by transnational terror groups because the Olympic Games had been the stage for these three forms of violence throughout the last third of its 20th century history.

Such fears and responsive strategies could also be witnessed at the 2000 Sydney Olympic Games, constituting the first in the new millennium. Even though Australia was considered a low security threat, the Sydney Games saw the largest security operation in Australia's history (Toohey and Taylor 2012). In contrast to previous approaches, the Australian authorities put great effort into surveilling Olympic visitors within and outside the Olympic venues. New surveillance cameras, computer networks, CCTV, satellites and other technologies were installed to undertake the surveillance efforts (Ibid.). From as early as 1997, individual groups were monitored. However, for the first time the security operations were also criticized heavily in the run up to the Olympic Games. Helen Lenskyj reports that the Australian anti-Olympic groupings were concerned about the surveillance and disturbing securization of Sydney's citizens (Lenskyj 2002). Whilst no significant security incidents occurred in Sydney, the surveillance infrastructure was kept after the Olympic Games (Toohey and Taylor 2012).

GLOBAL ISSUES AFFECT THE OLYMPICS

In retrospect, the security measures at the 2000 Sydney Olympic Games appear trivial compared to all following Olympic Games. The trigger for a significant rise in security operations at the Olympic Games were the 9/11 terror attacks on the World Trade Center in New York City. The attack came only a few months before the opening of the 2002 Winter Olympic Games in Salt Lake City that had, with nearly $200 million already in the early planning phase, the highest anticipated security budget of any Winter Olympic Games (IOC 2001). The 9/11 attacks shifted the fears surrounding the security of the Olympic Games back onto the global dimension. In response to the attacks, the IOC's Coordination Commission held an emergency meeting in October 2001, in which it concluded that security had to be made "extremely strong" but that sufficient standards were met for the Games to go ahead (IOC, 2002a). As a result, the 2002 Winter Olympic Games developed into the largest domestic security operation ever undertaken in the United States (Decker et al. 2005). In total, more than $310 million was spent on securing the event, meaning that the security budget in Salt Lake City more than doubled that of Atlanta in 1996.

Understandably, the 9/11 attacks also influenced the staging of the 2004 Athens Olympic Games in Greece. Athens had been more a romantic choice by the IOC than one of a belief in a flawless organization, but against the background of global terror threats, the Greek security operations were in the spotlight and required considerable expansion in the face of global fears of terror. This was regarded as a very negative development by the IOC, which had to acknowledge that "the need for more security (…) was sadly now a very significant part of the games budget" (IOC 2002b). Such rising costs proved an extreme challenge for a financially weak country like Greece. However, within the global environment of terror fears, Athens had no choice but to invest heavily in its security operations. After all, citizens from all over the globe were to be hosted in the Greek capital. On the organizational level, the Greek organizers built a global alliance with France, Germany, Israel, Spain, the United States, Great Britain, and Australia that together comprised an "Olympics Advisory Security Team" (Samatas 2007). The Greek authorities also decided to acquire state-of-the-art security and surveillance technology made in the United States. 70,000 military and security staff went on patrol by the start of the Olympic Games. The final security costs are estimated at $1.5 billion and therewith considerably higher than at any previous Olympic Games (Ibid). The age of big spending on security budgets had begun.

The security bill for the following Summer Olympic Games in Beijing, China, in 2008 is "widely believed to have topped the amount spent in Athens" (Yu, Klauser and Chan 2009). Some authors estimate that the security budget was more than an astonishing $6 billion (Sugden 2012). This is despite the fact that the 9/11 attacks did not have a direct impact on China (Samatas 2011). Instead the Chinese fears focused on Muslim separatists and the autonomy movement in Tibet. Such concerns proved reasonable when between March and August 2008 pro-Tibet and pro-Chinese government supporters and international human rights activists clashed during the Olympic torch relay (Horne and Whannel 2010). Not only the local organizers but the IOC and one of the Olympic Movement's most visible symbols, the Olympic fire, were heavily affected by the violence.

The security operations in Beijing focused on two main aspects: removals and military operations. *Human Rights Watch* documented that the Chinese governments increased detentions of political dissidents such as human rights activities and pro-Tibet campaigners. Other efforts included the removal of local criminals and robbers as well as the confiscation of illegal explosives, guns and ammunition (Yu, Klauser and Chan 2009). The centralized, national government-led security operations also led to the Olympic facilities becoming "overtly militarized" zones (Samatas 2011). A 100,000 person anti-terrorist unit had been installed with a specialized 300 person counter-terrorism unit. In contrast to Athens, the Chinese did not hesitate to make their military and security efforts visible. Despite their extent, the security operations in Athens in 2004 had been discreet. However, in Beijing, the tight security measures were clearly noticeable. For example, anti-aircraft missiles were employed at both Games: in Beijing they were located in close proximity to the Olympic Stadium, in Athens, situated a long distance away from the Olympic Park (Ibid.).

Global terror fears dominated the security preparations ahead of the 2012 London Olympic Games. British authorities recognized terrorism as the major threat to security, placing this ahead of local criminals, public disorder and national extremism (Spaaj 2016). A large part of the concerns was triggered by the terrorist bombings that occurred in London on July 7, 2005, killing 52 people and injuring more than 700. The attack took place the day after London had been awarded the 2012 Olympic Games and created a constant public link between terror and the Games. In view of such, it was almost impossible for critics to argue against supersize security to respond to the potential terror threats (Sugden 2012). Hence, there was little public opposition against the installation of wide-ranging surveillance and security operations. A total of 89,000 police officers were on duty every day during the Games (Fussey 2015). Air and maritime defenses were installed to combat potential external threats but for the first time in Olympic history there was also a high emphasis on IT security. Whilst potential threats could be controlled through the installed security measures and no major incidents occurred, the security budget again erupted. Some reports indicate that the total costs for securing the 2012 London Olympic Games were as high as $3.1 billion (Houlihan and Giulianotti 2012). This accounts for between 15 and 20 per cent of the total costs for staging the Olympic Games. The security situation ahead of the London Games caught a lot of public attention when the official security services provider G4S announced that it could not deliver the number of security personnel as originally agreed (Fussey 2015). As a consequence, an extra 3,500 military troops were deployed to secure the Games, leading to an increased perceived militarization of the event.

The attacks in Paris on November 13, 2015, which killed 130 people, have again triggered fears concerning safety at major sporting events ahead of the 2016 Rio de Janeiro Olympic Games (Spaaj 2016). However, the security preparations had already been well underway as the IOC and local Organizing Committee attempted to stage the first Olympic Games on the South American continent. Already in the official bidding documents, the Bidding Committee had shown much awareness for potential security concerns with great emphasis on promising "safe" Olympic Games" (Barbassa 2017). The fears focused in particular on potential domestic violence and local crimes. Brazil´s economic crisis and politically unstable situation led popular demonstrations and civil disturbances to become a major concern for the authorities (Visacro 2017). The need for wide-ranging safety procedures was on display when during the 2013 FIFA Confederations Cup, the first of three major international sporting events held in Brazil between 2013 and 2016, more than two million Brazilians demonstrated—partly violently—against corruption and police violence. In an attempt to combat the domestic violence, the City of Rio de Janeiro demolished residencies in unsafe areas, in particular within the Favelas (Freemann and Burgos 2017). The Rio Games also followed the trend to deploy a great number of security personnel for the event, including police forces and military personnel. In total, 88,000 safety professionals were working during Games time in Rio (Social Communication Secretariat of the Office of the President of Brazil 2016). In order to undertake preventive measures to combat terrorism, an "Antiterrorism Law" was sanctioned in March 2016 as Brazil did not have any regulatory instrument to define terrorism previously in place (Visacro 2017). The Brazilian authorities also continued the trend of growing IT security and online security checks for all spectators of Olympic events as the Brazilian government attempted to check all names against a database of people with alleged terrorism links (Gregory 2016).

The brief summaries of the security operations at the respective Summer Olympic Games in the 21st century demonstrate that the Olympic stakeholders' security fears rose dramatically due to international terror threats. Without question, the anti-terror operations required the biggest share of the ever-increasing security budget of Olympic hosts. Hence, the security costs exploded following the terror attacks in the United States, the United Kingdom and Spain in the 2000s. That said, it is equally important to consider the socio-political environments of host cities when discussing Olympic Games security operations.

CONSEQUENCES OF COST ERUPTIONS

Security investments are not sustainable and they do not produce any future economic revenues. However, they are indispensable to stage mega sport events in the present day and constitute a key concern for a sport organization such as the IOC already during the bidding process (Houlihan and Giulianotti 2012). Bidding cities must therefore calculate security costs in their original financial plans, leading to high projected costs for all involved stakeholders. The cost eruptions as a result of safety operations have led to new "fears" on staging the Olympic Games. In the last years, the majority of the population in potential host cities has rejected—when asked—the organization of the Olympic Games.

Coincidentally, as the site of the most devastating terror attack on the Olympic Games (1972) and the most politically misused Olympic Games (1936), Germany serves as an excellent example for the current climate of fear towards hosting costs. Amongst the top eight countries in all-time Olympic medals, Germany is the only nation that did not host either the winter or summer edition of the Olympic Games in the 21st century (France has been awarded the 2024 Olympic Games, which will be held in Paris). In fact, the 1972 Munich Olympic Games were the last Olympic Games hosted on German soil. Whilst the reasons for this are multifold, recent unsuccessful bids for the Olympic Games in Munich (winter, 2022) and Hamburg (summer, 2024) highlight that there is a climate of fear in the population that emerged mainly as a result of costs.

Munich attempted to bid twice for hosting the Winter Olympic Games in 2018 and 2022 respectively. For the Games in 2018, Munich's bid was defeated by the South Korean city of Pyeongchang by 63 to 25 votes (IOC 2011). However, the main concerns and public opposition against hosting the Olympics in Munich only formed for the city's second attempt to secure the event. Originally, Munich did not want to bid for the 2022 Olympic Games but once the United States Olympic Committee decided against a bid that would have been favored by the IOC, the German National Olympic Committee (DOSB) decided to put forward another bid in 2013 (Sueddeutsche Zeitung 2013). As the bid for 2018 had already experienced opposition due to ecological concerns amongst the population in Munich and the participating communities, the stakeholders behind the bid decided to seek a referendum to prove local backing for the bid (Coates and Wicker 2015). This decision backfired heavily when the residents of Munich voted against the city's bid in the referendum. A main reason constantly voiced by activists against the bid was that of the high security costs and the lack of transparency of the proposed security budget in the bidding documents. For the Munich 2018 bid, the Bidding Committee only included €31.7 million and referred to any additional costs to be bore by governmental agencies and therefore not to be included in the official bid books. This confirmed research that cost explosions in general and in particular *after* a successful bid as the main reasons for citizens participating in referenda not to endorse hosting the Olympic Games (Zervas 2012; Könecke, Schubert and Preuß 2016). In addition, the fears related to the high security costs, the concerns were also linked to recent major projects in Germany that created cost overruns and massive delays in completion.

Despite the rejection of the local population, the DOSB decided again to enter the race for Olympic Games in attempt to bring the 2024 Summer Olympic Games to Germany. Berlin and Hamburg both bid to become the German host city and the DOSB eventually decided to put Hamburg's application forward. From the beginning of the campaign, the DOSB and Hamburg highlighted that the German bid would focus on a decline of gigantism and reduced costs, demonstrating awareness of potential opposition due to high perceived costs. However, even such consciousness did not protect Hamburg's bid to be eventually rejected by its citizens based on the perception of excessive costs. 52% of the voters rejected the proposal, meaning that Hamburg pulled out of the race for hosting the 2024 Olympic Games.

The phenomenon of local citizens rejecting the hosting of Olympic Games cannot only be witnessed in Germany. In many democratic countries, it has, in recent years, become practice to hold a referendum in an attempt to demonstrate public support, due to that local populations are increasingly considered an important stakeholder of the bidding and hosting processes (Preuß 2013). The local residents in Austria (Innsbruck) and in Switzerland (Graubünden) recently voted against a bid for the 2026 Winter Olympic Games. For the same bidding process, the citizens of Calgary, Canada, rejected an Olympic bid. In all cases, fears about terror appear to be of little significance compared to the fear of increasing costs.

Summary

In this chapter, I set out to detail the links between the terror attacks on the 1972 Munich Olympic Games, rising security costs for Olympic Games Organizing Committees and public concerns to host Olympic Games in their countries. Without doubt, the existing threat posed by international and domestic extremists will continue to exist. Consequently, safety operations will also in the future include the usage of military forces and other wide-ranging security measures. This means that the security costs for the Olympic Games are expected to experience a further increase. Following the 2020 Tokyo Olympic Games that will require yet further safety dimensions through the staging in an earthquake-prone region, the Olympic Games will return to Europe and be held in Paris. Crucially, the site of the 2015 terror attacks in St. Denis will then be the location of the Olympic village, hosting Olympic athletes from all around the world. Fears of terror associated with the attacks from 2015 will certainly be present. However, it appears that the second dimension of fears explored in this chapter, those of excessive costs, will become an even more substantial challenge for the IOC in the future. The struggle to find host cities will require an alternative approach to address the concerns of local citizens that the IOC has yet to find. A return to the idea of a permanent Olympic site seems highly unlikely but it seems that the IOC is not ill-advised to bring this proposal back to the table.

REFERENCES

Albanidis, Evangelis, and Robert K. Barney. 2007. "In Search of an Olympic Sanctuary: The Quest to Permanently Host the Olympic Games in Greece." *Journal of Olympic History* 15(2): 28–39.

Andrews, David L. Jaime Schultz and Michael L. Silk. 2010. "The Olympics and terrorism." In *The Politics of the Olympics*, edited by Alan Bairner and Gyozo Molnar, 81–92. London: Routledge.

Barbassa, Juliana. 2017. "Safety for Whom? Securing Rio for the Olympics." In *Rio 2016: Olympic Myths, Hard Realities*, edited by Andrew Zimbalist, 153-178. Washington D.C.: Brookings.

Cho, Ji Hyun. 2009. "The Seoul Olympic Games and Korean Society: Causes, context, consequences." PhD diss., Loughborough University

Clément, Dominique. 2017. "The Transformation of Security Planning for the Olympics: The 1976 Montreal Games." *Terrorism and Political Violence* 29(1): 27–51.

Coates, Dennis, and Pamela Wicker. 2015. "Why Were Voters Against the 2022 Munich Winter Olympics in a Referendum?" *International Journal of Sport Finance*, 10(3): 267–83.

Decker, Scott H., Jack R. Greene, Vince Webb, Jeff Rojeck, Jack McDevitt, Tim Bynum, Sean Varano and Peter K. Manning. 2005. "Safety and Security at Special Events: The Case of the Salt Lake City Olympic Games." *Security Journal* 18(4):

Duckworth, Austin, and Thomas M. Hunt. 2016. "Protecting the Games. The International Olympic Committee and Security, 1972-1984." *Olympika* 25(1): 67–87.

Fascell, Dante B. 1988. "Letter to Juan Antonio Samaranch." March 3, 1988. Lausanne. IOC Archive.

Freeman, James, and Marcos Burgos. 2017. "Accumulation by Forced Removal: The Thinning of Rio de Janeiro's Favelas in Preparation for the Games." *Journal of Latin American Studies* 49(3): 349–77.

Fussey, Pete. 2015. "Command, control and contestation: negotiating security at the London 2012 Olympics." *The Geographical Journal* 181(3): 212–23.

Giulianotti, Richard, and Francisco Klauser. 2012. "Sport mega-events and 'terrorism': A critical analysis." *International Review for the Sociology of Sport* 47(3): 307–23.

Gregory, Sean. 2016. "Terror Threat Looms as Olympians Ready to Compete in Rio." *Time*, August 5, 2016. http://time.com/4438690/rio-2016-olympics-terrorism-security/.

Guttmann, Allen. 2002. *The Olympics. A History of the Modern Games*. Urbana and Chicago: University of Illinois Press.

Horne, John, and Garry Whannel. 2010. "The 'caged torch procession': celebrities, protesters and the 2008 Olympic torch relay in London, Paris and San Francisco." *Sport in Society* 13(5): 760–70.

Houlihan, Barrie, and Richard Giulianotti. 2012. "Politics and the London 2012 Olympics: the (in)security Games." *International Affairs* 88(4): 701–717.

International Olympic Committee. 1981a. *11th Olympic Congress in Baden-Baden 1981*. Lausanne: International Olympic Committee.

———. 1981b. Minutes of the 84th Session of the International Olympic Committee, held in Baden-Baden, September 29 - October 2, 1981. Lausanne. IOC Archive.

———. 1983. Minutes of the IOC Executive Board Meeting, held in Lausanne, November 24 and 25, 1983. Lausanne. IOC Archive.

———. 1991. Minutes of the 97th Session of the International Olympic Committee, held in Birmingham, June 13-16, 1991. Lausanne. IOC Archive.

———. 1992. Minutes of the 98th Session of the International Olympic Committee, held in Courchevel, February 5 and 6, 1992. Lausanne. IOC Archive.

———. 2001. Minutes of the 112th Session of the International Olympic Committee, held in Moscow, July 13-16, 2001. Lausanne. IOC Archive.

———. 2002a. Minutes of the 113th Session of the International Olympic Committee, held in Salt Lake City, February 4-6 and 23, 2002. Lausanne. IOC Archive.

———. 2002b. Minutes of the 114th Session of the International Olympic Committee, held in Mexico City, November 28 and 29, 2002. Lausanne. IOC Archive.

———. 2011. Minutes of the 123rd Session of the International Olympic Committee, held in Durban, July 6-9, 2011. Lausanne. IOC Archive.

Könecke, Thomas, Matthias Schubert and Holger Preuss. 2016. "(N)Olympia in Germany? An analysis of the referendum against Munich 2022." *Sportwissenschaft* 46(1): 15–24.

Krüger, Michael. 1997. "Olympische Spiele in Deutschland: ausgefallen, mißbraucht, überschattet, gescheitert." In *Olympischer Sport: Rückblick und Perspektiven*, edited by Ommo Grupe, 71–84. Schorndorf: Hofmann.

Kumar, Ashwini. 1988. "Report: Security at the Seoul Olympics 1988—A Review." Lausanne. IOC Archive.

———. 1989. "Letter to Juan Antonio Samaranch: A Critique of Project Follow-Up Report." November 30, 1989. Lausanne. IOC Archive.

———. 1996. "Letter to Juan Antonio Samaranch: Dear President Samaranch." February 20, 1996. Lausanne. IOC Archive.

Lee, Jung Woo, 2010. "The Olympics and Post Soviet Era. The case of two Koreas". In *The Politics of the Olympics*, edited by Alan Bairner and Gyozo Molnar, 117–128. London: Routledge.

Lenskyj, Helen Jefferson. 2002. *The Best Olympics Ever? Social Impacts of Sydney 2000*. New York: State University of New York Press.

Lindsey, R. 1984. "THE OLYMPICS: LOS ANGELES '84; SECURITY IS CALLED LARGEST IN PEACETIME." *New York Times*, July 26, 1984. https://www.nytimes.com/1984/07/26/sports/the-olympics-los-angeles-84-security-is-called-largest-in-peacetime.html.

Organizing Committee of the 1976 Montreal Olympic Games. 1978. *Games of the XXI Olympiad, Montreal 1976: Official Report, Volume 2*. Montreal: Organizing Committee of the 1976 Montreal Olympic Games.

Pfahl-Traughber, Armin. 2016. "Terrorismus—Merkmale, Formen und Abgrenzungsprobleme." *Aus Politik und Zeitgeschichte* 66(24–25): 10–19.

Preuss, Holger. 2013. „Olympische Spiele der Neuzeit als Wirtschaftsfaktor—Wer profitiert von den Olympischen Spielen?" In *Sport—Recht—Gesellschaft: Vol. 4. Olympische Spiele*, edited by Wolfram Höfling, Johannes Horst and Martin Nolte, 27–56. Tübingen: Mohr Siebeck.

Radchenko, Sergey. 2011. "Sport and Politics on the Korean Peninsula: North Korea and the 1988 Seoul Olympics." *North Korea International Documentation Project*. Accessed December 14, 2018. https://www.wilsoncenter.org/sites/default/files/NKIDP_eDossier_3_North_Korea_and_the_1988_Seoul_Olympics.pdf.

Riding, Alan. 1992. "OLYMPICS; Keeping Terrorism at Bay in Barcelona." *New York Times*, July 21, 1992. https://www.nytimes.com/1992/07/11/sports/olympics-keeping-terrorism-at-bay-in-barcelona.html.

Samaranch, Juan Antonio. 1996. "Letter to IOC Members." July 27, 1996. Lausanne. IOC Archive.

Samatas, Minas. 2007. "Security and Surveillance in the Athens 2004 Olympics. Some Lessons From a Troubled Story." *International Criminal Justice Review* 17(3): 220–38.

———. 2011. "Surveillance in Athens 2004 and Beijing 2008: A Comparison of the Olympic Surveillance Modalities and Legacies in Two Different Olympic Host Regimes." *Urban Studies* 48(15): 3347–66.

Schiller, Kay, and Christopher Young. 2010. *The 1972 Munich Olympics and the Making of Modern Germany*. Oakland: University of California Press.

Social Communication Secretariat of the Office of the President of Brazil. 2016. "Security in the Rio 2016 Olympic and Paralympic Games". Last Modified July 18, 2016. http://www.brasil2016.gov.br/en/presskit/files/fact-sheet-security.

Spaaij, Ramón. 2016. "Terrorism and Security at the Olympics: Empirical Trends and Evolving Research Agendas." *The International Journal of the History of Sport* 33(4): 451–68.

Sueddeutsche Zeitung. 2013. "DOSB befürwortet Münchner Olympia-Bewerbung." *Sueddeutsche Zeitung*, September, 30 2013. http://www.sueddeutsche.de/muenchen/olympische-winterspiele-dosb-befuerwortet-muenchner-olympia-bewerbung-1.1784366.

Sugden, John. 2012. "Watched by the Games: Surveillance and Security at the Olympics". In *Watching the Olympics. Politics, Power and Representation*, edited by Alan Tomlinson and John Sugden, 228–241. London: Routledge.

Torres, Cesar R., and Mark Dyreson. 2005. "The Cold War Games." In *Global Olympics: Historical and Sociological Studies of the Modern Games*, edited by Kevin Young and Kevin B. Wamsley, 59–82. Amsterdam and Oxford: Elsevier.

Visacro, Alessandro. 2017. "Brazilian Organization for Combating Terrorism during the Rio 2016 Olympic Games and Paralympic Games." *Military Review* September-October 2017, 94–104.

Yan, Holly, Julia Jones, and Shasta Darlington. 2016. "Brazilian police arrest 12 suspected of planning terrorist acts during Olympics." *CNN*, July 25, 2016. https://edition.cnn.com/2016/07/21/americas/brazil-olympics-terror-arrests/index.html.

Ying, Yu, Francisco Klauser and Gerald Chan. 2009. "Governing Security at the 2008 Beijing Olympics." *The International Journal of the History of Sport* 26(3): 389–405.

Zervas, Konstantinos. 2012. "Anti-Olympic Campaigns." In *The Palgrave Handbook of Olympic Studies*, edited by Helen Jefferson Lenskyj and Stephen Wagg, 533–48. New York: Palgrave MacMillan.

Dark Sides of Sport

CHAPTER 5

The Human Rights Impacts of Olympic Games

Daniela Heerdt[1]

INTRODUCTION

The 2024 and 2028 Summer Olympic Games will be the first Olympic Games ever for which the protection of and respect for human rights forms an integral part of the Host City Contract (International Olympic Committee 2017c). The introduction of these measures follows increasing pressure from civil society and other stakeholders on the International Olympic Committee, to address the adverse human rights impacts of these events. Most recently, the 2016 Summer Olympic Games in Rio de Janeiro, and the 2018 Winter Olympic Games in Pyeongchang sparked critique. Thousands of people had to make room for the large scale construction projects connected to hosting the Olympics in Rio (World Cup and Olympics Popular Committee 2015, 20). Similar construction projects were carried out in Pyeongchang, which came at the expense of workers' rights and even workers' lives (Building and Wood Workers' International and the Korean Federation of Construction Industry Trade Unions 2018).

The occurrence of human rights violations is not exclusively related to organizing and staging the Olympic Games. In fact, reports on adverse human rights impacts arose in the context of the majority of mega-sporting event (MSE) hosted in the past decades. Other events likely to bring about human rights abuses are the FIFA World Cup, the Commonwealth Games and other World Championships (Amis and Morrison 2017, 136). Furthermore, the hosting of regional sport events, like the European Games in Azerbaijan in 2015, bear numerous human rights risks. The dangers associated with these events do not only affect people living in and around MSE-venues, or those involved in the MSE supply chain. Human rights of athletes are also at stake, not only at the time of these events but throughout the entire Olympiad.[2] Discrimination of athletes based on gender or ethnic background, sexual abuse and other exploitation of child athletes, or substandard working conditions for women athletes are common human rights risks in sports (Kidd and Donnelly 2000).

---

[1] I gratefully acknowledge the support and feedback on earlier drafts of this chapter provided by Prof. Nicola Jägers, professor of human rights law at Tilburg University and Commissioner at The Netherlands Institute for Human Rights, and Prof. Mark James, professor of Sports Law and Director of Research at Manchester Law School.
[2] The term 'Olympiad' refers to the four years cycle in between the Games.

Dark Sides of Sport

This chapter intends to demonstrate how adverse human rights impacts are structurally linked to the delivery of MSEs, with a focus on the impact on those individuals living in and around MSE venues and those involved in their organization. For this purpose, the chapter draws primarily on examples from hosting the Olympic Games and occasionally mentions additional examples from hosting the FIFA World Cup. When speaking of human rights and human rights violations, this Chapter refers to internationally-recognized human rights standards, as can be found in the international bill of human rights.[3] To grasp the wide range of human rights affected by these events, this chapter first provides a brief historical overview of the human rights issues that arose in the context of all Olympic Games hosted in the past decade. Subsequently, it conducts a life-cycle analysis of these events to highlight the human rights risks that lie in each stage of the cycle and to underline the argument that these impacts are indeed a structural problem connected to hosting these events. In the final part, the chapter takes an excursion into human rights-related measures adopted by the IOC in recent years and reflects on the potential of these measures to mitigate and eventually prevent these adverse impacts altogether.

THE HISTORY OF OLYMPIC GAMES AND HUMAN RIGHTS

Since the Beijing Olympic Games in 2008, the number of reports and initiatives highlighting and condemning the negative effect of staging these events have been piling up (Worden 2013). In the course of the preparations for the Beijing Games, an estimated number of 1.5 million residents were evicted to make room for Olympic Games-related constructions. Those employed on these sites faced harsh working conditions. Accidents, including fatal ones, occurred regularly (Perelman 2012, 9, 13–16; Beck 2007; Worden 2008, 183). Furthermore, reports showed that child labour has been used in the factories producing official Olympic merchandise (Worden 2008, 184).

In the course of the Vancouver Winter Olympic Games in 2010, different human rights issues and abuses emerged. The greatest concerns related to the far-reaching security measures that were taken, as well as gentrification and environmental damages (Shaw 2008, 205 ff.). Members of the Vancouver police and the Vancouver Integrated Security Unit allegedly intimidated and harassed those who opposed the hosting of the Games (Robinson 2009). Additional human rights risks appeared in connection with the rise in human trafficking and prostitution (Wallace 2010). Furthermore, the discrimination of female athletes was a publicly discussed issue, triggered by the failed attempt of a group of female ski jumpers to overturn the IOC's decision of 2006 to not allow women's ski jumping at the Olympics (Robinson 2009).

In the context of the 2012 London Olympic Games somewhat different human rights issues were at stake. They arose in particular out of the legislation passed in the

---

[3] The International Bill of Human Rights consists of the Universal Declaration of Human Rights (1948), the International Covenant on Civil and Political Right (1966), and the International Covenant on Economic, Social, and Cultural Rights (1966)

run-up to the event, which secured land for Olympic venues and introduced strict anti-ambush marketing policies, stricter than those of previous Games (James and Osborn 2016, 102–5). People were forced out of business, due to harsh sanctions for using the Olympic logo or Olympic Games-related language for advertising their businesses without a licence (Girginov 2014, 162; James and Osborn 2011, 413–15, 427). In addition, allegations of cases of child labour in the supply chain for Olympic logo goods, mascot toys, or other Olympic merchandise occurred in the run up to the event (Brackenridge et al. 2013, 14)

The Sochi Winter Olympic Games in 2014 received stronger critcism for its adverse human rights impacts than any previous Olympic Games. The critiques uncovered issues such as exploitative working conditions, discriminatory legal acts, the silencing and detention of activists and peaceful protestors, as well as forced evictions (Davidson and McDonald 2017; Human Rights Watch 2014). Some of the evicted families have not been offered compensation, nor temporary accommodation at the time their houses were demolished (Human Rights Watch 2012).

Large-scale evictions were also one of the main problems ahead of the 2016 Summer Olympic Games in Rio de Janeiro. In total, more than 77000 people living in and around Rio de Janeiro have been displaced between 2009 and 2015 to make room for construction projects related to the 2014 FIFA World Cup and the 2016 Summer Olympic Games (World Cup and Olympics Popular Committee 2015, 20). Further issues arose in relation to the excessive security measures and increased use of violence by the police, which not only affected problematic neighbourhoods in Rio, but also occurred in connection with the many protests that took place in the run-up to the events. Amnesty International reported that in the months leading up to the event, violence and police killings increased every month. In the first week of the 2016 Olympics, almost twice as many armed shootouts were registered compared to the week before (Amnesty International 2016a).

Pyeongchang hosted the latest Olympic Games in 2018. The information on the human rights impacts of this event is rather scarce. Nevertheless, a number of human rights-related concerns became known, most of them concerning violations of workers' rights such as cases of delayed or unpaid wages. Some of those speaking up against these issues have been arrested (Building and and Wood Workers' International and the Korean Federation of Construction Industry Trade Unions 2018, 4,6). Moreover, insufficient safety standards caused severe injuries and even deaths of workers on Olympic construction sites (Building and Wood Workers' International and the Korean Federation of Construction Industry Trade Unions 2018, 5).

Two conclusions can be drawn from this brief historical overview. First, it becomes visible that all editions of the Games struggled with human rights issues and while the type of human rights issues and the scale of abuses differ for each event, it still implies that adverse human rights impacts are a structural problem linked to these events. The most common types of violations are in respect of worker's rights, infringements on freedom of speech and the right to protest, and cases of forced evictions. A study from the Centre on Housing Rights and Evictions on housing impacts of Summer Olympic Games shows that for the Seoul, Barcelona, Atlanta, Sydney, Athens, Beijing, and London events of more than two million families and individuals have been displaced or forcefully evicted due to construction projects directly and indirectly linked to the events (Centre on Housing Rights and Evictions 2007, 217). These projects run on a tight schedule and require a large amount of labour, which triggers the influx of migrant workers, who are often most vulnerable to labour rights violations. In addition, the regulations of the Olympic Games prohibit any demonstrations in or around Olympic venues and areas (*Olympic Charter* 2018, Rule 50(2); International Olympic Committee 2017a, Principle 23).

Secondly, the overview demonstrates that human rights risks associated with Olympic Games have not decreased. In fact, the increase in reports and information available on adverse human rights impacts of MSEs are hints for the opposite. Adverse human rights impacts of MSEs might be increasing, which is not surprising given that hosting these events become more and more attractive for states with rather questionable human rights records. Tokyo is up next to host the Summer Olympic Games and Beijing will stage the 2022 Winter Olympic Games. In the same year, Qatar is hosting the FIFA World Cup. The preparations for these events are well underway and human rights concerns have already been raised concerning the treatment of migrant workers, the discrimination of minority groups and forced evictions and displacements of homeless people (Suzuki, Ogawa, and Inaba 2018, 89; Business & Human Rights Resource Centre 2018; Amnesty International 2016b).

HUMAN RIGHTS IN THE MSE LIFE-CYCLE

The total life-cycle of an MSE lies between ten and 20 years, depending on the host nation and cities. During these years, the event runs through various stages, starting with the vision and concept, moving to the actual bidding and planning, the income generation and sustainable sourcing, to the construction phase, the delivery stage, the actual competition, and ending with the legacy (Mega-Sporting Events Platform 2018). From a human rights risk perspective, these eight stages can be conflated into four: the bidding and planning stage, the construction stage, the delivery and operations stage, and finally the event's legacy. The following four sections discuss each of these four stages in detail by identifying the operations taken and the associated human rights risks that emerge. To better illustrate these risks, concrete examples of cases of human rights violations that occurred in the context of past and upcoming Olympic Games and Football World Cups are provided for each stage.

Stage 1: Bidding and Planning

Even before a city moves forward with an official candidature, plans are made and concrete actions are taken to prepare the city for the possibility of hosting an MSE (Mega-Sporting Events Platform for Human Rights 2016, 16). The Chinese authorities started their preparation works for the bid for the 2008 Summer Olympic Games in the early 1990s, even though the official bidding procedure only started in the late 1990s and the IOC awarded the event to Beijing only in 2001 (Worden 2008, 181). Most of the pre-bid actions concentrate on preparing the city for the bidding process, which includes reaching internal agreements and starting organizational processes, as well as planning of infrastructure changes and drafting of legislation (Gauthier 2015, 115ff.).

Interestingly, some candidate cities do not only draft and plan Olympic-related legislation in the bidding stage, but already adopt parts of it, which the IOC generally appreciates (Spalding 2016, 5). For example, the Brazilian national and regional government adopted several acts before it was decided that Rio would be hosting the next Summer Olympic Games (International Olympic Committee n.d., 48). Depending on the host in question, the amount of legal guarantees required by the Sports Governing Bodies changes. Most of these guarantees concern financial guarantees, intellectual property, or marketing. According to research conducted by Spalding, the Rio bid committee only had to demonstrate that appropriate legal protections are in place concerning the general execution of the Games and intellectual property and marketing. No guarantees were needed for legislation on ethical concerns, such as anti-corruption or anti-bribery, let alone human rights (Spalding 2016, 13).

The drafting and adoption of so-called 'Olympic Acts' does not pose human rights risks per se. However, these legislative acts often undermine or suspend rights and mandatory processes that would usually apply (Corrarino 2014). Therefore, the failure to factor human rights in can turn into a real risk as soon as a city is elected as a host city. At that point, all commitments made during the bidding stage, including those on legislative acts, automatically transform into contractual obligations (International Olympic Committee 2017b, Principle 1.1). As Corrarino observed, construction workers on World Cup building sites in Brazil were told that their normal collective bargaining rights have been suspended due to the exceptional circumstances that the hosting of the MSE creates (Corrarino 2014, 180).

The greatest human rights risks in the bidding and planning stage are the far-reaching measures taken to ensure that the city makes a good impression as a candidate, in particular when the visits of the Evaluation Commissions lie ahead. Before the visit by the IOC Evaluation Committee to Beijing in February 2001, the government ordered thousands of workers to wash and scrub the city (Broudehoux 2004, 198). This 'beautification program' also entailed a total of 26 million square meters to be freshly painted in the weeks before the visit (Hessler 2001). Constructions were also halted and heating was reduced in a number of office buildings, "to reduce the smoke and dust" in the city (Hessler 2001). Moreover, and most problematic from a human rights perspective, as part of these improvements of the city's outer appearance, the Chinese police scared off and arrested numerous homeless people, beggars, informal vendors and even children that were living on the streets just before the visit of the IOC's Evaluation Committee (Broudehoux 2004, 198; Eckholm 2001; Watts 2008). Further reports claim that human rights activists were kept under house arrest to prevent them from getting in contact with the IOC delegation during their visit (CNN 2001).[4]

---

[4] Arbitrary arrests are prohibited by Article 9 of the Universal Declaration of Human Rights and Article 9(1) of the International Covenant on Civil and Political Rights.

Stage 2: Construction and Event-Preparation

Once the decision fell for a host city or country, the involved stakeholders waste no time with starting the preparations for the upcoming event. This stage commences with signing the Host City Contract (HCC), which binds the IOC, the National Olympic Committee, and the respective city representatives. The latter two agree to set up a Local Organizing Committee (LOC), which bears primary responsibility for the organization of the event and therefore plays a lead role in this stage.

From a human rights perspective, the construction and execution stage is the most precarious stage of the entire MSE life-cycle. In particular the large-scale construction projects related to the event carry severe human rights risks, not only for those living in or around MSE venues but also for the workers hired to build Olympic-Games related infrastructure. In many cases, an influx of migrant workers are needed to finish the great amount of MSE-related construction projects, due to strict deadlines and requirements from the sports organizing bodies. In those countries where worker's rights already constitute a problem due to insufficient legal protection and exploitative practices, the hosting of these events can increase the number of migrant workers present and thereby the amount and scale of violations. In relation to the Winter Olympics in Sochi 2014, migrant workers that predominantly came from countries like Armenia, Serbia, Ukraine, or Uzbekistan, faced a series of abuses, including severe delays in payment of wages or no payment of wages at all, excessive working hours, lack of employment contracts, and inadequate housing (Human Rights Watch 2013a). Japan's foreign trainee worker program has also been criticized in connection with the construction works for the Tokyo Olympics 2020, for the fact that under this program Japanese companies attract "inexpensive workers for less attractive jobs", while the rights of these workers were not protected (Cyrus R. Vance Center For International Justice 2018). More concrete stories became public in connection with the preparations for the 2022 FIFA World Cup in Qatar. Up to 50 degrees Celsius outside temperature and no breaks, nor access to drinking water create hazardous and inhuman working conditions (Human Rights Watch 2017; Gibson and Pattisson 2014).

Those people living in and around MSE venues face an increased risk of being evicted.[5] In many cases, it is the city hall that works together with urban planners and decides on which neighborhoods have to give way to event-related infrastructure (World Cup and Olympics Popular Committee 2015). While some form of urban restructuring is necessary for every event, some host cities require more restructuring than others, making cases of forced evictions more likely to occur. The problem is also that due to time pressure and expectations of stakeholders, procedural and

---

[5] As such, displacements do not necessarily amount to human rights violations, even though they generally may only be justified in most exceptional circumstances. Displacements are illegal as long as no adequate compensation is secured for the loss of property and even more so if they are carried out. Forced evictions are considered to be gross violations of human rights and protected under the right to adequate housing as enshrined in article 11 of the International Covenant on Economic, Social, and Cultural Rights and the right to adequate standard of living in article 25 of the Universal Declaration of Human Rights.

substantive human rights as Corrarino calls them, such as rights to information, to be notified, to receive alternative housing or compensation, are suspended for the time being and 'exceptional legal regimes' take over (Corrarino 2014). Such violations occurred on a large scale in the run-up to the Olympic Summer Games in Rio in 2016 (Agencia Publica 2016a). In many cases, those evictions took place before residents were moved to other housing (Philipps 2011). The community reporting initiative 'RioOnWatch' identified four patterns of abuses in the course of these displacements cases: lack of notification, violent and intimidating eviction tactics, unfair or no compensation, and the lack of justifiable reasons for eviction (Tapley 2012).

In addition, forced evictions can trigger further infringements of rights, as evictions not only mean a change of housing and a change of living environment; in most cases, people are forced to change their daily routines completely. For the two MSEs that took place in Brazil, people were moved to places as far as 28km away from their previous homes (Agencia Publica 2016b). Moreover, being forced to leave your house against your will can have tremendous psychological impacts (Alvad 2016).

Stage 3: Delivery

The official start of an event usually comes with an increased presence of police and other security personnel in the respective host cities. While their purpose is to maintain peace and order during the event, the increase in security bears numerous human rights risks. For instance, similar to what happens in the bidding stage, it can lead to a rise in in arbitrary arrests of beggars, street traders, street children, and other homeless people. In addition, police and other security personnel resort to violent measures more easily, in particular against already marginalized groups of society. The Brazilian World Cup and Olympics Popular Committee observed that the staging of the two MSEs:

> "represent a new period of expansion, standardisation and aggravation of these structures, which function as an instrument of the black "genocide" policy and the repression in shantytowns and the suburbs, emphasising further the criminalisation of social movements" (World Cup and Olympics Popular Committee 2015, 101).

The increase in security measures and propensity to violence on the side of authorities is also problematic for the many protests that take place in hosting cities just before and during these events. In the days before the start of the Sochi Olympics, the silencing of human rights and environmental activists intensified, through numerous arrests by the Russian police and accelerated convictions in front of Russian courts (Human Rights Watch 2014, 2013b). Thousands of Brazilians protested against the corruption and high costs associated with staging the Olympic Games and the World Cup, which the police heavily repressed, by making use of lethal weapons and detaining hundreds of people, including minors (Amnesty International 2016a). While compliance with event regulations that in fact prohibit any demonstrations close to or at Olympic sites might drive the local police, their actions do not comply with human rights law and principles on freedom of speech and the right to protest.[6] Interestingly, a federal court in Brazil had ruled that banning people from Olympic venues for displaying political statements constitutes an infringement of their right to freedom of expression (BBC News 2016).

Stage 4: Legacy

The legacy rhetoric around MSEs can take place in positive and negative terms. On the positive side, the potential that hosting MSEs can have for improving urban infrastructure and living conditions for citizens is an often-used argument from bid supporters. In terms of sustainability and environmental aspects, the negative short- and long-term effects of hosting MSEs have been highlighted in various studies (see e.g. Collins, Jones, and Munday 2009; Flyvbjerg, Stewart, and Budzier 2016). However, the fact that also the human rights legacy of these events features more strongly on the negative side has to a certain extent been overlooked. A reason for this might be that human rights risks in the legacy stage are not a consequence of actions or operations taken after the closure of an event. Instead, they are the result of continuing human rights violations, which have their origin in earlier stages. For example, many of the people that have been displaced to make room for an Olympic Games or World Cup venue in Brazil have never been compensated adequately (Agencia Publica 2016b). People were displaced to far-off areas with lower living standards and no easy access to the city, their work place, school, or their previous social life, which can trigger additional abuses. Other examples of continuing human rights violations relate to cases of exploitation at the work place, in particular when workers suffered injuries and have not been compensated, or when relatives of workers that died have never received any explanation of the cause of death, nor any form of compensation (Wintour 2017).

Hence, the main concern for human rights risks in the legacy stage is that most of the MSE-related cases of human rights violations are currently not being addressed, due to a lack of available and effective remedy mechanisms. This constitutes a violation of a victims' right to remedy.[7] The remedy question is in particular

---

[6] Restrictions on freedom of speech and protest are a violation of the right to peaceful protest or assembly, as stipulated by Article 20 of the Universal Declaration for Human Rights, Article 21 of the International Covenant on Civil and Political Rights and Articles from regional human rights documents such as Article 11 of the European Convention on Human Rights. The right to freedom of expression is guaranteed by Article 19 of both, the Universal Declaration for Human Rights and the International Covenant on Civil and Political Rights, as well as by Article 10 of the European Convention on Human Rights and Article 13 of the American Convention on Human Rights.

[7] The right to an effective remedy can be found in a number of international and regional human rights instruments, such as Article 8, Universal Declaration of Human Rights; Article 2 (3), International Covenant on Civil and Political Rights; Article 2, International Covenant on Economic, Social and Cultural Rights, or Article 13, European Convention for the Protection of Human Rights and Fundamental Freedoms; Article 25, American Convention on Human Rights, Article 7(1)(a), African Charter on Human and Peoples' Rights

problematic in the MSE-context due to the multiple operations and actors that contribute to adverse human rights impacts. Identifying the actors responsible and holding them accountable is a complex undertaking, given that these violations are often a result of joint efforts taken by various actors, some of which even cease to exist once the event is over, as is the case with the LOC.

THE IOC AND HUMAN RIGHTS

In 2009, the IOC obtained observer status in the *United Nations*, for its efforts in and support of initiatives for humanitarian aid, education, peace, gender equality, environment, and the fight against HIV/AIDS (Perelman 2012, 17). This seems rather contradictory, considering the structural link between human rights violations and the IOC's main events, and considering that it took the IOC another five years to react to the growing awareness of Olympics-related human rights abuses and the resulting pressure from civil society. In 2014, the IOC adopted the Olympic Agenda 2020, a set of reforms aimed at reshaping the future of the Olympic Movement and consisting of 40 recommendations concerning the candidature process, reducing the costs of bidding, adapting and further strengthening principles of good governance, and placing athletes in the center of attention of all recommendations (International Olympic Committee 2014). From a human rights perspective, the most relevant recommendations are recommendations 14 and 18, which call for a strengthened support to athletes and a new wording of the sixth Fundamental Principle of Olympism, to include sexual orientation as grounds for non-discrimination, in line with the Universal Declaration of Human Rights.

In 2015 the Olympic Charter was amended following these reforms (International Olympic Committee 2015). However, up until today human rights remain to be mentioned only in the context of the practice of sport being a human right (International Olympic Committee 2017d). In the spring of 2017, the IOC adopted new bidding and hosting regulations for the 2026 Winter Olympic Games and the 2024 and 2028 Summer Olympic Games. With this new approach, the IOC reacts to the increased awareness of the adverse human rights impacts that MSEs entail, as well as to pressure and advocacy from civil society and other actors, for instance exercised through multi-stakeholder initiatives such as the Centre for Sport and Human Rights (Centre for Sports and Human Rights 2019). The candidature process for the 2026 Olympic Winter Games now includes human rights as core guarantees that candidates have to submit together with the Candidature File. According to Principle 13 of the new Host City Contracts, the host city, the National Olympic Committee, and the Organizing Committee of the Olympic Games agree to

> "protect and respect human rights and ensure any violation of human rights is remedied in a manner consistent with international agreements, laws and regulations applicable in the Host Country and in a manner consistent with all internationally-recognized human rights standards and principles [...] applicable in the Host Country" (International Olympic Committee 2017b).

In addition to these regulatory changes, the IOC also introduced a reporting tool for journalists and media representatives before the Summer Olympic Games in Rio in 2016. This tool can be used to file a complaint concerning violations of press freedom. The mechanism can be used by anyone working on Olympic Games-related issues.

With regard to a strengthened support of athletes, the IOC implemented a number of concrete measures. Shortly after Agenda 2020 was adopted, the IOC launched an integrity and compliance hotline. The web-based hotline is open to all athletes, coaches, referees and the public, to report on cases of violations of the IOC's Code of Ethics, and the manipulation of competition in particular. The hotline can also be used to report cases of harassment or abuse in sport.

In the run-up to the Winter Olympic Games in Pyeongchang in 2018, the IOC launched a safeguarding toolkit to support International Sport Federations and National Olympic Committees in adopting measures for the protection of athletes. It is a step-by-step guide that calls for the development of policies and procedures, prevention mechanisms, and management of reports of harassment and abuse. The IOC itself states that this toolkit helps to comply with recommendation 18 of the Olympic Agenda 2020 (International Olympic Committee 2018c, 10 and 19). For the Olympics in Pyeongchang an IOC Safeguarding Officer was on site to deal with incidents in a confidential procedure.

The most recent measures taken by the IOC were the adoption of the Athlete's Rights and Responsibilities Declaration in October 2018 and its announcement to have a Human Rights Advisory Committee in place for the 2024 Olympic Games in Paris. The Athlete's Declaration holds 22 principles, divided into twelve principles on athlete's rights and ten principles on athletes responsibilities (International Olympic Committee 2018a). While the IOC presents this declaration as being athlete-driven and supported by thousands of athletes worldwide (International Olympic Committee n.d.), its adoption has been strongly criticized by several national athlete bodies, non-governmental organizations and players unions, such as the World Players Association and the Sport & Rights Alliance. Their key points of critique were the limited engagement and consultation with athletes, as well as the IOC's failure to acknowledge its leverage over internationally-recognized human rights. Furthermore, the declaration seems to strengthen the IOC's control over athlete's rights more than it embraces human rights of athletes and effectively represents their best interest. These points led the World Players Association to denounce the IOC's attempt "to unilaterally redefine the internationally-recognized human rights of the very people who sit at the heart of sport—the athletes" (UNIGlobalUnion 2018).

Finally, the IOC's decision to set up a Human Rights Advisory Committee can be traced back to the Olympic Agenda 2020, as well as to the inclusion of human rights provisions in the new Host City Contracts Games (International Olympic Committee 2018b). The Committee will be chaired by former UN Commissioner for Human Rights, Prince Zeid Ra'ad Al Hussein and six to nine other experts in human rights and sports. The Committee will report to the IOC Executive Board and the IOC President. However, as the IOC's press release announcing the decision to set up the Advisory Committee makes clear, regular public reporting should not be expected (International Olympic Committee 2018b).

It becomes evident that in the past years the IOC undertook efforts aimed at mitigating the adverse human rights impacts of the Olympic Games and the Olympic Movement as a whole. However, these efforts should only be complimented with caution, for mainly two reasons. First, while the concrete measures and tools adopted mainly address athletes, the rights of people affected through the organization and staging of the Olympic Games are only dealt with marginally through regulatory changes in bidding and hosting guidelines and it is disputable how effective and enforceable these provisions really are. The fact that the obligation to respect and protect human rights standards is limited to those standards "applicable in the Host Country" can limit the application of internationally-recognized human rights standards in case the host country did not ratify relevant human rights treaties (International Olympic Committee 2017b). This problem becomes apparent when considering the hosts of the Olympic Games in 2024 and 2028, Paris and Los Angeles. Both France and the USA have not ratified the International Convention on the Protection of the Rights of All Migrant Workers and Members of their Families. The IOC might even prefer to award the Games to countries with only a few human rights commitments as this would mean that the LOC has fewer regulations to comply with. Hence, it is questionable to what extent these provisions will help to prevent cases of forced evictions, excessive policing or exploitation of migrant workers.

The other reason is not less alarming. The IOC´s increased action to implement human rights-related measures demonstrates that the organization recognizes the growing pressure on sports governing bodies to adapt their rules and regulations to make them more human rights compliant. At the same time, the IOC is lagging behind when compared to other sports governing bodies, and it can best be described as slow adaptation, rather than mitigation or prevention. The Fédération Internationale de Football Association recently adopted a human rights policy, included human rights into their Statutes and introduced new bidding regulations that require bidders to respect human rights and conduct a human rights impact assessment for their bids. Similar efforts have been made by the Union of European Football Associations and the Commonwealth Games Federation.

CONCLUSION

This chapter's aim was to demonstrate that the adverse human rights impacts of delivering mega-sporting events, such as the Olympic Games, are a structural problem related to the organization and staging of these events. While the cases of human rights abuses used as examples to support this argument only present a fraction of the human rights issues related to these events, they suffice to convey that one of the main problems of MSEs is the fact that the same human rights issues are recurring year after year (Amis and Morrison 2017, 137).

The historical overview clarified that not all events raise the same human rights issues or bear identical human rights risks. Indeed, the risk for occurrence of human rights violations seems to increase when these events take place in countries with negative human rights records. However, arguing that the occurrence and scale of MSE-related human rights abuses solely depends on the hosting country would ignore the fact that a number of these adverse impacts are structurally linked to the tasks and operations necessary for delivering MSEs like the Olympic Games.

The life-cycle analysis highlighted that in the bidding and planning stage, most human rights violations concern participatory rights, the adoption of special legislation and the various efforts taken to prepare cities for the candidacy, including the visits of the evaluation commission of the respective sports organizing. During the construction and event-preparation stage, the greatest human rights risks emerge from large-scale infrastructure and construction projects. These affect the rights of people living in and around Olympic venues and heavily influence the rights of workers on the sites. Once the event is well underway, excessive use of violence by public and private security personnel, but also restrictions on freedom of speech, the right to protest and press freedom bear the greatest risks. Finally, in the legacy stage most event-related human rights risks are a continuation of the violations that occurred during the previous stages. Forced evictions in particular have long-term effects and continue to be a violation of human rights law if they are not compensated adequately.

The excursion into the IOC's recent human rights efforts pointed out that the measures taken until now fail to create a dense system of human rights risk mitigation and prevention of violations. What seems to be missing in particular is a statutory human rights commitment that binds the IOC to respect and protect human rights in all areas of their work. To draw level with other major sports governing bodies, the IOC needs to show a more genuine commitment to internationally-recognized human rights standards and instruments such as the international bill of human rights and other relevant instruments, like the UN Guiding Principles on Business and Human Rights.[8]

Finally, the potential of MSEs to actually promote human rights should not be ignored. Hosting an MSE can have various positive effects by creating jobs, raising living standards and improving urban infrastructure. It can help to institutionalize internationally-recognized human rights standards in certain countries and regions. Ever since the FIFA World Cup has been awarded to Qatar, amendments of Qatar's labour laws have been implemented, which are small steps taken towards a greater respect for and protection of internationally-recognized labour standards. Furthermore, in August 2018, the municipal government in Tokyo adopted a law that prohibits discrimination against lesbian, gay, bisexual, and transgender people, thereby demonstrating its commitment to equal rights of all and upholding the principle as stated in the Olympic Charter, to which the new law makes explicit reference (Knight 2018). However, currently these potential positive impacts still remain overshadowed by the negative impacts. It is time to make more effective use

---

[8] The UN Guiding Principles on Business and Human Rights is a set of principles developed by the Special Representative of the Secretary-General and endorsed by the Human Rights Council in June 2011. The principles rest on the 'Protect, Respect, and Remedy' framework and provide guidance on the issue of human rights and transnational corporations and other business enterprises. Numerous sport initiatives and sport governing bodies have committed to these guidelines and by now, they became the commonly accepted benchmark for human rights responsibilities in the world of sports.

of this potential and structurally link the respect for and promotion of human rights to hosting MSEs like the Olympic Games.

REFERENCES

Agencia Publica. 2016a. "Project 100 - 100 Stories. 100 Removals. 100 Houses Destroyed by the 2016 Olympic Games. Jorge Santos." 2016. http://apublica.org/100/?p=1530&lang=en.

———. 2016b. "Project 100 - What We Found out—100 Stories. 100 Removals. 100 Houses Destroyed by the 2016 Olympic Games." 2016. http://apublica.org/100/?page_id=22&lang=en.

Alvad, Stine. 2016. "A Live Database of Olympic Evictions." Play the Game. 2016. http://www.playthegame.org/news/news-articles/2016/0226_a-live-database-of-olympic-evictions/.

Amis, Lucy, and John Morrison. 2017. "Mega-Sporting Events and Human Rights—A Time for More Teamwork?" *Business and Human Rights Journal* 2 (01). Cambridge University Press: 135–41. https://doi.org/10.1017/bhj.2016.29.

Amnesty International. 2016a. "Brazil: Rio's Olympic Legacy Shattered with No Let-up in Killings by Police." https://www.amnesty.org/en/latest/news/2016/08/brazil-rio-s-olympic-legacy-shattered-with-no-let-up-in-killings-by-police/.

———. 2016b. "New Name, Old System? Qatar's New Employment Law and Abuse of Migrant Workers." file:///C:/Users/U1256077/Downloads/MDE2252422016ENGLISH.PDF.

Beck, Lindsay. 2007. "Beijing to Evict 1.5 Million for Olympics." Reuters. 2007. https://www.reuters.com/article/us-olympics-beijing-housing-idUSPEK12263220070605.

Brackenridge, Celia, Sarah Palmer-Felgate, Daniel Rhind, Laura Hills, Tess Kay, Anne Tiivas, Lucy Faulkner, and Iain Lindsay. 2013. "Child Exploitation and the FIFA World Cup: A Review of Risks and Protective Interventions."

Broudehoux, Anne-Marie. 2004. *The Making and Selling of Post-Mao Beijing*. Routledge.

Building and and Wood Workers' International and the Korean Federation of Construction Industry Trade Unions. 2018. "PyeongChang 2018 Winter Olympics - Construction Workers' Rights Violations." www.bwint.org.

Business & Human Rights Resource Centre. 2018. "Tokyo 2020 Olympic and Paralympic Games." 2018. https://www.business-humanrights.org/en/major-sporting-events/tokyo-2020-olympic-and-paralympic-games.

Centre for Sports and Human Rights. 2019. "Overview." 2019. https://www.sporthumanrights.org/en/about/overview.

Centre on Housing Rights and Evictions. 2007. "Fair Play for Housing Rights." Geneva. https://doi.org/10.2307/914451.

CNN. 2001. "China Jails Activist over Olympic Appeal." CNN.Com/WORLD. 2001. http://edition.cnn.com/2001/WORLD/asiapcf/east/02/22/china.ioc.jail/index.html.

Collins, Andrea, Calvin Jones, and Max Munday. 2009. "Assessing the Environmental Impacts of Mega Sporting Events: Two Options?" *Tourism Management* 30 (6). Pergamon: 828–37. https://doi.org/10.1016/J.TOURMAN.2008.12.006.

Corrarino, Megan. 2014. "'Law Exclusion Zones': Mega-Events as Sites of Procedural and Substantive Human Rights Violations." *Yale Human Rights and Development Law Journal* 17: 180–204.

Cyrus R. Vance Center For International Justice. 2018. "Vance Center Hosts Discussion on Human Rights Impact of Olympics." News. 2018. https://www.vancecenter.org/business-and-human-rights/.

Davidson, Judy, and Mary G. McDonald. 2017. "Rethinking Human Rights: The 2014 Sochi Winter Olympics, LGBT Protections and the Limits of Cosmopolitanism." *Leisure Studies* 37 (1). Routledge: 64–76. https://doi.org/10.1080/02614367.2017.1310284.

Eckholm, Erik. 2001. "Beijing Is Given an Olympian Burnish." *The New York Times*, 2001. http://www.nytimes.com/2001/02/21/world/beijing-is-given-an-olympian-burnish.html.

Flyvbjerg, Bent, Allison Stewart, and Alexander Budzier. 2016. "The Oxford Olympics Study 2016: Cost and Cost Overrun at the Games." *Saïd Business School Working Paper*, no. 20. https://doi.org/10.2139/ssrn.2804554.

Gauthier, Ryan. 2015. *The International Olympic Committee's Accountability for Harmful Consequences of the Olympic Games: A Multi-Method International Legal Analysis*. Rotterdam.

Gibson, Owen, and Pete Pattisson. 2014. "Death Toll among Qatar's 2022 World Cup Workers Revealed." The Guardian. 2014. https://www.theguardian.com/world/2014/dec/23/qatar-nepal-workers-world-cup-2022-death-toll-doha.

Girginov, Vassil. 2014. *Handbook of the London 2012 Olympic and Paralympic Games Volume Two: Celebrating the Games*. 2nd ed. New York: Routledge.

Hessler, Peter. 2001. "Great Sprint Forward." *The New Yorker*, 2001. https://www.newyorker.com/magazine/2001/05/07/great-sprint-forward.

Human Rights Watch. 2012. "Russia: Halt Forced Eviction for Olympics Road." 2012. https://www.hrw.org/news/2012/10/22/russia-halt-forced-eviction-olympics-road.

———. 2013a. "Race to the Bottom - Exploitation of Migrant Workers Ahead of Russia's 2014 Winter Olympic Games in Sochi." https://www.hrw.org/report/2013/02/06/race-bottom/exploitation-migrant-workers-ahead-russias-2014-winter-olympic-games.

———. 2013b. "Russia: Silencing Activists, Journalists Ahead of Sochi Games | Human Rights Watch." 2013. https://www.hrw.org/news/2013/08/07/russia-silencing-activists-journalists-ahead-sochi-games.

———. 2014. "Russia: Silencing Sochi Critics Intensifies on Eve of Olympics." 2014. https://www.hrw.org/news/2014/01/14/russia-silencing-sochi-critics-intensifies-eve-olympics.

———. 2017. "Qatar: Take Urgent Action to Protect Construction Workers." 2017.

International Olympic Committee. n.d. "Athletes' Declaration Document: Athlete365." 2018. Accessed November 14, 2018a. https://www.olympic.org/athlete365/athletesdeclaration/.

———. n.d. "Report of the 2016 IOC Evaluation Commission." Accessed March 20, 2017b. https://stillmed.olympic.org/media/Document Library/OlympicOrg/IOC/Olympic_Games/Olympic_Games_Candidature_Process/Past_Candidature_Processes/2016_Host_City_Election/EN_2016_Evaluation_Commission_report.pdf.

———. 2014. "OLYMPIC AGENDA 2020 20+20 RECOMMENDATIONS." https://stillmed.olympic.org/Documents/Olympic_Agenda_2020/Olympic_Agenda_2020-20-20_Recommendations-ENG.pdf.

———. 2015. *Olympic Charter*.

———. 2017a. "HOST CITY CONTRACT PRINCIPLES GAMES OF THE XXXIII OLYMPIAD IN 2024." https://stillmed.olympic.org/Documents/Host_city_elections/Host_City_Contract_Principles.pdf.

———. 2017b. "HOST CITY CONTRACT PRINCIPLES GAMES OF THE XXXIV OLYMPIAD IN 2028." https://stillmed.olympic.org/media/Document Library/OlympicOrg/Documents/Host-City-Elections/XXXIV-Olympiad-2028/Host-City-Contract-2028-Principles.pdf.

———. 2017c. "IOC Strengthens Its Stance in Favour of Human Rights and against Corruption in New Host City Contract." 2017. https://www.olympic.org/news/ioc-strengthens-its-stance-in-favour-of-human-rights-and-against-corruption-in-new-host-city-contract.

———. 2017d. *Olympic Charter*.

———. 2018a. "Athletes' Rights and Responsibilities Declaration." 2018. https://d2g8uwgn11fzhj.cloudfront.net/wp-content/uploads/2018/10/09134729/Athletes-Rights-and-Responsibilities-Declaration_2018.10.07.pdf?utm_source=hootsuite&utm_medium=social&utm_campaign=entourage.

———. 2018b. "IOC Sets up Advisory Committee on Human Rights Chaired by HRH Prince Zeid Ra'ad Al Hussein." Olympic News. 2018. https://www.olympic.org/news/ioc-sets-up-advisory-committee-on-human-rights-chaired-by-hrh-prince-zeid-ra-ad-al-hussein.

———. 2018c. "Safeguarding Athletes from Harassment and Abuse in Sport - IOC Toolkit for IFs and NOCs." https://d2g8uwgn11fzhj.cloudfront.net/wp-content/uploads/2017/10/18105952/IOC_Safeguarding_Toolkit_ENG_Screen_Full1.pdf.

James, Mark, and Guy Osborn. 2011. "London 2012 and the Impact of the UK's Olympic and Paralympic Legislation: Protecting Commerce or Preserving Culture?" *The Modern Law Review* 74 (3). Wiley/Blackwell (10.1111): 410–29. https://doi.org/10.1111/j.1468-2230.2011.00853.x.

———. 2016. "The Olympics, Transnational Law and Legal Transplants: The International Olympic Committee, Ambush Marketing and Ticket Touting." *Legal Studies* 36 (01). Cambridge University Press: 93–110. https://doi.org/10.1111/lest.12095.

Kidd, Bruce, and Peter Donnelly. 2000. "Human Rights in Sports." *International Review for the Sociology of Sport* 35 (2). SAGE Publications: 131–48. https://doi.org/10.1177/101269000035002001.

Knight, Kyle. 2018. "Tokyo's 'Olympic' LGBT Non-Discrimination Law." Human Rights Watch. 2018. https://www.hrw.org/news/2018/10/11/tokyos-olympic-lgbt-non-discrimination-law.

Mega-Sporting Events Platform. 2018. "The Mega-Sporting Event Lifecycle - Embedding Human Rights From Vision to Legacy." www.ihrb.org.

Mega-Sporting Events Platform for Human Rights. 2016. "The Sporting Chance Forum: Collective Action on Mega-Sporting Events and Human Rights." https://www.ihrb.org/uploads/meeting-reports/IHRB_et_al%2C_Sporting_Chance_Forum_Meeting_Report%2C_Dec_2016.pdf.

News, BBC. 2016. "Rio 2016: Brazil Judge Allows Political Protest at Olympics." BBC News. 2016. https://www.bbc.com/news/world-latin-america-37023425.

Olympic Charter. 2018. www.olympic.org.

Perelman, Marc. 2012. *Barbaric Sport : A Global Plague*. London, New York: Verso.

Philipps, Tom. 2011. "Rio World Cup Demolitions Leave Favela Families Trapped in Ghost Town." *The Guardian*, 2011. https://www.theguardian.com/world/2011/apr/26/favela-ghost-town-rio-world-cup.

Robinson, Laura. 2009. "Human Rights Are No Game." Play the Game. 2009. http://www.playthegame.org/news/news-articles/2009/human-rights-are-no-game/.

Shaw, Christopher A. 2008. *Five Ring Circus : Myths and Realities of the Olympic Games*. New Society Publishers.

Spalding, Andy. 2016. "Chapter 3: The Olympic Governance Framework: The IOC Brazil's Olympic Organizations, and the Contract Between Them." In *Olympic Anti-Corruption Report: Brazil and the Rio 2016 Summer Games*, edited by Andy Spalding. http://law.richmond.edu/olympics/.

Suzuki, Naofumi, Tetsuo Ogawa, and Nanako Inaba. 2018. "The Right to Adequate Housing: Evictions of the Homeless and the Elderly Caused by the 2020 Summer Olympics in Tokyo." *Leisure Studies* 37 (1). Routledge: 89–96. https://doi.org/10.1080/02614367.2017.1355408.

Tapley, Erica. 2012. "Rio Olympic Evictions Roundup." RioOnWatch - Community Reporting. 2012. http://www.rioonwatch.org/?p=4599.

UNIGlobalUnion. 2018. "Player Unions Denounce IOC Athletes' Declaration | UNI Global Union." 2018. https://www.uniglobalunion.org/fr/node/39568.

Wallace, Kathie. 2010. "Human Trafficking Alive and Well for the 2010 Olympics." *Vancouver Observer*, 2010. https://www.vancouverobserver.com/politics/commentary/2010/02/02/human-trafficking-alive-and-well-2010-olympics.

Watts, Jonathan. 2008. "Beijing to Evict 'undesirables' before Games." The Guardian. 2008. https://www.theguardian.com/world/2008/jan/24/china.international.

Wintour, Patrick. 2017. "Qatar World Cup Bosses Offer No Explanation for British Worker's Death." *The Guardian*, 2017. https://www.theguardian.com/world/2017/nov/11/qatar-world-cup-bosses-offer-no-explanation-for-british-worker-death-zac-cox.

Worden, Minky. 2008. *China's Great Leap : The Beijing Games and Olympian Human Rights Challenges*. Seven Stories Press.

———. 2013. "The Olympics' Leadership Mess." *The New York Times*, 2013.

http://www.nytimes.com/2013/08/13/opinion/the-olympics-leadership-mess.html.

World Cup and Olympics Popular Committee. 2015. "Mega-Events and Human Rights Violations in Rio de Janeiro Dossier - Rio Olympics: The Exclusion Games." http://www.childrenwin.org/wp-content/uploads/2015/12/DossieComiteRio2015_ENG_web_ok_low.pdf.

CHAPTER 6

Environment and Sustainability: Ecological Thought and the Olympic Games

Alberto Aragón-Pérez

Greenwashing refers deceptively to techniques of marketing that companies and organizations carry out to promote the perception that they follow eco-friendly practices and policies. Among a variety of negative aspects of sport, the issue of greenwashing and environmental damage should be at the core of the present chapter. This topic is investigated from a socio-historical perspective, with the focus being on the sport political level by tracing the roots of environmental protection in the Olympic Games, the largest contemporaneous sport event. The assumption of eco-friendly guidelines by organizations of the Olympic Movement like Olympic organizing committees (OCOGs) and, mostly, the IOC, has coexisted since the decade of the nineties with the increasing gigantism of the Games and its consequences in local ecosystems. Planned legacies have become a central subject for managers of multi-sport events in the last decades because this entails building positive images about the organizational capacity. Such professional attitude towards the post-Games period of the host city and the aim of gaining benefits from its Olympic investment tends to include sustainable and environmental approaches: "Legacy is also linked to [the] third strand of Olympism, the environment, which implies that any developments made in the name of the Olympic Games should be sustainable" (Cashman 2003, 39).

However, environmental objectives are not very often in the primary vision of legacy planners. Thanks to the Olympic Games, host cities tend to expect long-term tangible and intangible outcomes, economic benefits, urban modernization and continuous utilization of sport facilities. Generally, this has been the platform on which to argue for the very high expenditure of the entire event (Hiller 2006). Parallel to the increasing complexity of managing an Olympic event, planned urban legacies are ever more important, so positive legacies are a priority at the present time for local and national political authorities. Likewise, urban development and regeneration are basic goals for political leaders and citizens when bidding for the Games in order to overcome potential undesirable impacts (Long 2016). In connection with the concept of legacy, sustainability appears as a key idea because it means consuming present resources (natural but also social and economic) at a rate that will allow long-term development[1].

Therefore, it is necessary to analyze the symbiosis of environmental measures, sustainable aims, planned legacies and ecological negative impacts while hosting the Olympics. In theory, green initiatives and avoiding ecological impacts are mandatory targets for Olympic host cities and their OCOGs. But the reality evidences that the efficacy of standards on green legacies are uncertain because organizers are challenged by some complexities when trying to carry out eco-friendly Games. Firstly, ecological goals can be hardly achieved if, simultaneously, there are demands for magnificent sport facilities and other infrastructures. Secondly, the inclusion of environmental goals within a post-Olympic planned legacy does not guarantee holistic ambitious policies with successful outcomes (Boykoff 2017). At this point, we must clear up the different impacts caused by the Winter Games, involving mountain regions and creating numerous potentially damaging consequences in those natural ecosystems, in contrast to the Summer Games, mostly celebrated in urban scenarios (except for a few sports such as sailing, canoeing and rowing) (Chappelet 2003).

This chapter proposes a discussion about the relation of ecological issues and the Olympic Games, offering an interaction between a variety of voices that talk about the assumption of green concerns into the Olympic Movement in general or in specific editions of the Games. It calls for a methodology based on literature review, which allows discussions between authors following the chronological development of the research topic. The research is essentially supported by the existing theoretical framework and critical scholarly visions in order to build a comprehensive perspective on handicaps, misunderstandings and accomplishments of the Olympic environmental dimension.

Briefly, we can assert that the relevant literature usually explains that the relationship between Olympism and ecology has been implemented since the nineties through events like the IOC's collaboration with UNEP in 1994, the new Sport and Environment Commission in 1995 and an environmental paragraph added to the Olympic Charter of 1996 (Roper 2006). An article of DaCosta in 1997 about the steps that the Olympic Movement had to follow for making effective its announced ecological awareness was one of the first papers on the relation between ecology and the Olympics (DaCosta 1997). Since then, different authors have discussed the communication and practical origins of the so-called Olympic green dimension. For instance, the Albertville 1992 Winter Olympic Games caused controversy among ecologist groups, so the environmental measures of the Lillehammer 1994 OCOG were used by the IOC to defend a green-oriented communication strategy (Cantelon and Letters 2010). Lillehammer 1994 is often mentioned as the pioneering Games in implementing a global eco-friendly management structure. Additionally, it is also

---

[1] Concerning the recent guidelines on sustainability of the IOC, the 4th recommendation of Agenda 2020 proposes: "Develop a sustainability strategy to enable potential and actual Olympic Games organizers to integrate and implement sustainability measures that encompass economic, social and environmental spheres in all stages of their project" (IOC 2014, 12).

common to highlight Sydney 2000 as the first Games that were completely planned following the new IOC green guidelines in collaboration with NGOs.

In order to achieve an enriching discussion and present the results of the study, this chapter is structured into sections. The first section provides a historical overview of a few cases of ecological issues at the Olympic Games during the 20th century. The next section provides a description of the rapid adoption of an ecological framework by the IOC in the nineties. The third section examines some lights and shades produced by the development of an Olympic green dimension. Finally, the chapter ends with a discussion about the significance of the Olympic Movement's adoption of environmental policies.

HISTORICAL APPROACH OF THE OLYMPIC MOVEMENT TO ECOLOGY

Although the *Olympic Charter* currently states that one of the missions of the IOC is "to encourage and support a responsible concern for environmental issues, to promote sustainable development in sport" (IOC 2017, 17), it was not always like this. The origins of this issue suppose a brief historical overview because there are very few significant examples before the last three decades of the 20th century. Pierre de Coubertin wrote an extensive philosophical and pedagogical bibliography but he only mentioned once potential risks in natural ecosystems caused by sport practice. The Frenchman recognized natural damage caused by sport, especially cycling and motor races throughout the countryside, in an article that the *Olympic Review* published in 1907. He urged for the need to keep those sites clean without trash, arguing ethical and aesthetic motives (DaCosta 1997). Some years after this theoretical precedent, "the Lake Placid Games [in 1932] were the first to raise environmental questions" (Chappelet 2008, 1887). The construction of the bobsleigh run was planned in the Adirondack State Park, a protected landscape. The state of New York forbade this location after a local conservationist complained about the felling of trees, so the venue had to be built in a less controversial place.

It is widely accepted that the ecologist movement achieved its maturity in the decade of the seventies, when the environmental degradation already gained social awareness and started to become a political issue in some Western countries (Dobson 2007, 25). The growth of ecologism was based in ongoing scientific works that studied the limits to growth of contemporaneous human activities. Two notable works, the Rachel Carson's book *Silent Spring* published in 1965 and *The Limits to Growth* report in 1972, marked the pursuit of the ecology as science for greater consciousness within the society. It was reflected in one of the most universal phenomena of the modern times, the Olympic Games. Environmental criticism of this multi-sports event started with the Winter Games held in Sapporo in 1972 and the planned Games in Denver in 1976 (replaced by Innsbruck). It provoked the Lake Placid 1980 OCOG to apply an environmental impact study for the first time (Chappelet 2003). Those problems would pave the way for a later increasing presence of the environment within the Olympic Movement.

The bidding process for the 1972 Winter Olympics was influenced by the controversial candidature of Banff, in the Canadian oldest national park, as environmental groups intensely opposed this bid (mostly to some planned venues, such as one near Lake Louise). Consequently, the IOC awarded the event to Sapporo, which was also a controversial decision because this Japanese city had to replant trees that were cut down in order to create a downhill run on the slopes of Shikotsu National Park (Chappelet 2008). In the same year, Munich 1972 was a pioneer Summer Olympic edition because it openly developed a legacy plan for the urban ecosystem. This host city took advantage of the Games for regenerating an area of the city thanks to the construction of the *Olympiapark*, a completely new park in the second largest city in Germany after creating hills and dales and laying out a lake with green shores (Diem and Knoesel 1974, 29).

Those cases occurred in countries like Canada, Japan, West Germany and the United States, with considerable ecological sensitiveness. In fact, Denver rejected via referendum to host the 1976 Winter Games, after having already having been awarded them. Economic fears and environmental risks were two of the main questions that motivated this public vote (Karamichas 2013). Certainly, worries about financial, urban and natural undesirable legacies intensified among public authorities and citizens after the referendum in Denver and the severe debt caused by the organization of the 1976 Summer Games in Montreal: There were very few bidding applications for the next Olympic Games (Chappelet and Kübler-Mabbott 2008). As we have seen, the United States led the way in the prevention of ecological damage caused by hosting Olympic Games, which explains why the first impact study related to environmental issues dates from 1980 in Lake Placid (DaCosta and Carvalhedo Reis 2011). Meanwhile, this process arose in the seventies without the participation of the IOC, an institution that was extremely slow in adapting green policies. As Karamichas (2013, 95) notes, "It took two decades for the IOC to make the environmental dimension a necessary requirement for awarding the Games."

Juan Antonio Samaranch succeeded Lord Killanin in 1980 as IOC President and the Olympic Movement started a new period (Miller 1990). It was a challenging period for the increasing cost of organizing the Games and the problems associated to gigantism in the venues plans. Thus, the notion of Olympic Games legacies became progressively worthy. Planned legacies achieved enough visibility in this period as the Los Angeles 1984 and Calgary 1988 OCOGs demonstrated, since they aimed "that an Olympic fund was proposed prior to the Games in the bidding process (…) and continuous upkeep of the facilities" (Leopkey and Parent 2012, 936). Furthermore, the Los Angeles 1984 OCOG changed the location of the rowing and canoeing events because the originally proposed venue, the Lake Balboa Park, was rejected by a coalition of homeowners and environmentalists (Burbank et al. 2001).

This decade also saw an evident increase in environmental political support in certain European and Anglo-Saxon countries, mostly where ecologist movements were quite strong (Karamichas 2013). There was a progressive growth of legislation and social awareness, during the years after the 1972 United Nations Conference on the Human Environment, and some countries created national agencies and organisms with an implicit environmental mission. A milestone of this approach of public institutions to ecology was the World Commission on Environment and Development (Savery and Gilbert 2011; Strong 1994). This commission, headed by the Norwegian

Prime Minister Gro Harlem Brundtland, published in 1987 the report *Our Common Future* (submitted to the General Assembly of the United Nations), which proposed the concept 'sustainable development'.

The commitment of Norway to ecological protection supposes that the deliberation on a potential candidature of Lillehammer for the 1992 Winter Olympic Games (later on, for the 1994 Games) should include a program for the protection of the natural environment. Further, this program attracted the support and encouragement of the national government and Brundtland herself (Cantelon and Letters 2010). This occurrence was during a time when scientific evidences like climate change, the greenhouse problem and the ozone depletion were firming up social consciousness (Roper 2006). The era of an ecological rift into the Western society and economic-political establishment rooted the future interest of the IOC for 'soft' approaches to environmental issues such as sustainability and post-Olympic green legacies (Karamichas 2013).

CONSTRUCTION OF AN OLYMPIC GREEN DIMENSION

The IOC became directly interested in ecology in the early nineties because of the first Olympic event that took place in the decade. The 1992 Albertville Games stirred more criticism than ever following a series of circumstances, while interest in ecology rose in Western societies. First of all, these Olympics were hosted in the heart of the Alps, one of the most treasured ecosystems in Europe. Never before had the Winter Olympics been so regionalized, with the competition sites in more than ten Alpine communities. The criticism was in relation to "reports [which] confirmed that construction was on a scale that would result in the irrevocable transformation of the natural environment" (Cantelon and Letters 2010, 423). The environmental damage caused by the construction of new sporting venues altered the natural landscape, but there were other negative impacts as well. The inhabitants of La Plagne, the site of the luge and bobsleigh events, "wore gas masks (...) against the risk (...) of the 40 tonnes of ammonia needed to freeze the bobsleigh track" (Newlands 2011, 155–156).

Although the organizing committee recognized some ecological damage, it was always in order to reinforce their positive measures, even asserting that Albertville'92 were pioneers implementing green projects at the Olympics: "Even we did not manage to avoid errors altogether, something has been proved: the pre-definition of environmental objectives from the outset" (Barnier 1993, 26). Further than these attempts to stop the critics, negative environmental impacts on the host Alpine region were getting considerable public attention. Ecologist groups were mature in France and, specifically, in the Alps, so they prepared a protest march right before the opening ceremony. The negative image of Albertville 1992 reached the Council of Europe, which voted for a resolution promoting ecologically-concerned sports and condemning the environmental controversies of these Winter Games (DaCosta 1997).

This controversy arose in a period when other scandals (doping, bribery or patronage of IOC members) were questioned by publications like *The Lords of the Rings* (Simson and Jennings 1992) and damaged the public image of the Olympic Movement. Simultaneously, the United Nations Conference on Environment and

Development (known also as the Earth Summit and, in Brazil, as Eco-92) took place in Rio de Janeiro after decades of maturation of ecological thought. Environmental awareness had emerged in many countries, meaning that some social sectors and countries were already talking about global warming. In June 1992, the Earth Summit was a high-level meeting that marked global society's attitude towards ecology. Since the environment was emerging as an issue of global significance, the IOC felt pressure because of the controversies concerning Albertville 1992: "The IOC was identified as Albertville and it had to be seen to be doing something" (Cantelon and Letters 2010, 425). It is true that Lausanne was already paying attention to political summits on ecology, i.e. Samaranch and the IOC Executive Board attended discussions about sustainability at the 1991 Davos World Economic Forum (Chappelet 2008).

Furthermore, sustainability and ecology became a major issue for the IOC members starting in the 96th and 97th IOC Sessions (in Tokyo in September 1990 and in Birmingham in June 1991, respectively). These sessions hosted detailed discussions about the subject for the first time in Olympic history (IOC 1992). Publications like the *Olympic Magazine* aimed to defend that "the IOC has been working (...) towards the implementation of a long-term protection policy", revealing that the 98th Session in Courchevel gave some steps towards practical environmental procedures (Gunz 1993, 40). Demonstrators protesting against Albertville'92 months before the Earth Summit showed that something had to be done. Actually, a delegation of the IOC participated at the Earth Summit in Rio as an NGO and delivered a speech entitled *The Olympic Movement and the Environment, by the International Olympic Committee*. Therewith, the speech, already announced that the IOC had just decided to include the environment as an additional topic at its 1994 Centennial Congress in Paris (IOC 1992).[2] On behalf of the IOC Executive Board, Richard Pound explained the participation at the UN Conference as follows:

> Perhaps the most difficult task for the IOC has been to determine the extent of its role in [the] protection of the environment. The enormity of the problem has been identified by many national and international organizations. Conferences have been held; laws have been enacted; books have been written. (...) It has required courage and responsibility (...) to raise the problem to the level of public consciousness. (Pound 1993, 14)

A few weeks after this international event in Rio, the 1992 Summer Olympic Games took place in Spain. Barcelona 1992 sought to yield benefits such as a strategically planned legacy through urban regeneration. Without external standards but following the local political agenda, these Games were planned by municipal authorities with

---

[2] The speech declared that "the IOC is an international non-governmental organisation whose actions and measures in favour of the environment are projected without political purposes" (IOC 1992). It also informed that the new IOC headquarters and a new Olympic Museum in Lausanne were built respecting the trees in Vidy Park, specifically an old oak.

certain ideas in mind, such as the building of sustainable facilities, the city's redevelopment, a coastal regeneration and new green areas (Bohigas 1992). This strategy gradually introduced environmentally-oriented policies that responded to environmental laws decreed by the European Economic Community. On one hand, Barcelona City Council and the organizing committee COOB'92 worked together on the real-time monitoring of concentrations of several pollutants in the atmosphere. On the other hand, both organisms also monitored the concentration of several pollutants on the seacoasts. This control of seawater pollution met the requirements of the Yacht Racing Union (the federation of sailing) and was part of the plan for shoreline regeneration (Plasència 1994; Aragón-Pérez 2018).

Thus, Barcelona 1992 implemented those few practical initiatives in such a critical year. The operation was based on protecting the athletes during the Games and thinking of longer-term urban public health (Aragón-Pérez 2018). There were some communication initiatives too, mostly the Earth Pledge (a pledge wall) at the Barcelona's Olympic Village empowered by the IOC itself (Tarschys 2000). Although Barcelona 1992 is not considered a major milestone for the Olympic green dimension and literature does not acknowledge it, the IOC accepts that these early initiatives hosted at the 1992 Games made considerable progress in the imminent adoption of green decisions into the Olympic Movement, together with the importance of the Earth Summit (IOC 2012).

At the same time, Norway was organizing the 1994 Winter Olympics, which are commonly accepted as the first Games guided by green criteria. As Leopkey and Parent (2012, 933) wrote, ecology were incorporated into the Games' core because "it was the Lillehammer Games in 1994 (…) that brought the issue to the forefront." Norwegian society was very mobilized in defending nature and the environment, with its political leaders having promoted sustainable policies on the national and international levels (e.g., Brundtland and the report *Our Common Future*). In such context, avoiding ecological damage arose as a priority to host the Games (Karamichas 2013). Lillehammer'94 implemented a holistic environmental project thanks to the intense conviction of the host country towards green issues much more than as a reaction of the Olympic Movement after the discredit caused by the previous Winter Olympics.

Lillehammer 1994 based its green management on the need to ensure the conservation of Gudbrandsdalen, the host region, and its high-value mountainous ecosystem. The potential impact of these Winter Games in this area caused social alarm, on account of the city being sparsely inhabited (the city of Lillehammer has 25,000 inhabitants) but expecting a total of 100,000 visitors to arrive for the Games (LOOC 1992). The functional area for environment of the organizing committee LOOC worked together with *Naturvernforbund* (a Norwegian ecologist association) for planning a series of goals that followed five fundamental ideas. Those purposes were the environmental protection of Gudbrandsdalen, the application of sustainable development guidelines, the maintenance of environmental health standards during the event, the development of certain environmental guidelines (energy efficiency, use of renewable energy sources, recycling and integration architecture in the landscape) and the promotion of ecological awareness (LOOC 1992). A key for guaranteeing such simultaneous regional development and environmental protection was the utilization of existing and distant venues, in order to minimize potential environmental threats (Kovác 2003).

In consonance, the 1994 Games were a turning point because it succeeded in implementing an environmental program. It allowed the leaders of the Olympic Movement to recognize the environment as the third dimension of Olympism following the soft ecological thought that UNEP (the environmental United Nations' agency) had encouraged worldwide after the Earth Summit: "UNEP has worked very closely with the IOC since" (Oben 2011, 27). The proclamation at the 1994 Centennial Congress in Paris (103rd IOC Session) that the environment is an essential element of the Olympic Movement was formally accepted. A mention to ecological responsibility was added in the Olympic Charter in 1995 and the IOC inaugurated a Sport and Environment Commission a few months later (Boykoff 2017). After one hundred years of history, the modern Olympism was suddenly assimilating eco-friendly goals such as promoting education or giving priority to activities related to the environment and sustainability. This enthusiasm has produced statements such as: "It is important to ensure that respect for the environment and the active promotion of sustainable development are incorporated in the spirit and practice [of Olympism]" (IOC 2007, 41). The IOC itself offers a positive point of view about the achievements of its green dimension defending that it has strengthened sport activities and ecologically respectful facilities:

> The Olympic Movement has regarded the environment as the third pillar of Olympism. (…) As a result, it has developed a proactive environmental defense policy which has found expression in the 'Earth Pact', joint activities with the UNEP, the 'greening' of the Olympic Games, and the holding of world and regional conferences on Sport and the Environment. This Agenda 21 places the environmental defense policy of the Olympic Movement in the broader context of sustainable development. (Tarradellas 2003, 76)

However, that passionate green approach proclaimed at the Centennial Congress that appeared right after the criticism generated around Albertville 1992 has also incited less optimistic feedbacks. Some voices have stressed the speed of the IOC's adoption of environmental criteria. They emphasize the short period taken by the IOC to adapt to the global ecological agenda, in contrast with other historical controversies such as amateurism. Therefore, many environmental contradictions of the Olympic Games were not solved in depth yet: "The IOC's environmental adaptation has proved the capacity-building (…) when exposed to external pressures, but equally suggests a lack of strength for resolving internal controversies" (DaCosta 1997, 102). For instance, Stubbs (2011) argues that environment and sustainability challenges are continually moving and, consequently, effective Olympic policies should be flexible.

DEVELOPMENT OF AN OLYMPIC GREEN DIMENSION

The 2000 Games became a milestone that integrated environmental management systems into the preparation and staging of the event. Australia was a pioneering country in the adoption of green policies. As an example, the first green political party in the world was born in Australia in 1971. In consonance, it was the first Olympic organization monitored by the IOC for an effective introduction of green plans. The Lillehammer 1994 OCOG followed its own local agenda, while the Sydney Olympics were also the result of the green dimension recently adopted by the Olympic Movement. The Sydney 2000 OCOG (SOCOG) achieved several environmental improvements: an ambitious nationwide tree-planting goal and native species were planted near sport venues as part of a land-care program; recycling was extensively assumed; there were measures to save on water use; the Games allowed a major clean-up at Homebush Bay and former industrial and wasteland areas were regenerated creating new parks, and a special program led to the restoration of wetlands (Stubbs 2001). As Lillehammer'94 did, there was a functional area explicitly devoted to manage actions derived from ecological thought (SOCOG 1999).

Since Sydney was chosen in 1993 as host city of the 2000 Olympics, one year before the Centennial Congress, both the IOC and the Australian organizers aimed for the event to be "dubbed the Green Games" (Stubbs 2001, 3). Thus, a communication strategy became essential in parallel with the mentioned green programs. Despite these green projects, the huge dimensions of the Olympic Games connoted potential impacts (such as energy consumption or waste production) that had to be compensated with the Environment Information Office, a department within SOCOG that informed journalists and media. The magnificent motto of the 'Green Games' was censured as an unrealistic term and, according to some opinions, "Sydney 2000 failed to appreciate the significance of what they had achieved" (Stubbs 2001, 27).

Therefore, SOCOG reinforced a message of enthusiasm publicizing that those Games would leave an eco-friendly legacy after the IOC established the requirement of adopting more environmentally responsible approaches: "The rhetoric employed in the media leading up to Sydney 2000 revealed great enthusiasm" (Coaffee 2010, 3638). Since then, most organizing committees promote an environmental image and aim to be mentioned as 'Green Games' too. The organizers of the 2004 Summer Games in Athens promised that this event would only use clean and renewable energy sources and environmentally friendly technologies and materials. But these words were a long way off coming into existence. International NGOs like Greenpeace demonstrated that "nearly all environmental recommendations were ignored" in the construction of the Olympic Village in Athens (Coaffee 2010, 3684).

Actually, Greenpeace itself and SOCOG developed a fruitful collaboration for strengthening the environmental measures and projects of Sydney 2000. Although the 2000 Summer Olympics are widely known as the "the greenest Olympics ever" (Mol 2010, 511), some Australian ecologist groups reported lack of commitment against environmental pollution and transport congestion or complained about some standards of the 'ecologic Olympic Village'. Athens 2004 also announced the assistance of another ecologist NGO, in this case World Wild Fund for Nature (Maslova 2010). However, this approach was much less effective and the 2004 Olympics were accused of greenwashing. One of the very few accomplishments of these Games was the improvement of social awareness towards ecology in Greece, which quickly decreased in the context of the Greek economic downturn (Karamichas 2013).

Western populations usually perceive China as a leading polluter state, with limitations in transparency. Indeed, Chinese large urban areas like Beijing, host city of the 2008 Games, historically suffer severe environmental problems; mainly very high levels of atmospheric pollution. In these circumstances, the IOC introduced Olympic Games Impact studies during the preparations of Beijing 2008 in order to prevent potential risks (IOC 2012). Additionally, the Chinese authorities had the ambition to transform the country's international image thanks to the catalyst effect of the Games, and good environmental quality certainly constituting part of such a new modern image. Beijing'08 included the environment in the design of the Olympics already at the candidature. Ecology was necessary even for the success of the event because "environmentalists, medical specialists and athletes in many countries were concerned about China's environmental problems" (Mol 2010, 517–518). The truth is that the organizers of the 2008 Games lived up to most green promises and these efforts resulted in better environmental quality in Beijing. For example, there were clear improvements in air quality indicators in the years up to Beijing 2008. Nevertheless, the harmful conditions of the urban ecosystem of the Chinese capital did not disappear, so there was ecological "concern for Olympic organizers, competitors and observers, as well as for the citizens of Beijing" (Mol 2010, 519).

Regarding the Winter Olympics, Turin 2006 implemented new strategies for environmental management but ecologist groups disapproved of some other decisions. This mostly consisted of the construction of infrastructure in the Alps (Burnside-Lawry and Ariemma 2014). While the world of sport (international federations, managers of facilities and events, etc.) has lately been adopting sustainability in a holistic way (Dolf 2011), it is particularly intense in some countries like Canada. This explains why the Vancouver 2010 organizing committee implemented sustainable concepts under a very mature perspective: reduction of carbon footprint; initiatives for conserving biodiversity; use of renewable energy, and moderating waste, water consumption and pollution. Also, constructions incorporated technologies that minimized environmental impacts, according to "Canadian green building standards for the new sport venues" (Duffy 2011, 95). In contrast with "Games in the last two decades (…) [being] presented as 'green', with an emphasis on eco-efficiency rather than a more complex approach to sustainability", DaCosta and Carvalhedo Reis (2011, 167) emphasize that the Vancouver 2010 Winter Games were a holistic sustainable mega-event because they involved more than just eco-friendly procedures. Therein, it is claimed that the Games also incorporated social and economic goals.

Presenting the urban regeneration of Barcelona 1992 and the environmental achievements of Sydney'00 as role models, the managers of the London 2012 Olympics also insisted on delivering "the greenest Games in history" (Coaffee 2010, 3726). London'12 already promised in its bid the creation of a large new urban parkland and five main sustainable pillars: carbon footprint, waste, biodiversity, healthy living and inclusion. But these exemplary environmental standards lacked a comprehensive plan and the main institutional stakeholders executed projects that were sometimes disconnected. Therefore, the organizing committee LOCOG and the local authorities decided to promote a single Commission for a Sustainable London 2012, which set up a Sustainability Plan (McCarthy 2011; Roper 2006).

Despite the 2014 Winter Games in Sochi, in which environmental goals were a secondary priority for the Russian authorities, Rio 2016 continued the tradition of presenting a candidature with ambitious ecological promises. As an example, the bid assured that sanitation upgrade systems at Barra-Jacarepagua and Guanabara Bay would result in more than 80% of overall sewage collected and treated when the Games would take place. However, this and other promises were not achieved in 2016 and caused the Rio Games to be accused of greenwashing (Boykoff 2017). Despite many accomplishments, such as the regeneration of Lake Rodrigo de Freitas (venue of canoeing and rowing), other goals failed, impacting the targeted good image about the environmental management of Rio'16. This occurred even when considering that the organizers of this Olympic edition fulfilled most of the environmental criteria that the IOC had recommended:

> The awarding of the sustainability certificate to Rio 2016 symbolizes the disjointed relationship that can develop between internal environmental practices and wider sustainability goals. Creating international standards (…) is clearly not enough. (Boykoff 2017, 197)

CONCLUSION: CONTRADICTIONS, ACHIEVEMENTS AND CHALLENGES OF AN ECO-FRIENDLY OLYMPISM

As stated in the introduction, the Olympic Games are an exceptional project for host cities because they allow for urban entrepreneurialism and regeneration goals, which require a solid planned legacy (Tomlinson 2010). Legacies are, today, something systematically planned since positive benefits are commonly put forth as reasons to justify hosting the Games. Those general benefits always contain references to sustainable long-term legacies, but the huge dimensions of a mega-event like the Olympics shows that green goals are sometimes unrealistic and even sometimes concepts of marketing. This also happens in cases that are thought to be successful: "Sydney was said to be a 'Green Games', but to what degree 'greenwashing' occurred merits additional review" (Leopkey and Parent 2012, 938). Olympism, a phenomenon based on a philosophy of altruism and purity that welcomes most aims of the ecological thought, brings at the same time a wonderful platform for marketing messages. This message has been used by candidate and host cities to promote their Games as the 'greenest event ever', a promotional rhetoric helpful for winning bids but not necessarily for environmental or sustainable tangible legacies (Ward 2010).

In consonance with the above, the issue of greenwashing arises. If environmental damage is always undesirable, a cynical utilization of ineffective and futile green slogans tends to normalize such damage. How does the IOC and the rest of the Olympic Movement deal with such a dark side within their main product, the Games? Some voices claim that ecological considerations play a full role in the decision-making process to choose Olympic host cities. On the other hand, these considerations have often been criticized as inefficient because of the construction of gigantic new facilities with little use afterwards, the waste generated at the Olympics and the consequences in surrounding natural landscapes (Mol 2010). Fairly, the Olympic mega-event does not appear to be a sustainable activity for its unavoidable consequences: energy use, international transportation and carbon footprint, waste, etc. At the same time, the catalyzing potential of the Olympics brings enough resources to deliver sustainable and long-term gains (Stubbs 2011). Therefore, is ecology a dark aspect within the most popular sport phenomenon?

Rocha Araujo (2015) thinks that the sustainable guidelines that the IOC adopted in 1994 lacked a more holistic and applicable approach because it only reinforced a pure environmental perspective, dismissing economic and social elements. Indeed, we have already analyzed that most Olympic Games after Lillehammer 1994 (with very few exceptions, like Vancouver 2010) did not accomplish a totally satisfactory ecological management. Jägemann (2013) considers that there is a central problem since recommendations proclaimed by the IOC are not mandatory nor decisive for choosing an Olympic city. Furthermore, the required outstanding new infrastructure or the low weight of environmental criteria on the evaluation of candidate cities implies that actual sustainability is hardly addressed because "the IOC's environmental concept is not comprehensive. It addresses significant aspects, but not all the important ones" (Jägemann 2013, 253–254). Following this last line of reasoning, we could deduce that the Olympic Movement sets itself up for charges of greenwashing by failing to introduce oversight mechanisms and concrete standards:

> Beyond mutually beneficial blackslappery, the problem also emerges from the verbal arms race to offer the grandest, most robust environmental promises during the bid phase in order to both impress IOC members and to attract support from local populations. (…) This dialect of escalation can lead to overhyped environmental pledges that are difficult (…) to meet. (Boykoff 2017, 196)

Nevertheless, institutionalizing environmental sustainability in all phases of the Olympic Games process made it possible for green measures to have become a key factor in global networks and flows. It is a positive outcome of the Olympic green dimension that, thanks to this, many actors (international official sponsors and suppliers, local stakeholders, sport federations, etc.) have kept in close touch (Mol 2010). In this sense, 'soft' environmentalists welcome partial achievements through global phenomena like sport or multinational organizations, so limited steps can also bring about a more sustainable environment (Dobson 2007). Concern for the environment can be translated into simple measures and decisions or into ambitious plans for ecological protection. There are differences both within and between host countries because ecosystems, needs, risks and demographic contexts are variables. Thus, "these marked variations have played an important role in assessing the environmental concern (…) exhibited by the populations of Olympic host nations" (Karamichas 2013, 44). The environmental conditions in the Alps or a pollutant megalopolis like Beijing are different; also the social awareness in Australia, Greece or China. In agreement with this, an environmental strategy within the management of OCOGs may take into consideration the local and national ecological circumstances.

A sport mega-event with the magnitude of the Olympic Games is an excellent opportunity for encouraging global awareness of the human impact on the Earth and for developing solid eco-friendly measures. In this sense, activities like the Olympics have the strength to change behaviors and to implement good practices. However, even considering that sport events are far from being a main cause of ecological damage, greenwashing, white elephants, carbon emissions, waste production or ignored environmental goals are some of the negative ecological effects of hosting the Games. But those dark sides can be avoided and attempts to combat them are possible if an appropriate ecological management system is planned and applied. Further, one must consider that it is difficult to decide whether a legacy is positive or negative because sometimes it is both, depending on the stakeholder under observation (Preuss 2015).

This means that every strategy for a green legacy and for preventing environmental threats must be unique according to the needs of each host city (Gratton and Preuss 2008). Adaptability to the local ecosystem and its circumstances and a holistic approach to sustainability (as Agenda 2020 does, approved by the IOC in 2014) become indispensable. We are not owners of this planet, just its guests, so a phenomenon based on universal values and principles like Olympism should not be an activity that regularly provokes ecological scandals and undesirable impacts. On the contrary, the Games should be used for implementing the promises of OCOGs and the IOC to protect and care for our surroundings.

References

Aragón-Pérez, Alberto. 2018. "The Construction of an Ecological Thought during the Olympic Games of Barcelona 1992: Elements of Sustainability, Environmental Health and Diffusion. " PhD diss., Universitat Autònoma de Barcelona.

Barnier, Michel. 1993. "L'environnement en Jeux... = The Environment at Stake." *Message Olympique = Olympic Message* 35: 23–26.

Boykoff, Jules. 2017. "Green Games: The Olympics, Sustainability, and Rio 2016." In *Rio 2016: Olympic Myths, Hard Realities*, by Andrew Zimbalist, 179–206. Washington: Brookings Instituion Press.

Burbank, Matthew, Gregory Andranovich, and Charles H Heying. 2001. *Olympic Dreams: The Impact of Mega-Events on Local Politics*. Boulder, Colo.: Lynne Rienner Publishers.

Burnside-Lawry, J., and Ariemma, L. 2014. "Global governance and communicative action: a study of democratic participation during planning for the Lyon–Turin rail link". In *Journal of Public Affairs*.

Cantelon, Hart, and Michael Letters. 2010. "The Making of the IOC Environmental Policy as the Third Dimension of the Olympic Movement." In *The Olympics : A Critical Reader*, edited by Vassil Girginov, 419–29. London: Routledge.

Cashman, Richard. 2003. "What Is 'Olympic Legacy'?." In *The Legacy of the Olympic Games, 1984-2000: International Symposium, Lausanne, 14th, 15th and 16th November 2002*, edited by Miquel Moragas Spà, Christopher Kennett, and Nuria Puig, 31–42. Lausanne: International Olympic Committee.

Chappelet, Jean-Loup. 2008. "Olympic Environmental Concerns as a Legacy of the Winter Games." *International Journal of the History of Sport* 25 (14): 1884–1902.

Coaffee, Jon. 2010. "Urban Regeneration and Renewal." In *Olympic Cities: City Agendas, Planning, and the World's Games, 1896 - 2016*, edited by John R. Gold and Margaret M. Gold. Routledge. Kindle.
DaCosta, Lamartine. 1997. "The Olympic Movement Today and the Environment Protection." *International Olympic Academy Session* 37: 100–106.
DaCosta, Lamartine, and Arianne Carvalhedo Reis. 2011. "Is the Booming Sustainability of Olympic and Paralympic Games Here to Stay?" In *Sustainability and Sport*, edited by Jill. Savery and Keith Gilbert, 167–76. Champaign, Ill.: Common Ground.
Diem, Liselott, and Ernst Knoesel, eds. 1974. *Die Spiele : The Official Report of the Organizing Committee for the Games of the XXth Olympiad Munich 1972 : The Organization*. Vol. 1. Munich: Organisationskomitee fur die Spiele der XXth Olympiade München 1972.
Dobson, Andrew. 2007. *Green Political Thought*. London; New York: Routledge.
Dolf, Matt. 2011. "SSeting Up Sport with Tools for Sustainability." In *Sustainability and Sport*, edited by Jill. Savery and Keith Gilbert, 33–42. Champaign, Ill.: Common Ground.
Duffy, Ann. 2011. "Vancouver 2010 : Raing the Bar for Sustainable Olympic and Paralympic Winter Games." In *Sustainability and Sport*, edited by Jill. Savery and Keith Gilbert, 91–102. Champaign, Ill.: Common Ground.
Gunz, Jean-Michel. 1993. "Environnement et Villes Candidates = Environment and Candidate Cities." *Message Olympique = Olympic Message* 35: 40–44.
Hiller, Harry. 2006. "Post-Event Outcomes and the Post-Modern Turn: The Olympics and Urban Transformations." *European Sport Management Quarterly* 6 (4): 317–32.
International Olympic Committee. 1992. *Conferencia de las Naciones Unidas sobre el Medio Ambiente y el Desarrollo: El Movimiento Olímpico y el medio ambiente, por el Comité Olímpico Internacional* [Document]. International organizations Files. Lausanne: Centre d'Études Olympiques.
———. 2007. *IOC Guide on Sport, Environment and Sustainable Development*. Lausanne: International Olympic Committee.
———. 2012. *Sustainability through Sport : Implementing the Olympic Movement's Agenda 21*. Lausanne: International Olympic Committee.
———. 2014. *Olympic Agenda 2020 : Context and Background*. Lausanne: International Olympic Committee.
———. 2017. *Olympic Charter: In force as from 15 September 2017*. Lausanne: International Olympic Committee.
Jägemann, Hans. 2013. "The Olympic Games and Sustainability." In *Olympics : Past & Present*, edited by Andreas Amendt, Christian Wacker, and Stephan Wassong, 251–56. Munich: Qatar Olympic & Sports Museum : Prestel.
Karamichas, John. 2013. *The Olympic Games and the Environment*. Houndmills, Basingstoke, Hampshire; New York: Palgrave Macmillan.
Kovác, Igor. 2003. "The Olympic Territory : A Way to an Ideal Olympic Scene." In *The Legacy of the Olympic Games, 1984-2000: International Symposium, Lausanne, 14th, 15th and 16th November 2002*, edited by Miquel Moragas Spà, Christopher Kennett, and Nuria Puig, 110–17. Lausanne: International Olympic Committee.
Leopkey, Becca, and Milena M. Parent. 2012. "Olympic Legacy: From General Benefits to Sustainable Long-Term Legacy." *The International Journal of the History of Sport* 29 (6): 924–43.
LOOC. 1992. *Olympic Games with a Green Profile : Environmental Goals for the XVII Olympic Winter Games*. Lillehammer: Lillehammer OL'94 AS.
Maslova, Nadezhda. 2010. "Green Olympics: Intentions and Reality." Estocolmo: Royal Institute of Technology.

McCarthy, Shaun. 2011. "Sustainable Olympics - Assuring a Legacy: The Commission for a Sustainable London 2012." In *Sustainability and Sport*, edited by Jill. Savery and Keith Gilbert, 133–44. Champaign, Ill.: Common Ground.

Miller, David. 1990. "Evolution of the Olympic Movement." In *De Moscou À Lausanne = From Moscow to Lausanne*, by IOC, 9–24. Lausanne.

Mol, Andrew P. J. 2010. "Sustainability as Global Attractor: The Greening of the 2008 Beijing Olympics." *Global Networks* 10 (4): 510–28.

Newlands, Maxine. 2011. "Deconstructing 'Team Green Britain' and the London 2012 Olympic and Paralympic Games." In *Sustainability and Sport*, edited by Jill. Savery and Keith Gilbert, 153–66. Champaign, Ill.: Common Ground.

Oben, Theodore. 2011. "Sport and the Environment: An UNEP Perspective." In *Sustainability and Sport*, edited by Jill. Savery and Keith Gilbert, 25–33. Champaign, Ill.: Common Ground.

Plasència, Antoni, ed. 1994. *La Salut pública en els Jocs Olímpics de Barcelona'92 = La salud pública en los Juegos Olímpicos de Barcelona'92*. Barcelona: Ajuntament de Barcelona.

Pound, Richard W. 1993. "Le C.I.O. et L'environment = The IOC and the Environment." *Message Olympique = Olympic Message* 35: 14–22.

Preuss, Holger. 2015. "The Legacy Framework of Olympic Games." In *O Futuro dos Mega-eventos Esportivos = The Future of Sports Mega-events*, edited by Andrea Deslandes, Lamartine DaCosta, and Ana Miragaya, 61–91. Rio de Janeiro: Engenho.

Rocha Araujo, Carla Isabel. 2015. "Sustentabilidade e Desenvolvimento Sustentável nos Jogos Olímpicos do futuro: uma revisão da Agenda 2020 do Comitê Olímpico Internacional." In *O Futuro dos Mega-eventos Esportivos = The Future of Sports Mega-events*, edited by Andrea Deslandes, Lamartine DaCosta, and Ana Miragaya, 242–58. Rio de Janeiro: Engenho.

Roper, Tom. 2006. "Producing Environmentally Sustainable Olympic Games and 'Greening' Major Public Events." *Global Urban Development* 2 (1): 1–5.

Savery, Jill, and Keith Gilbert. 2011. *Sustainability and Sport*. Champaign, Ill.: Common Ground.

Simson, Vyv, and Andrew Jennings. 1992. *Los Señores de Los Anillos: Poder, Dinero Y Doping En Los Juegos Olímpicos*. Barcelona: Transparència.

SOCOG. 1999. *Environment Report: Turning Green into Gold: Making an Environmental Vision a Reality*. Sydney: SOCOG.

Strong, Maurice F. 1994. "Conferencia de las Naciones Unidas sobre Medio Ambiente y Desarrollo." In *La Diplomacia ambiental: México y la Conferencia de las Naciones Unidas sobre Medio Ambiente y Desarrollo*, edited by Alberto I. Glender Rivas and Víctor Lichtinger, 19–44. México: Fondo de Cultura Económica - Secretaría de Relaciones Exteriores.

Stubbs, David. 2001. *Sydney Olympic Games 2000: The Environmental Games: A Review of the Environmental Achievements of the "Best Olympic Games Ever."* Dorking: Committed to Green Foundation.

———. 2011. "The Olympic Movement as a Leader of Sustainability." In *Sustainability and Sport*, edited by Jill. Savery and Keith Gilbert, 117–22. Champaign, Ill.: Common Ground.

Tarradellas, Josep. 2003. "The Olympic Games and Sustainability." In *The Legacy of the Olympic Games, 1984-2000: International Symposium, Lausanne, 14th, 15th and 16th November 2002*, edited by Miquel Moragas Spà, Christopher Kennett, and Nuria Puig, 74–80. Lausanne: International Olympic Committee.

Tarschys, Daniel, ed. 2000. *Sports de pleine nature et protection de l'environnement / actes du colloque organisé à l'initiative du Centre de droit et d'économie du sport (CDES)*. Limoges: Pulim.

Tomlinson, Richard. 2010. "Whose Accolades? An Alternative Perspective on Motivations for Hosting the Olympics." *Urban Forum* 21: 139–52.

Ward, Stephen V. 2010. "Promoting the Olympic City." In *Olympic Cities: City Agendas, Planning, and the World's Games, 1896 - 2016*, edited by John R. Gold and Margaret M. Gold. Routledge. Kindle.

Dark Sides of Sport

CHAPTER 7

The Russian Doping Scandal in the Context of Global Political Relations

Thomas M. Hunt and Austin Duckworth

RUSSIAN DOPING, CONTEMPORARY AFFAIRS, AND THE DARK SIDE OF SPORT

The ongoing Russian doping scandal constitutes perhaps the single most prominent controversy in recent sports history. Occurring as it did after a world record setting performance at the 1988 Olympics in Seoul, Ben Johnson's positive test for steroids perhaps equaled it terms of dramatic revelation (see Francis and Coplon 1990; and Moore 2012). The same might be said of the admittance by Lance Armstrong of his use of performance-enhancing substances in seven Tour de France victories (see Albergotti and O'Connell 2013; and Dimeo 2014). None of these, however, featured the type of state involvement which appears to have taken place in Russia. Indeed, only the Cold War case of the Soviet Union and its satellite system in Eastern Europe (see Franke and Berendonk 1997; Ungerleider 2001; Hunt 2011; Dennis and Grix 2012; Krüger, Becker, and Nielsen 2015) seems to offer a meaningful point of comparison. The return to Great Power competition that is now under way in global political relations (Mankoff 2011; Feldman 2013; Coker 2015) imparts a great deal of meaning to this fact. In recently describing the dynamics at play in the current scandal, a Russian-American research team composed of scholars Sergey Altukhov and John Nauright went so far as to invoke the specter of last century's era of superpower rivalry. In doing so, they declared that no less than a "New Sporting Cold War" was at hand (Altukhov and Nauright 2018, 1; see also Hunt 2017b).

While too early to predict how matters will play out in the coming years, it is nevertheless clear at this point that the contemporary doping scandal reveals much about Russia's complicated relationship with the wider world. It is one marked by individual self-interest as well as geopolitical trends and nationalist ambitions. With much to criticize on all sides of the matter, this is very much a story about the dark side of sports.

EARLY STAGES OF THE DOPING SCANDAL

While evidence existed prior to 2014 that a sizable number of Russian athletes were using performance-enhancing substances ("CAS Dismisses Russian Skier's Doping Appeal" 2010), it wasn't until that year that the true dimensions of their usage began to be revealed. The previous year, the International Association of Athletics Federations (IAAF) banned Russian middle-distance runner Yuliya Stepanova, who later admitted long-term involvement with testosterone and the blood-boosting hormone Erythropoietin. With the input of her husband, an anti-doping official named Vitaly, she resolved to respond by unveiling all that she could about what was happening in Russia. In a July 2018 written statement to the U.S. Commission on Security and Cooperation in Europe (also known as the Helsinki Commission), she described the decision: "I could act like most of my teammates did—cry a little and continue to listen to the lies of the Russian sports officials and while being sanctioned continue to get paid by the Russian Police, Russian Ministry of Sports and Russian Regional sports organizations. Or we could try to fight the system together" (Stepanova 2018, 2).

With the 2014 Winter Olympics set to soon open in the Russian resort town of Sochi, there was much then going on in the Russian sport system. By using her cell phone, Stepanova secretly recorded the words and actions of a sizable number of Russian coaches, athletes, staff, and training personnel—most of whom were involved in disciplines related to track-and-field. The records were in time turned over to a German investigative journalist named Hajo Seppelt. Through the German media group ARD, he released the following December an hour-long documentary film based on these and other materials (Seppelt 2014; see also Bonesteel 2014). In the documentary, Russian discus thrower Evgenia Pecherina says at one point that nearly 100 percent of the elite athletes from her country were doping. Even if it's a gross overestimation this is an astonishing number. Even so, it is a statement by Seppelt at the 35-minute mark of the film that gives a true sense of its content:

> I found coach[es] and doctors who authorize doping, athletes who admit to it, an Act of Government of the State which hinders controls, a laboratory which seems to help with the cover-up, an anti-doping agency, which apparently provides appointments for controls. And a management that does not want to talk. And then I realize, that still was not everything (ARD 2014, 21).

RESPONSE OF THE SPORTS WORLD

The reactions of several individuals connected to the World Anti-Doping Agency (WADA) were captured in the ARD documentary. The still-highly influential former head of the organization Richard Pound (for background on his ideas about doping, see Pound 2008) declared that "if something of this nature is being organized by any country it is a very serious problem for the credibility of international sport and the credibility of anti-doping efforts" (ARD 2014, 28). WADA director David Howman added that "when you combine everything and you look at the facts of this documentation and oft [*sic*] the other things, that I have heard and seen, of course it is shocking. What we have gotta do is to be fearless in approaching [these] issues and make sure that those who are suffering from fear are protected" (ARD 2014, 28).

On December 16, WADA announced that an independent investigation would be conducted by a three-person commission under the direction of Pound (Press Association 2014); the other members who took part in the inquiry were Canadian law professor Richard McLaren and German cyber-crime expert Günter Younger. Among the numerous findings of endemic doping expressed in the body's final report, the following passage perhaps best distills its conclusions about the state of the Russian sports system:

> A Deeply Rooted Culture of Cheating—The investigation indicates that the acceptance of cheating at all levels is widespread and of long standing. Many of the more egregious offenders appear to be coaches who, themselves, were once athletes and who work in connection with medical personnel. This 'win at all costs' mentality was then passed to current athletes, whether willing to participate or not. An athlete's decision not to participate is likely to leave him or her without access to top calibre coaches and thus the opportunity to excel. This acceptance and, at times, expectation of cheating and disregard for testing and other globally accepted anti-doping efforts, indicate a fundamentally flawed mindset that is deeply ingrained in all levels of Russian athletics. The mindset is "justified" on the theory that everyone else is cheating as well (WADA Independent Commission 2015, 10–11).

Russian athletes, coaches, medical staff were all implicated in the document (WADA Independent Commission 2015). Members of Russia's infamous Federal Security Service were in addition asserted as having maintained a regular and intimidating presence at Russia's WADA-accredited anti-doping laboratory (2015, 196–97). It should be noted that along with its director, Dr. Grigory Rodchenkov, this facility received perhaps the single largest dose of criticism from the commission. Its report described bribes to ensure that positive test results were hidden as well as the submission by sports officials of bogus "clean" urine on behalf of athletes who were likely to otherwise fail their tests (2015, 275). Another passage described the destruction of some 1,400 lab samples just days prior to a WADA visit despite the fact that Rodchenkov had been ordered to preserve everything until the allegations made in the ARD documentary could be investigated (2015, 203).

In response to the report, WADA suspended the Russian Anti-Doping Laboratory, called for the removal of Rodchenkov, initiated a review process of the Russian Anti-Doping Agency (RUSADA), and recommended that the IAAF suspend its Russian track-and-field affiliate—an organization called the All Russian Athletics Federation ("WADA Takes Immediate Action on Key Recommendations of Independent Commission" 2015). Perhaps motivated by the fact that it itself had not escaped critique by Pound's commission (WADA Independent Commission 2015, 12; see, for additional background Krieger 2018, 8–10), the IAAF in short order confirmed that it would at least provisionally take the suggested step ("IAAF Provisionally Suspends Russian Member Federation ARAF" 2015).

As Pound later explained, however, the commission had failed to find definitive indications of a true state-sponsored doping program:

> While our Independent Commission's Report suggested that doping in Russia was likely not restricted to athletics, and that the Russian secret services (FSB) were present within the Sochi and Moscow laboratories, the Commission did not uncover concrete evidence to the effect that the Russian state was manipulating the doping control process." The Pound Commission leveraged all information that the whistleblowers had provided; and yet, there was no concrete evidence to support State manipulation ("WADA Statement Clarifies Timing of McLaren Investigation Report and States Facts Related to Investigations into Russian Matters" 2016).

Matters would soon change on the issue. As captivatingly asserted in the Academy-award-winning documentary *Icarus* (Fogel 2017), the pressure which ensued in the aftermath of the Independent Report was reportedly so intense as to cause Rodchenkov to flee the country through the assistance of the primary maker of the film, Bryan Fogel. A measure of skepticism is warranted when watching these events; and, in fact, the same should be said for virtually everything Rodchenkov says—whether in the film or otherwise. Throughout the documentary and in later statements to the media and to governmental officials, the former laboratory director has made a number of contradictory claims. A 2017 review of *Icarus* in *The Guardian* captures this point perfectly:

> Certainly it's clear that Fogel has been won over by the ebullient Rodchenkov from the pair's very first meeting over Skype. You can see why: he's charismatic, makes for a great subject and is always willing to divulge a bit of devastating inside info to camera. At the same time though, there's an inescapable slipperiness to Rodchenkov's character that makes his testimony slightly hard to swallow. At points, he exhibits remorse at his actions, lamenting that Russia's medal haul at Sochi might have emboldened Putin in his decision to meddle in the Ukraine; other times he seems mischievously gleeful at his own nefarious deeds (Mumford 2017).

This is all to say that one would do well to consider Rodchenkov's words carefully—and as part of a much larger body of information.

In a May 2016 appearance on CBS's *60 Minutes* television program, the Stepanovas disclosed the contents of a recent discussion with the former laboratory director which they had secretly recorded. They recalled that Rodchenkov had "bragged he was in possession of what he called 'the Sochi list,' the Russians who competed dirty at the games." He moreover had claimed "that some FSB agents worked as doping control officers during the [recently concluded] Sochi games. That FSB tried to control every single step of the anti-doping process in Sochi" ("Russian

Doping at Sochi Winter Olympics Exposed" 2016). Here again, the former laboratory director came across as less than trustworthy. Even so, something clearly was going on in the Russian sports sytem.

A few days after the Stepanovas' interview the *New York Times* published an article based on an intensive three-day round of interviews with Rodchenkov himself (Ruiz and Schwirtz 2016; additional documentary support was later supplied by Rodchenkov, as covered in Ruiz 2017). The efforts to enhance the performance-levels of Russian athletes had been going on for years, he said. Moreover, he claimed that everything was done at the behest of the Russian government's Ministry of Sport and its leader, bureaucrat Vitaly Mutko (Ruiz and Schwirtz 2016; for more background on Mutko, see Critchley 2015). One aspect of the program was Rodchenkov's provision of "a cocktail of three anabolic steroids" soaked in alcohol to ministry officials that would pass drug tests if taken properly. He in addition outlined a clandestine effort to circumvent anti-doping protocols at the 2014 Winter Olympic Games in Sochi. One of his more striking remarks was that a shadowy individual whom he strongly suspected to be an FSB agent had prior to the competitions found a way to remove the tamperproof caps of the bottles in which backup samples of athletes' urine were stored. "When I first time saw that bottle is open, I did not believe my eyes," Rodchenkov said. He and his team were thus given the ability to swap clean urine in for all Russian athletes who might test positive. They did so by means a small cutout in the wall of the sample storage room which otherwise hidden from view by a storage cabinet (Ruiz and Schwirtz 2016).

In light of these disclosures, WADA felt it necessary to initiate a second round of independent investigation. Perhaps to cut off criticisms of a conflict of interest on the matter (Keating 2016), WADA turned to McLaren rather than Pound to lead the new inquiry ("WADA Names Richard McLaren to Sochi Investigation Team" 2016). The Canadian legal scholar issued his report only a short time before the commencement of the 2016 Summer Games in Rio de Janeiro. Its executive summary noted that the inquiry:

> [confirmed] the general veracity of the published information concerning the sample swapping that went on at the Sochi Laboratory during the Sochi Games. The surprise result of the Sochi investigation was the revelation of the extent of State oversight and directed control of the Moscow Laboratory in processing, and covering up urine samples of Russian athletes from virtually all sports before and after the Sochi Games. (McLaren 2016, 6)

The IOC Executive Board briefly considered the idea of outright banning Russia from international competition, though it soon backed off and left the various international federations to decide what should happen in their respective disciplines (Ingle 2016). In announcing this conclusion, the body asserted that it felt compelled to balance the reality of the evidence that had been gathered against the fact that individual Russian athletes had a right to be heard:

> On the basis of the Findings of the IP [McLaren's] Report all Russian athletes seeking entry to the Olympic Games Rio 2016 are considered to be affected by a system subverting and manipulating the anti-doping system...
>
> Under these exceptional circumstances, Russian athletes in any of the 28 Olympic summer sports have to assume the consequences of what amounts to a collective responsibility in order to protect the credibility of the Olympic competitions, and the "presumption of innocence" cannot be applied to them.
>
> On the other hand, according to the rules of natural justice, individual justice, to which every human being is entitled, has to be applied. This means that each affected athlete must be given the opportunity to rebut the applicability of collective responsibility in his or her individual case...
>
> Entry will be accepted by the IOC only if an athlete is able to provide evidence to the full satisfaction of his or her International Federation (IOC 2016).

While this outcome greatly disappointed the anti-doping community (Slater 2016; for a critique by a legal scholar, see also Cuffey 2017), the end result was that considerable portion of the Russian Olympic team (including, at the decision of the IAAF (Duval 2017, 179–84), every single member of the track-and-field squad) was disqualified from the competitions in Rio (Ruiz 2016); in addition, the result of an even harsher ruling by the International Paralympic Committee was that nobody at all from the country would be allowed to participate in the Paralympic Games to be held in the city immediately afterwards (*BBC Sport* 2016).

The Russian government was apoplectic about what had happened. President Vladimir Putin himself interjected on the matter, exclaiming from the halls of the Kremlin that the episode constituted no less than:

> an attempt to bring the rules of world politics into the world of sport....The targeted campaign our athletes became the victim of included notorious double standards, a principle of collective responsibility and a cancellation of the presumption of innocence, which are incompatible with sport, or with justice, elementary legal norms...We're talking about a threat and discrediting of the principles of equality, justice, mutual respect and the rights of so-called clean athletes," Putin said. "In essence, this is a revision or at least an attempt to revise the ideas of Pierre de Coubertin, the founder of the modern Olympic Games (Luhn 2016).

Ensuing events would prove no more satisfactory. In November 2017, an IOC disciplinary commission charged with re-testing samples from Sochi began to issue its conclusions; in time 43 athletes would be disqualified through its decisions (International Olympic Committee 2017a), although twenty-eight would eventually make successful appeals to the Court of Arbitration for Sport (Homewood 2018). Of equal or greater import, the IOC received in early December the results of a separate investigation that it had commissioned on the involvement of the Russian State—particularly the federal Ministry of Sport—in the ongoing doping scandal. The document cautioned that the investigation had failed to find "any documented, independent and impartial evidence confirming the support or the knowledge of this system by the highest State authority." Even so, it was made clear in the report that "the operational side of the fight against doping, regulation and practical terms, was under the authority of the Russian Ministry of Sport, according to the governmental structure; therefore, the then Minister of Sport has to bear the major part of the administrative responsibility" (Schmid 2017, 24, 28).

The document was enough to convince the IOC to immediately suspend the Russian National Olympic Committee (ROC) in a ruling that officially barred the country's Olympic team from the 2018 Winter Games soon to begin in PyeongChang, South Korea—though Russian leaders could take limited satisfaction from the fact that individual athletes would have the chance to participate under a neutral flag should they pass a rigorous set of qualifying principles (Ruiz and Panja 2017). In the end, 168 such individuals competed under the designation "Olympic athlete from Russia" (Maese 2018). Notably absent as a result of the IOC's decree, however, were representatives of the country's Ministry of Sport as well as the national flag and anthem (International Olympic Committee 2017b).

Before the competitions in PyeongChang had even begun, the Russian government exhibited a notably gentler line on the issue of its status. In late January 2018, Putin himself admitted that "There were instances of doping use, true — I want the audience to know this and the whole country to know this" (Hodge 2018). The change in tone bore almost immediate fruit. Just after the closing of the event, the IOC announced lifting of its suspension of the Russian Olympic Committee (International Olympic Committee 2018). "It seems to me that this is a page which we should turn," Putin happily noted (Reevell 2018). The country would nevertheless need RUSADA to be reinstated before it could hope to win additional rights to host a major international athletics competition. Negotiations on the topic accelerated when Moscow: 1) promised to make the documents of its anti-doping lab available to WADA investigators; and 2) made a very slight and grudging acknowledgment of McLaren's findings (World Anti-Doping Agency 2018). Moreover, as this volume was going into final editing, the Russian Paralympic Committee was only days away from a similar declaration (International Paralympic Committee 2019). Once this takes place, the Russian track-and-field team will be the sole component of the country's sports system still waiting for clearance.

The Doping Scandal in the Context of Russia's Broader Foreign and Domestic Behavior

The way in which Russia has acted in the doping scandal reflects a number of patterns in its broader internal and external behavior. In recent years the country has time and again sought to test the boundaries of various international norms. In February 2017, it fielded a new cruise missile weapons system whose technological aspects, according to U.S. authorities, violated the terms of the 1987 Intermediate Range Nuclear Forces Treaty ("Russia: Missiles Allegedly Deployed in Violation of 1987 Treaty" 2017). Its incursions in Eastern Europe also cut against longstanding treaty obligations (see Cooley 2017; *The Guardian* 2018). The fact that Russia's 2014 invasion of the Crimean region of Ukraine began only three days after that year's Winter Games in Sochi had concluded in Sochi seems in hindsight particularly meaningful as to Moscow's perception of the political importance of sport (Marten 2014; see also Hunt 2017d). Russian interference in the 2016 U.S. presidential election provides yet another example of Moscow's willingness to push the envelope of international norms (Ohlin 2017). It is perhaps noteworthy on this point that one of the two Russia-based groups reported to have hacked the email system of the U.S. Democratic National Committee during the run-up to the election—has been implicated in the doping scandal. In September, Fancy Bears (as the group calls itself) published the therapeutic use exemptions of several prominent American athletes after hacking into the electronic databases of WADA (Greenberg 2016). Moreover, just after Russia was banned from the 2018 Winter Games, the group released several emails from IOC and United States Olympic Committee officials (Matsakis 2018). Given the far lower stakes involved on the Olympic fields, it should perhaps not surprise that the International Convention Against Doping in Sports likewise proved ineffective (this argument is made in Hunt 2017a).

At the domestic level, those who revealed information about the doping program risked potentially severe retaliation from Russian authorities. Moscow, they knew, possessed a well-earned reputation for committing violent acts against those who opposed its wishes—especially those citizens whom it saw as treasonous (See Kramer 2016). In a recent representative case, British authorities announced in March 2018 that a former Russian spy (and longstanding British informant) named Sergei V. Skripal had along with his daughter been poisoned with a highly lethal nerve agent outside his home in London—almost certainly at the hands of Russian agents (Barry and Pérez-Peña 2018). For her part Yuliya Stepanova has expressed a long-held belief that such a risk exists for those who revealed anything about doping in her home country. "If something happens to us," she said in August 2016, "then you should know that it is not an accident" (Stubbs 2016). More recently, Stepanova (2018, 2, 3) has explained:

> The Russian doping system does not hate people that stay in the system and get caught. It hates people that fight the system. And we decided to fight it. We are now traitors to Russia...
>
> ....From the beginning, it was our hope that we would be able to get people to tell the truth. But we understand why others have not become whistleblowers and are still inside of the system as the fight against doping and corruption in Russian sports is not easy. You will lose your job, your career and even fear for the safety of you and your family.

The words of an anonymous Russian coach also resonate from this perspective: "When you talk about such things, it can be very dangerous. An accident can happen, you know. Anything could happen" (ARD 2014, 27).

Given this context, one might have trouble questioning Rodchenkov's assertions that a fear of such an ending led him to flee to the United States and enter into witness protection. The same can also be said of the former lab director's claimed suspicions that his friend Nikita Kamaev had been murdered after deciding to write a book based on his time as executive director of the Russian Anti-Doping Agency (see Green 2016; Fogel 2017; and Hunt 2017c). Kamaev, one should remember, was the second of two former RUSADA officials to die in the span of only a few weeks; the other was Vyacheslav Sinev—the founding chairman of the organization (Associated Press 2016). A November 2017 statement by former head of the Russian Olympic Committee (still honorary president of the organization) Leonid Tyagachev is instructive as well on the potential risks faced by those who revealed information on the Russian doping program. "Rodchenkov should be shot for lying, like Stalin would have done," he exclaimed (Walker 2017).

CONCLUSION

International relations scholar Victor D. Cha, a former director of Asian Affairs at the U.S. National Security Council (for additional information, see "Victor D. Cha Biographical Information" 2019), is virtually alone among high-level members of the American foreign policy establishment who have thought deeply about the place of sport within the global political system. A series of works (Cha 2008, 2009, 2013, 2016) which he has published on the topic thus merit special consideration among those hoping to understand the political insights that that might be gleaned through an examination of the Russian doping scandal. In his view:

> Sport, national pride, and international prestige are inextricably intertwined. The desire to host major events like the Olympics and to perform well is intimately related to a nation's sense of its self-image and pride of its citizens. Participation and performance in global sport are also related to a country's international prestige and the message that a government wants to send to the world about its country. (Cha 2016, 141)

Moreover, according to Cha, authoritarian regimes hold a unique perception of these linkages. Although his thoughts on the matter specifically relate to the hosting of "mega" sporting events, they also hold lessons for the participation in international sport by such countries more generally. He writes that:

> the difference in regime types of the host country correlates with different politics that surround sport. To put it simply, Liberal regimes tend to want to put on a good show when it is their turn to host the Olympics. But illiberal regimes want to do much more. They seek to leverage the games as a way to

make political statements to both external and internal audiences. (Cha 2013, 1293)

Western observers of contemporary Russia are largely in agreement as to the increasingly authoritarian nature of its political system (see, for instance, Zimmerman 2014; Gel'man 2015). In light of this reality, one would do well to contemplate the meaning of Cha's ruminations on the political meaning of sport for such regimes. A 2015 article in Britain's *The Guardian* newspaper is noteworthy for what it says along these lines. "[F]or Putin," it argued, "sport is more than a pastime. It serves an ideological function. It's an essential part of his maximal vision of Russia as a revived Great Power" (Harding and Luhn 2015). In line with Cha's thinking, the authors of the piece moreover noted both an external and an internal dimension to such thinking. Athletic success on the one hand is seen as a means of signaling strength to the nation's rivals abroad. At the same time, it offers a useful mechanism through which to boost the type of nationalist sentiments at home that are the lifeblood of any authoritarian regime.

Through its reflection of these characteristics, the Cold War casts a long shadow over the contemporary Russian doping scandal. In directly tracing just such a lineage, former Soviet-bloc exercise scientist Michael Kalinski 2017a, 3, see as well 2017b) recently asserted that "In reality, since the old times of former Soviet Union, the goal was to create dominant sports teams by any price, reap the benefits from Olympic victories, convince the world of the superiority of the sport system and to resurrect Russia's greatness." These words will no doubt remind many of the state-sponsored doping program which existed in the former German Democratic Republic (see Franke and Berendonk 1997; Ungerleider 2001; Dennis and Grix 2012; and Krüger, Becker, and Nielsen 2015). The war against drugs in sport may itself be unethical—and in the end hopeless (for a compelling case for such an interpretation, see Dimeo and Møller 2018). Even so, the fact that East Germany comes to mind as an apt comparison to recent events is emblematic of something rotten. The Russian doping scandal is indeed a dark chapter in the modern history of sports.

REFERENCES

Albergotti, Reed, and Vanessa O'Connell. 2013. *Wheelmen: Lance Armstrong, the Tour de France, and the Greatest Sports Conspiracy Ever*. Penguin.

Altukhov, Sergey, and John Nauright. 2018. "The New Sporting Cold War: Implications of the Russian Doping Allegations for International Relations and Sport." *Sport in Society* 21 (8): 1120–36. doi:10.1080/17430437.2018.1442194.

ARD. 2014. "English Script of the ARD-Documentary 'Top-Secret Doping: How Russia Makes Its Winners.'" https://presse.wdr.de/plounge/tv/das_erste/2014/12/_pdf/English-Skript.pdf.

Associated Press. 2016. "Leading Russian Anti-Doping Official Dies Suddenly." *Daily Mail*, February 15, online edition. https://www.dailymail.co.uk/wires/ap/article-3447497/Leading-Russian-anti-doping-official-dies-suddenly.html.

Barry, Ellen, and Richard Pérez-Peña. 2018. "Britain Blames Moscow for Poisoning of Former Russian Spy." *The New York Times*, March 12, sec. World. https://www.nytimes.com/2018/03/12/world/europe/uk-russia-spy-poisoning.html.

BBC Sport. 2016. "Rio Paralympics 2016: Russia Banned after Losing Appeal," August 23, sec. Disability Sport. https://www.bbc.com/sport/disability-sport/37165427.

Bonesteel, Matt. 2014. "German TV Documentary Alleges That '99 Percent' of Russian Olympic Athletes Are Doping." *Washington Post*, December 4. https://www.washingtonpost.com/news/early-lead/wp/2014/12/04/german-tv-documentary-alleges-that-99-percent-of-russian-olympic-athletes-are-doping/.

"CAS Dismisses Russian Skier's Doping Appeal." 2010. *ESPN.Com*. October 2. http://www.espn.com/olympics/skiing/news/story?id=5639124.

Cha, Victor D. 2008. *Beyond the Final Score: The Politics of Sport in Asia*. New York: Columbia University Press.

———. 2009. "A Theory of Sport and Politics." *International Journal of the History of Sport* 26 (11): 1581–1610. doi:10.1080/09523360903132972.

———. 2013. "Winning Is Not Enough: Sport and Politics in East Asia and Beyond." *The International Journal of the History of Sport* 30 (11): 1287–98. doi:10.1080/09523367.2013.793177.

———. 2016. "Role of Sport in International Relations: National Rebirth and Renewal." *Asian Economic Policy Review* 11 (1): 139–55. doi:10.1111/aepr.12127.

Coker, Christopher. 2015. *The Improbable War: China, the United States and the Continuing Logic of Great Power Conflict*. Oxford University Press.

Cooley, Alexander. 2017. "Whose Rules, Whose Sphere? Russian Governance and Influence in Post-Soviet States." Task Force White Paper. Carnegie Endowment for International Peace. https://carnegieendowment.org/2017/06/30/whose-rules-whose-sphere-russian-governance-and-influence-in-post-soviet-states-pub-71403.

Critchley, Mark. 2015. "Who Is Vitaly Mutko, the Man Who Once Claimed 97 Breakfasts on His Expenses?" *The Independent*, November 10. http://www.independent.co.uk/sport/general/athletics/russia-doping-crisis-who-is-vitaly-mutko-russias-minister-of-sport-at-the-centre-of-wadas-report-a6728936.html.

Cuffey, Saroja. 2017. "Passing the Baton: The Effect of the International Olympic Committee's Weak Anti-Doping Laws in Dealing with the 2016 Russian Olympic Team Notes." *Brooklyn Journal of International Law* 43 (2): 665–90.

Dennis, Mike, and Jonathan Grix. 2012. *Sport Under Communism: Behind the East German "Miracle."* Palgrave Macmillan.

Dimeo, Paul. 2014. "Why Lance Armstrong? Historical Context and Key Turning Points in the 'Cleaning Up' of Professional Cycling." *The International Journal of the History of Sport* 31 (8): 951–68. doi:10.1080/09523367.2013.879858.

Dimeo, Paul, and Verner Møller. 2018. *The Anti-Doping Crisis in Sport : Causes, Consequences, Solutions*. London: Routledge. doi:10.4324/9781315545677.

Duval, Antoine. 2017. "The Russian Doping Scandal at the Court of Arbitration for Sport: Lessons for the World Anti-Doping System." *The International Sports Law Journal* 16 (3): 177–97. doi:10.1007/s40318-017-0107-6.

Feldman, Noah. 2013. *Cool War: The Future of Global Competition*. Random House.

Fogel, Bryan. 2017. *Icarus*. Netflix. http://www.imdb.com/title/tt6333060/.

Francis, Charlie, and Jeff Coplon. 1990. *Speed Trap: Inside the Biggest Scandal in Olympic History*. New York: St. Martin's.

Franke, Werner W., and Brigitte Berendonk. 1997. "Hormonal Doping and Androgenization of Athletes: A Secret Program of the German Democratic Republic Government." *Clinical Chemistry* 43 (7): 1262–79.

Gel'man, Vladimir. 2015. *Authoritarian Russia: Analyzing Post-Soviet Regime Changes*. University of Pittsburgh Press.

Green, Elon. 2016. "Russian Olympic Doping Scandal: How It Happened." *Rolling Stone*. July 28. https://www.rollingstone.com/culture/culture-sports/russian-olympic-doping-scandal-how-it-happened-98340/.

Greenberg, Andy. 2016. "Russian Hackers Get Bolder in Anti-Doping Agency Attack." *Wired*, September 14. https://www.wired.com/2016/09/anti-doping-agency-attack-shows-russian-hackers-getting-bolder/.

Harding, Luke, and and Alec Luhn. 2015. "Sport, Doping and Putin's Vision of Russia as a Revived World Power." *The Guardian*, November 13, sec. Sport. https://www.theguardian.com/sport/2015/nov/13/sport-doping-putin-russia-world-power-wada.

Hodge, Nathan. 2018. "Putin Admits 'instances of Doping' in Russian Athletes." *CNN*. January 30. https://edition.cnn.com/2018/01/30/sport/vladimir-putin-russia-winter-olympics-doping/index.html.

Homewood, Brian. 2018. "CAS Overturns Doping Bans on 28 Russian Athletes." *Reuters*, February 1. https://www.reuters.com/article/us-doping-olympics-russia-idUSKBN1FL4ET.

Hunt, Thomas M. 2011. *Drug Games: The International Olympic Committee and the Politics of Doping, 1960–2008*. University of Texas Press.

———. 2017a. "Russia: Playing to Win, No Matter the Cost." *Stratfor*. April 10. https://worldview.stratfor.com/article/russia-playing-win-no-matter-cost.

———. 2017b. "A Cold War Echo Reverberates in Rio." *Stratfor*. May 8. https://worldview.stratfor.com/article/cold-war-echo-reverberates-rio.

———. 2017c. "A Filmmaker's Journey Into the Heart of an Olympic Drug Scandal." *Stratfor*. December 11. https://worldview.stratfor.com/article/filmmakers-journey-heart-olympic-drug-scandal.

———. 2017d. "The Kremlin's Weapon of Mass Distraction." *Stratfor*. July 3. https://worldview.stratfor.com/article/kremlins-weapon-mass-distraction.

"IAAF Provisionally Suspends Russian Member Federation ARAF." 2015. *IAAF*. November 13. https://www.iaaf.org/news/press-release/iaaf-araf-suspended.

Ingle, Sean. 2016. "Russia's Athletes Escape Blanket IOC Ban for Rio Olympic Games." *The Guardian*, July 24, Online edition, sec. Sport. https://www.theguardian.com/sport/2016/jul/24/russia-team-escape-blanket-ban-ioc-rio-olympic-games.

International Olympic Committee. 2016. "Decision of the IOC Executive Board Concerning the Participation of Russian Athletes in the Olympic Games Rio 2016." *International Olympic Committee*. July 24. https://www.olympic.org/news/decision-of-the-ioc-executive-board-concerning-the-participation-of-russian-athletes-in-the-olympic-games-rio-2016.

International Olympic Committee. 2017a. "[Fact Sheet] IOC RE-ANALYSIS PROGRAMME -SOCHI 2014." https://stillmed.olympic.org/media/Document%20Library/OlympicOrg/IOC/Who-We-Are/Commissions/Disciplinary-Commission/2017/IOC-re-analysis-programme-Sochi-2014-22-december-2017-1.pdf#_ga=2.175109034.927894473.1551735999-945774857.1549064860.

———. 2017b. "IOC Suspends Russian NOC and Creates a Path for Clean Individual Athletes to Compete in PyeongChang 2018 under the Olympic Flag." *International Olympic Committee*. December 5. https://www.olympic.org/news/ioc-suspends-russian-noc-and-creates-a-path-for-clean-individual-athletes-to-compete-in-pyeongchang-2018-under-the-olympic-flag.

———. 2018. "IOC Statement." *International Olympic Committee*. February 28. https://www.olympic.org/news/ioc-statement-2018-02-28.

International Paralympic Committee. 2019. "IPC to Lift Russia Suspension." *International Paralympic Committee*. February 8. https://www.paralympic.org/news/ipc-lift-russia-suspension.

Kalinski, Michael. 2017a. "'State-Sponsored' Doping: A Transition from the Former Soviet Union to Present Day Russia." *BLDE University Journal of Health Sciences* 2 (1): 1–3.

———. 2017b. "State-Sponsored Doping System in Russia: A Grand Failure of the Largest Institutional Conspiracy in History of Sport." *Annals of Sports Medicine and Research* 4 (4): 1–3.

Keating, Steve. 2016. "WADA Seeks More Independence for Sochi Investigation Team." *Reuters*, May 19. https://www.reuters.com/article/us-sport-doping-wada-conflict-idUSKCN0YA33G.

Kramer, Andrew E. 2016. "More of Kremlin's Opponents Are Ending Up Dead." *The New York Times*, August 20, sec. World. https://www.nytimes.com/2016/08/21/world/europe/moscow-kremlin-silence-critics-poison.html.

Krieger, Jörg. 2018. "Manipulation in Athletics: Historical and Contemporary Ties between On- and Off-Field Corruption in the International Association of Athletics Federations (IAAF)." *The International Journal of the History of Sport* preprint (March): 1–16. doi:10.1080/09523367.2018.1432601.

Krüger, Michael, Christian Becker, and Stefan Nielsen. 2015. *German Sports, Doping, and Politics: A History of Performance Enhancement*. Rowman & Littlefield.

Luhn, Alec. 2016. "Vladimir Putin Says Banned Russian Athletes Are Victims of 'Discrimination.'" *The Guardian*, July 27, Online edition, sec. Sport. https://www.theguardian.com/sport/2016/jul/27/vladimir-putin-russian-president-russia-athletes-rio-olympic-games-discrimination.

Maese, Rick. 2018. "Russian Athletes' 11th-Hour Appeal Denied by Court of Arbitration for Sport." *Washington Post*, February 8. https://www.washingtonpost.com/sports/olympics/russian-athletes-11th-hour-appeal-denied-by-court-of-arbitration-for-sport/2018/02/08/76648a96-0c9a-11e8-8b0d-891602206fb7_story.html.

Mankoff, Jeffrey. 2011. *Russian Foreign Policy: The Return of Great Power Politics*. Rowman & Littlefield.

Marten, Kimberly. 2014. "Crimea: Putin's Olympic Diversion." *Washington Post*, March 26. https://www.washingtonpost.com/news/monkey.../crimea-putins-olympic-diversion/.

Matsakis, Louise. 2018. "Hack Brief: Russian Hackers Release Apparent IOC Emails in Wake of Olympics Ban." *Wired*, January 10. https://www.wired.com/story/russian-fancy-bears-hackers-release-apparent-ioc-emails/.

McLaren, Richard H. 2016. "The Independent Person Report." Montreal, Canada: World Anti-Doping Agency. https://www.wada-ama.org/sites/default/files/resources/files/20160718_ip_report_new final.pdf.

Moore, Richard. 2012. *The Dirtiest Race in History: Ben Johnson, Carl Lewis and the 1988 Olympic 100m Final*. Wisden Sports Writing. London: Bloomsbury.

Mumford, Gwilym. 2017. "Icarus Review—Netflix Doping Scandal Doc Is Flawed but Fascinating." *The Guardian*, August 4, sec. Film. https://www.theguardian.com/film/2017/aug/04/icarus-review-netflix-doping-wada-russia.

Ohlin, Jens David. 2017. "Did Russian Cyber Interference in the 2016 Election Violate International Law." *Texas Law Review* 95 (7): 1579–98.

Pound, Richard W. 2008. *Inside Dope: How Drugs Are the Biggest Threat to Sports, Why You Should Care, and What Can Be Done About Them*. Mississauga, Ontario: John Wiley & Sons.

Press Association. 2014. "Former Wada President Dick Pound to Investigate Russian Doping Allegations." *The Guardian*, December 16, sec. Sport. https://www.theguardian.com/sport/2014/dec/16/wada-dick-pound-investigate-russia-doping.

Reevell, Patrick. 2018. "Putin Honors Russian Olympic Medalists, as IOC Lifts Doping Ban - ABC News." *ABC News*. February 28. https://abcnews.go.com/International/putin-honors-russian-olympic-medalists-ioc-lifts-doping/story?id=53414693.

Ruiz, Rebecca R. 2016. "Olympic Officials Set Russia's Roster; More Than 100 Are Barred for Doping." *The New York Times*, August 4, sec. Sports. https://www.nytimes.com/2016/08/05/sports/olympics/rio-russians-barred-doping.html.

———. 2017. "Olympic Doping Diaries: Chemist's Notes Bolster Case Against Russia." *The New York Times*, November 28, sec. Sports. https://www.nytimes.com/2017/11/28/sports/olympics/russia-doping.html.

Ruiz, Rebecca R., and Tariq Panja. 2017. "Russia Banned From Winter Olympics by I.O.C." *The New York Times*, December 5, sec. Sports. https://www.nytimes.com/2017/12/05/sports/olympics/ioc-russia-winter-olympics.html.

Ruiz, Rebecca R., and Michael Schwirtz. 2016. "Russian Insider Says State-Run Doping Fueled Olympic Gold." *The New York Times*, May 12, sec. Sports. https://www.nytimes.com/2016/05/13/sports/russia-doping-sochi-olympics-2014.html.

"Russia: Missiles Allegedly Deployed in Violation of 1987 Treaty." 2017. *Stratfor*. February 15. https://worldview.stratfor.com/article/russia-missiles-allegedly-deployed-violation-1987-treaty.

"Russian Doping at Sochi Winter Olympics Exposed." 2016. *60 Minutes*. May 8. https://www.cbsnews.com/news/60-minutes-russian-doping-at-sochi-winter-olympics-exposed/.

Schmid, Samuel. 2017. "IOC Disciplinary Commission's Report to the IOC Executive Board." Lausanne, Switzerland: International Olympic Committee.

Seppelt, Hajo. 2014. *Geheimsache Doping - Wie Russland Seine Sieger Macht*. http://www.imdb.com/title/tt5922854/.

Slater, Matt. 2016. "Rio 2016: IOC Decision Condemned after Deciding Not to Impose Ban on Russia." *The Independent*, July 25, Online edition, sec. Sport. https://www.independent.co.uk/sport/olympics/rio-2016-russia-doping-ioc-decision-condemned-after-deciding-not-to-impose-ban-a7154241.html.

Stepanova, Yuliya. 2018. *Yuliya Stepanova Written Statement*. https://www.csce.gov/sites/helsinkicommission.house.gov/files/III.%20Testimony%20III.%20Yuliya%20Stepanova.pdf.

Stubbs, Jack. 2016. "Russia's Stepanova - 'No Accident' If Something Happens to Me." *Reuters*, August 15. https://uk.reuters.com/article/uk-olympics-rio-russia-stepanova-idUKKCN10Q1VE.

The Guardian. 2018. "Mattis Condemns Russia for Treaty Violations and Election Interference," December 1, sec. World news. https://www.theguardian.com/world/2018/dec/01/russia-ukraine-ships-jim-mattis-trump-administrtion.

Ungerleider, Steven. 2001. *Faust's Gold: Inside the East German Doping Machine*. Macmillan.

"Victor D. Cha Biographical Information." 2019. *Georgetown University*. Accessed February 21. https://gufaculty360.georgetown.edu/s/contact/00336000014RXwoAAG/victor-cha.

WADA Independent Commission. 2015. "Independent Commission Report #1." Montreal, Canada: World Anti-Doping Agency. https://www.wada-ama.org/sites/default/files/resources/files/wada_independent_commission_report_1_en.pdf.

"WADA Names Richard McLaren to Sochi Investigation Team." 2016. *World Anti-Doping Agency*. May 19. https://www.wada-ama.org/en/media/news/2016-05/wada-names-richard-mclaren-to-sochi-investigation-team.

"WADA Statement Clarifies Timing of McLaren Investigation Report and States Facts Related to Investigations into Russian Matters." 2016. *World Anti-Doping Agency*. August 1. https://www.wada-ama.org/en/media/news/2016-08/wada-statement-clarifies-timing-of-mclaren-investigation-report-and-states-facts.

"WADA Takes Immediate Action on Key Recommendations of Independent Commission." 2015. *World Anti-Doping Agency*. November 13. https://www.wada-ama.org/en/media/news/2015-11/wada-takes-immediate-action-on-key-recommendations-of-independent-commission.

Walker, Shaun. 2017. "Russian Olympic Official Says Doping Whistleblower Should Be Executed." *The Guardian*, November 17, sec. Sport. https://www.theguardian.com/sport/2017/nov/17/russian-olympic-official-says-doping-whistleblower-should-be-executed.

World Anti-Doping Agency. 2018. "WADA Executive Committee Decides to Reinstate RUSADA Subject to Strict Conditions (20 September 2018)." *World Anti-Doping Agency*. September 20. https://www.wada-ama.org/en/media/news/2018-09/wada-executive-committee-decides-to-reinstate-rusada-subject-to-strict-conditions.

Zimmerman, William. 2014. *Ruling Russia: Authoritarianism from the Revolution to Putin*. Princeton, NJ: Princeton University Press.

CHAPTER 8

Sex Testing in Sport

Lindsay Parks Pieper

Mandatory sex testing of women athletes commenced in 1966. Sport leaders enacted the policy due to the fear that strong, powerful female athletes were actually male imposters. Yet, after decades of enlisting different scientific techniques to verify women's sex, sport officials failed to uncover a single male masquerader. Sex testing instead reaffirmed gendered assumptions in sport, harmed women athletes, and disregarded the ethics of elite sport.

Ewa Kłobukowska's story illustrates the inherent problems of sex testing in sport. In 1964, the Polish runner won the 100-meter race at the European Athletics Junior Championships. She gained national adoration with the victory, but it was during the 1964 Tokyo Olympics where she garnered international recognition. After earning bronze in the 100-meter race, Kłobukowska anchored the 4x100 meters relay for the Polish squad. She crossed the finish line three tenths of a second ahead of US runner Edith McGuire to claim gold and set a new world record. The eighteen-year-old returned to Poland a national hero.

Two years after the 1964 Olympics, the International Association of Athletics Federation (IAAF) introduced compulsory sex testing for all female athletes. IAAF Rule 141 stipulated that for Area Games or Championships, women had to be examined by a panel of three female doctors before competition (Pieper 2016). As noted by Arne Ljungqvist (2011, 183), an IAAF member in the 1970s, "sport had no other means of asserting the gender of participants other than having them parade naked in front of a panel of doctors." The IAAF debuted the policy at the 1966 British Empire & Commonwealth Games in Kingston, Jamaica.

The track and field federation believed the "nude parade" was effective in deterring the participation of male imposters and masculine women. According to IAAF President David Burghley (1967), the policy "has been successful in frightening the doubtful ones away." The IAAF continued the practice two weeks later at the 1966 European Athletics Championships in Budapest. Three female doctors visually inspected all 243 women participants, including Kłobukowska (Ferguson-Smith and Ferris 1991, 17). The Polish track star passed the physical exam and earned gold in the 100-meters, silver in the 200-meters, and another gold in the 4x100 meters relay.

Yet, female athletes disdained the intrusive nature of the physical inspection, which encouraged the IAAF to embrace the relatively new Barr body test, which identifies chromosomes, for verification purposes. The federation replaced the physical exam with a chromosomal check at the 1967 European Cup Track and Field Event in Kiev, Soviet Union. Three Hungarian and three Russian physicians swabbed the cheeks of all female competitors to identify sex chromosomes (Pieper 2016). The test showed that Kłobukowska possessed a "mosaic" of chromosomes ("Mosaic in X&Y" 1967, 74). The IAAF quickly disqualified her, erased her records, and released the results. Newspapers around the world publicized Kłobukowska's medical information, devastating her on a global stage (Rodda 1967, D1).

Polish Olympic Committee (POC) President Włodzimierz Reczek immediately lodged a complaint. He pointed out that the publication of Kłobukowska's medical records "fills one with indignation because it disaccords with elementary ethics" (Reczek 1967). Moreover, Reczek also foreshadowed fundamental issues with sex testing in sport when he argued that "there are no generally acceptable criteria of sex for women athletes and the lightminded arbitrariness in the interpretation of the results of examinations may harm the examined persons." Despite Reczek's poignant plea, the IAAF banned Kłobukowska from future competitions and continued to use the Barr body test for three decades. The International Olympic Committee (IOC) followed suit in 1968.

The mistreatment Kłobukowska experienced stemmed from the inherent problems of sex testing. As correctly pointed out in 1967 by POC President Reczek, sex-based policies are flawed for several reasons; this chapter identifies and explains three of the issues. First, sex control was, and continues to be, based on the assumption that athletic ability is a masculine trait and therefore an inappropriate quality for women to possess. Strong, powerful female athletes who did not uphold conventional notions of white femininity were the targets of the policy. Sex control criminalized successful women and hampered female athleticism.

Second, no single scientific criteria can neatly classify people by sex because sex exists as a spectrum rather than a binary. Sport officials nevertheless repeatedly attempted to find a concrete line of separation between men and women. Sport leaders mandated anatomical examinations in the interwar era, chromosomal checks during the Cold War, and hormonal analyses in the millennium. Yet, all of these techniques not only failed to divide men and women, but instead illustrated a range of biological characteristics. As sports writer David Epstein (2014, 58) surmises, "human biology does not break down into male and female as politely as sport governing bodies wish it would."

Finally, sex tests harmed women athletes. The policy failed to uncover a single male imposter but vilified intersex individuals. Like Kłobukowska, several women suffered public disparagement as a result of the practice. And, despite the introduction of non-disclosure protocols, biological estimations suggest that anywhere between sixteen and one hundred women either experienced difficulty with the examinations or were excluded outright (Fox 1993). The total number of women quietly removed from sport remains unknown. Founded upon conventional ideas of sex and gender, sex testing has historically reaffirmed a false belief in a sex binary and harmed women athletes.

MASCULINITY, FEMININITY, AND FAIRNESS IN SPORT

Modern sport developed in the mid-1800s (Guttmann 1978). Several Western countries experienced significant changes during this period due to industrialization. Industrialization, in turn, granted sport new social capital (Hargreaves 1994; Kimmel 1997; Putney 2003). While most women remained encumbered by a tradition of "separate spheres," a growing number demanded new rights, as embodied by the suffrage movement. This threat to the conventional gender order sparked a "crisis in masculinity" at the end of the century (Kimmel 1997). Sport thereby evolved into a space for men to stave off feminization, reassert dominance, and prove their manliness (Riess 1999). Women were either side-lined from sport completely or restricted to purposive exercises like calisthenics (Todd 1998).

As male sporting opportunities grew in the late-nineteenth century, affluent men founded amateur leagues and clubs. French aristocrat Pierre de Coubertin organized the modern Olympic Games to revitalize French masculinity, foster European camaraderie, and diminish the possibility of future warfare (Hoberman 1986, 33-36). Under his authority, the 1896 Athens Olympics was an event where men competed in athletics, cycling, fencing, gymnastics, shooting, swimming, tennis, weightlifting, and wrestling. Women were prohibited (Cahn 1994; Pieper 2016). Although Coubertin infamously argued against the inclusion of female athletes, the localized organization of the 1900 Paris Games, in connection with the World's Fair, permitted their participation. Female Olympians competed, however, they remained limited to croquet, golf, and tennis. Western society considered these events socially acceptable for white, upper-class women (Cahn 1994). Female Olympians tellingly remained barred from all other activities, including track and field.

Track and field was the most popular and prestigious of the Olympic sports. It was also considered the most masculine and therefore initially off limits to female athletes. Because the IOC did not include women's athletics in the Olympics, female sports organizations created alternative forums for women's track and field. The Fédération Sportive Féminine Internationale (FSFI) hosted the Women's Olympic Games in 1922, 1926, 1930, and 1934, which forced the IAAF and IOC to acquiesce on its ban (Carpentier and Lefévre 2006). The sport organizations agreed to accept women into Olympic track and field in 1928 if the FSFI agreed to drop the word "Olympic" from the event.

It was thus in track and field where concerns about sex, gender, and athleticism coalesced. Medical practitioners, sport officials, physical educators, and the media all believed the sport was too grueling, and therefore unacceptable, for women (Cahn 1994; Hargreaves 1994). Female runners, jumpers, and throwers faced disparagement for being masculine. White, middle-class western women abandoned the sport due to this stigma, which left a vacuum that was filled by white, working-class women and women of color. Athletics provided novel opportunities for these athletes, but their victories simultaneously reinforced the belief of athletics as a masculine pursuit (Lansbury 2014; Pieper 2016).

This notion was exacerbated during the Cold War when the Soviet women dominated track and field. The Cold War superpower usurped the United States in the Olympic medal count, largely due to the successes of its female athletes. For example, in the 1952 Games, the Soviet women claimed eleven of the possible twenty-seven medals in track and field while the United States earned one. The Western press did not applaud the Soviet victories. "The Russian women indeed are favored again over the American women," wrote *Washington Post* writer Shirley Povich before the 1956 Olympics, "mostly because they have muscles, big ones, in the places United States gals don't want 'em'" (Povich 1956, 53). Such concerns about the masculinizing effects of athletics plagued female track and field athletes and eventually encouraged the IAAF and IOC to introduce sex testing.

With sport constructed as a domain for men, and athletic skills tied to masculinity, women's eventual success in competitive physical endeavours—specifically track and field—caused angst. If sport existed as a forum to demonstrate male strength and superiority, what did it mean when women demonstrated athletic ability? Powerful female athletes challenged the notion of men as inherently faster and stronger than women. Many people therefore viewed muscular female competitors with suspicion and derision (Cahn 1994; Ritchie 2003; Schultz 2014). Prevailing beliefs suggested that women who excelled in sport by exhibiting strength and possessing muscles could not be "real" representatives of the "weaker" sex.

To diminish this threat, sport practitioners cast muscular women as unnatural freaks. For example, Jacques Thiebault, the French doctor who oversaw testing at the 1968 Winter Olympics, argued that a control was needed for "it is inevitable that sooner or later, the representatives of the weaker sex should feel persecuted and ask that the feminine records be awarded to them" (Thiebault 1968). Such statements reaffirmed the belief that athleticism and femininity were analogous. The IAAF and IOC introduced sex testing to establish a concrete line between men and women and preserve the status quo. Although each medico-scientific technique failed to find a dividing point between male and female athletes, and instead demonstrated the fallibility of using scientific criterion to determine sex in sport, officials remained dedicated to the task for decades.

SEX VERIFICATION METHODS USED IN SPORT

Medical practitioners recognize the diversity in human biology. As bioethicist Alice Domurat Dreger (1988, 3) explains, "humans come in a wonderful array of types: many sizes, many abilities, and many approaches to experiencing and organizing the world." Despite the existence of a "wonderful array of types," sport leaders repeatedly embraced new technologies to verify the sex of women athletes. All failed. In the interwar era, the IAAF and IOC embraced anatomical investigations. Deeming physical exams too intrusive, the two organizations turned to chromosomal checks during the Cold War. However, the test highlighted the various chromosomal compositions that exist in humans. After a brief hiatus from testing in the early 2000s, the IAAF and IOC next enacted hormonal assessments, a policy that as of this writing is still being discussed and debated.

The Nude Parade

During the nineteenth century, external anatomy was the preeminent feature in the determination of sex. Physicians prioritized reproductive organs when labeling a baby male or female (Vertinsky 1994) and gonads specifically held sway in the declaration or one's maleness or femaleness. According to Dreger (1998, 29), physicians "came to an agreement that every body's 'true' sex was marked by one thing and one thing only: the anatomical nature of the gonadal tissue as either ovarian or testicular." Sport practitioners embraced the importance of gonads in the identification of sex, particularly when coupled with outward appearance. Muscular women athletes who challenged the idea of sport as a male realm, specifically those who competed in track and field, were thus the first to experience anatomical investigations.

Women's track and field debuted at the 1928 Amsterdam Olympics. Sport officials immediately questioned the sex of one of the runners. Japanese runner Hitomi Kinue finished second in the 800-meters, the longest distance available to women at the time, becoming the first Japanese woman to earn an Olympic medal (Frost 2010). She was also likely the first woman to undergo a sex test during the Olympics. According to US journalist Grantland Rice (1936, A9), prior to the start of the 1928 Games, a "case concerned a Japanese girl in Amsterdam, where the investigating committee was out two hours before it decided predominant sex." Despite the lack of detail provided in the account, Rice insinuated that Hitomi's appearance convinced the IOC to conduct an exam to verify her sex. This type of inspection increased as women made strides in athletics.

Concerns heightened during the 1936 Summer Games. US sprinter Helen Stephens defeated world record holder Stanisława Walasiewicz in the 100-meter final. Because few people believed a woman could run as fast as Stephens did, some claimed she cheated (Hanson 2004) and a rumor that she was a man spread. A Polish writer suggested that "Miss Walasiewicz would have gained first place if she had competed only against women" (as cited in "Polish Writer Calls" 1936, A9). To quiet the suspicions, the Berlin Olympic organizers reported that Stephens had undergone an anatomical test prior to the start of the games. It is unclear when Stephens underwent the exam, what organization required it, and who conducted it. According to Stephens, a team physician checked her prior to competition. Newspaper accounts largely credited Berlin officials for requiring and overseeing the control once rumors surfaced (Pieper 2016).

Additional accounts insinuate that investigations of women's reproductive organs were somewhat frequently conducted on competitors who did not uphold conventional notions of gender. Stephens herself told the press to "check the facts with the Olympic committee physician who sex-tested all athletes prior to competition" (Hanson 2004, 96). US writer Paul Gallico (1937, 234) explained that the American Athletics Union had "Stephens frisked for sex" before departing for Berlin. Likewise, runner-up Walasiewicz reportedly underwent physical examinations, likely due to her muscular appearance and notable speed. According to her childhood friend Casimir Bielen, she "was medically examined by hundreds of doctors" and regularly "passed qualifying medical examinations" before competing (Tullis 2013).

The IAAF eventually changed from sporadic inspections to compulsory testing. At the 1966 British Empire & Commonwealth Games, the federation introduced obligatory checks. British pentathlete Mary Peters (1974, 56-57) recalled being told to lie down and pull up her knees for the exam. She compared the ordeal to a "grope' and described it as the "most crude and degrading experience I have ever known in my life." Despite the athletes' disdain of the process, the IAAF continued the examinations at the 1966 European Athletics Championship, 1966 Asian Games, and 1967 Pan American Games (Pieper 2016; Ritchie 2003).

Ultimately, the intrusive nature of the "nude parade," coupled with the inadequacy of anatomy as the sole determinant of sex, caused issues. The exams did not delineate sex. Most women have a clitoris, fallopian tubes, ovaries, and a vagina; however, each come in a variety of shapes and sizes, even in individuals considered anatomically "normal." The IAAF realized the error in utilizing anatomical features as the single criteria to verify sex and therefore turned to a technique considered more scientifically sound, the Barr body test.

The Barr Body Test

By the middle of the twentieth century, most medical professionals agreed that a person's sex was multifaceted and complex. However, geneticists initially championed chromosomes as the most significant element in sex determination. Chromosomes exist in the nucleus of cells and are comprised of DNA tightly coiled around proteins. Women typically have forty-four autosomal chromosomes and XX sex chromosomes (46,XX); men typically have forty-four autosomal chromosomes and XY sex chromosomes (46,XY). However, numerous chromosomal compositions exist, upending the idea that sex chromosomes alone indicate maleness or femaleness. For example, as psychologist David T. MacLaughlin and pediatric surgeon Patricia K. Donahoe (2004) show, individuals with Androgen Insensitivity Syndrome (AIS) demonstrate the impossibility of dividing men and women by chromosomes. A person with AIS is genetically 46,XY but does not respond to androgens. They typically present outwardly as female and are designated female at birth. Despite the known existence of chromosomal varieties, many people equated XX with women and XY with men. Or, as historian Sarah S. Richardson (2013, 9) explains, for many "X and Y came to represent the necessary alter ego of gender fluidity." During the Cold War, sport practitioners believed chromosomes were the answer.

The IAAF implemented the Barr body test in 1967. The Barr body test was a relatively new discovery that used cells to identify sex chromosomes. Although the inaccuracy of relying on chromosomes was on display immediately—in that Ewa Kłobukowska, who "failed" the chromosomal check had previously passed a physical inspection—the IAAF considered the technique a success. The IOC also interpreted the results positively and introduced the Barr body test in 1968 (Pieper 2016).

Protests regarding the singular use of the Barr body test to verify sex surfaced immediately. Scottish geneticist Malcolm Ferguson-Smith (1969) wrote to the organizers of the 1970 Edinburgh Commonwealth Games that the procedure was inaccurate for three reasons. First, a person's identity did not always correspond with his or her chromosomal makeup. Second, 7-out-of-1,000 people had some type of chromosomal difference. Third, a physical examination would be a better option if the IAAF truly intended to unmask male imposters. Ferguson Smith concluded that "It is not in the best interests of the individual competitors to have this test." Finnish geneticist Albert de la Chapelle was also vocal in his opposition. He (1982) argued that the use of the Barr body test was a "flagrant violation" of women's rights.

The protests increased after the 1985 World University Games. Spanish hurdler María José Martínez Patiño—who had previously passed the required sex test—forgot her "femininity certificate" at home. Without official documentation, the IAAF required she again undergo the Barr body test. This time, she "failed" (Carlson 1991). However, when the team doctor told Patiño to quietly retire from sport, she refused. She won the 60-meter hurdles the following year at the Spanish National Games and was consequently barred from sport. Unlike previous athletes who silently disappeared from competition, Patiño protested the IAAF's decision (Patiño 2005). Her public plight showcased the inherent flaws of the Barr body test and eventually forced change. The medical community increased their protests of the policy. In the wake of Patiño's publicity, the IAAF and IOC briefly abandoned compulsory sex testing. The IAAF halted the practice in 1992 and the IOC in 1999. The abatement was short.

Regulations on Female Hyperandrogenism

The IAAF stopped compulsory verification in 1992 and the IOC in 1999; however, both organizations maintained the right to verify the sex of any "suspicious" women athletes. South African runner Caster Semenya underwent a sex test based on this stipulation after the 2009 World Track and Field Championships. She defeated her competitors in the 800-meter final by two seconds; an impressive time gap between her and the runner-up, but still two seconds slower than the world record. Her speedy time, combined with racialized gender norms, convinced the IAAF to verify her sex. While women in general historically experienced ridicule for their participation in sport, women of color faced disparagement for not upholding white, western beauty standards. In other words, black female athletes faced additional scrutiny for not appearing feminine by white norms. Critics pointed to Semenya's muscular physique, cornrows, and deep voice as evidence of masculinity. For example, Italian runner Elisa Cusma hostilely commented that "these kinds of people should not run with us. For me, she's not a woman. She's a man" (Clarey and Kolata 2009). Influenced by Semenya's appearance and the suspicions she faced, the IAAF and IOC reintroduced testing in elite sport (IAAF 2011; IOC 2012).

The sport organizations focused on female athletes who naturally produced higher-than-average levels of testosterone, those with hyperandrogenemia. The IAAF outlined "Regulations Governing Eligibility of Females with Hyperandrogenism to Compete in Women's Competition" in 2011 and the IOC introduced "Regulations on Female Hyperandrogenism" in 2012 (IAAF 2011; IOC 2012). Similar to previous sex control efforts, the sport bodies focused on a single characteristic to determine sex, testosterone. Testosterone is a hormone present in men and women, albeit in different quantities, and oftentimes linked to athleticism. For example, scientists Francisco J. Sánchez, María José Martínez-Patiño, and Eric Vilain (2013, para. 12) argue that it is "a trait that is known to influence one's athletic performance and which happens to be sexually dimorphic." However, Vilain also admitted the arbitrary nature of separating men and women by testosterone level in that the amounts present in humans exist in a spectrum, not a binary. "You have to draw a line in the sand somewhere," he admitted (quoted in Macur 2012, para. 5).

According to the IAAF's and IOC's hyperandrogenism policies, women suspected of having hyperandrogenemia needed to be tested at specific reference centres. If diagnosed, the regulations mandated "treatment" to "normalize" her testosterone levels (IAAF 2011). At the 2012 London Olympics, officials sent four Olympic hopefuls to France for treatment (Littlefield 2014). The doctors performed surgeries that would "allow [the four women] to continue in elite sport in the female category," yet, held no medical benefit otherwise (Fénichel et al. 2013, 1056). In other words, the procedures were completed solely to permit participation in sport.

The IAAF and IOC embraced this method of sex control despite concerns raised by medical professionals. Those opposed to the new policy argued that testosterone is not the sole indicator of athletic ability and—like the other biological characteristics used for sex testing—hormone levels overlap in men and women. These concerns heightened in 2014. At the Commonwealth Games that year, the Sports Authority of India (SAI) prevented Indian runner Dutee Chand from competing based on the assumption that she had high levels of naturally-produced testosterone. After conducting a medical exam, the SAI deemed her ineligible (CAS 2014). However, Chand refused to undergo the required treatment and protested the hyperandrogenemism policy to the Court of Arbitration for Sport (CAS), a non-jurisdictional body that mediates disputes in sport.

The CAS ruled in 2014 that the IAAF failed to produce evidence about the degree of advantage hyperandrogenic women possess over non-hyperandrogenic women; the panel therefore suspended the regulations for two years. The temporary ban was enacted to provide the IAAF time to collect data regarding the quantitative degree of competitive advantage conferred by testosterone. If the sport organization could not produce evidence that the advantage justified excluding women with hyperandrogenmia from the women's category of sport, the regulations would be permanently suspended (CAS 2014). Debates about the ethics and validity of the hyperandrogenism policies therefore continue, as does the harming of women athletes in sport.

THE HARMING OF FEMALE ATHLETES

Since the first widely-publicized test in 1936, the IAAF and IOC have negatively impacted women athletes with their verification practices. Thousands of women underwent the compulsory control and an unknown number of athletes experienced difficulty with it. Not only was the revelation of anatomical, genetic, or hormonal differences in-and-of-itself devastating to women, but it oftentimes occurred prior to significant athletic events for which they had spent years training. Moreover, a handful of women faced cruel criticism when their test results were revealed to the public, such as Helen Stephens, María José Martínez Patiño, Santhi Soundarajan, and Caster Semenya. Taken together, sex tests were, and continue to be, harmful to female competitors.

As previously noted, Stephens underwent the first widely-reported sex test for the 1936 Berlin Olympics. The results of her exam appeared in newspapers around the world. Although the IOC allowed Stephens to run, not everyone was so easily convinced. Journalists harassed her in Germany. According to biographer Sharon Kinney Hanson (2004, 96), Stephens tried to ignore the cruelty, but "it upset her." The hostility continued when she returned home from the Olympics. Perhaps most notably, in February 1937, *Look* magazine featured a picture of Stephens in an unflattering pose with the words "What Do You Think? Is This a Man or a Woman?" emblazoned across the page. The nationally circulated photograph "caused people to whisper things deeply disturbing to Helen," notes Hanson (2004, 144). Although Stephens passed the sex test and competed in Berlin, the suspicions about her never wavered. "The almost maniacal, delinquent focus on sex delineations never let up, never let her be," explains Hanson (2004, 243). For the rest of her life, Stephens was besieged by curious strangers who demanded to know her "true" sex.

Spanish hurdler Patiño experienced similar mistreatment after she refused to quietly retire from sport. Her victory at the 1986 Spanish National Games ignited international criticism. Spanish sport officials immediately kicked her out of the athletes' residency, removed her sport scholarship, and erased her records. She compared the experience to being raped. "I'm sure it's the same sense of incredible shame and violation. The only difference is that, in my case, the whole world was watching," she said (Carlson 1991). The prohibitions also diminished Patiño's Olympic opportunities. She remained banned from the 1988 Olympics. While her protest forced the IAAF and IOC to terminate their compulsory sex test policies, it came at a cost. "I paid a high price," she wrote. "My story was told, dissected, and discussed in a very public way" (Patiño 2005, S38).

Although Patiño helped push the IAAF and IOC to stop compulsory verification, the termination proved only temporary and athletes continued to be harmed by sex control. Soundarajan grew up in India's lowest caste, the Dalits, previously known as the untouchables, and developed an impressive running ability. Yet, her speed earned her both awards and abuse. At the 2006 Asian Games, she won a silver medal in the 800-meter race and was required to undergo a sex test the next day (Bhowmick and Thottam 2009). Only when she returned home did she learn from a news report that she had "failed." "That was the end of my sports life," Soundarajan said. The IAAF immediately removed her medals and banned her from future events (Shapiro 2012). Traumatized and publicly humiliated, she fell into a severe depression. "Everyone was looking at me in this new way: Is she a man? Is she a transvestite?" she said through an interpreter. "It's very hurtful. It ruined my life" (Shapiro 2012). According to several reports, Soundarajan tried to commit suicide. Sex testing cost her a livelihood, created social ostracism, and desecrated her running career.

Three years after Soundarajan's devastating ordeal, Semenya faced comparable hostility after undergoing a publicized sex test. Her sex became an international topic of conversation. "If it wasn't for my family, I don't think I could have survived," she later explained (Smith 2015). She reportedly was placed on suicide watch. "I'm angry. I'm fuming. This girl has been castigated from day one, based on what?" intoned South Africa President Leonard Chuene. "You can't say somebody's child is not a girl" ("Runner Caster Semenya" 2009). Despite experiencing tremendous cruelty on an international stage, Semenya's athletic career blossomed. She withstood the pressure and won the silver medal in the 2012 London Olympics, which was later converted to gold when it was discovered the first-place finisher had doped. Semenya then defended her position at the top of the podium at the 2016 Rio Olympics. She refused to stop running, even when the IAAF introduced a new sex control policy in 2018 that seemed to target her directly.

Epilogue: Sex Testing Today

Semenya's dealings with sex testing are not over. In April 2018, the IAAF issued a new verification protocol, the "Eligibility Regulations for Female Classification." As required by the 2014 CAS decision, the IAAF collected data on the degree of advantage afforded to women with hyperandrogenia to justify the policy. The updated regulations are based primarily on a 2017 study that examined the influence of testosterone on athletic performance. Stéphane Bermon, Director of the IAAF Health & Science Department, and Pierre Yves Garnier (2017) analysed women's times at the 2011 and 2013 IAAF World Championships and compared them against their testosterone levels. The study found statistically significant athletic advantages in five events: 400-meters (2.73%), 400-meters hurdles (2.78%), 800-meters (1.78%), hammer throw (4.53%), and pole vault (2.94%).

The IAAF's new regulations apply only to women who compete on the track in distances from 400-meters to the mile, including hurdles and combined events over those distances. Competitors in these events, who are receptive to the biological effects of testosterone, with levels over 5 nmol/L must (1) be recognized as female or intersex by law, (2) reduce their hormone level below 5 nmol/L for six months, and (3) keep their hormone level below 5 nmol/L continuously (IAAF 2018).

The policy is not only problematic, but it is seemingly aimed at Semenya. Shot putters and pole vaulters remain curiously outside of the policy's control, despite the fact that the 2017 study indicated it is in these two events where women with hyperandrogenia possess the greatest advantage. Supporters of the policy argue that shot put and pole vault were not included because hyperandrogenic women from "rural areas in developing nations" were unlikely to succeed in these two events due to various constraints, specifically citing their lack of access to high-caliber coaching (Harper et al. 2018). Rather than serve as a valid reason for the exclusion of shot put and pole vault, this defense seems to support critics' concerns that the policy targets women of color from the global south. Moreover, the 1,500-meters was also included in the guidelines, even though the study did not indicate any advantage in this event for women with hyperandrogenia. It is important to note that Semenya won bronze in the 1,500-meters at the 2017 World Championships and gold at the 2018 Commonwealth Games. Finally, several scientists have criticized the study's methodology and selective sample size, which possibly included female athletes who had doped (Sönksen et al. 2018; Menier 2018; Franklin, Betancurt and Camporesi 2018). Chand is not able to challenge the guidelines as she competes in events not included in it; however Semenya announced in June 2018 that she is challenging the IAAF's policy to the CAS.

Polish Olympic Committee President Włodzimierz Reczek foreshadowed the inherent flaws in sex testing in 1967. Sex-based policies are founded upon a belief in sport as a male domain. It was the appearances of strong, muscular women that fostered the concerns, which, in turn, convinced sport authorities to institute verification methods. However, despite repeated efforts to identify a technique to separate men and women, no single biological characteristic can identify one' sex. Anatomical investigations, chromosomal checks, and hormonal analyses all demonstrated the spectrum of human biology. Finally, and perhaps most importantly, sex testing harmed women. All elite female athletes experienced the control from 1968 to 1999, and an unknown number were forced to quietly retire or face public backlash.

REFERENCES

Bermon, Stéphane, and Pierre-Yves Garnier. 2017. "Serum Androgen Levels and Their Relations To Performance in Track and Field: Mass Spectrometry Results from 2127 Observations in Male and Female Elite Athletes." *British Journal of Sports Medicine* 51 (17): 1309-1314.

Bhowmick, Nilanjania, and Jjoti Thottam. 2009. "Gender and Athletics: India's Own Caster Semenya." *Time*, September 1, 2009. http://www.time.com/time/world/article/0,8599,1919562,00.html.

Burghley, David. 1967. Letter to Johann Westerhoff. January 10, 1967. Biography and Correspondence of David Burghley, Olympic Studies Centre Archives. Lausanne, Switzerland.

Cahn, Susan K. 1994. *Coming on Strong: Gender and Sexuality in Twentieth-Century Women's Sport*. Cambridge: Harvard University Press.

Carpentier, Florence, and Jean-Pierre Lefévre. 2006. "The Modern Olympic Movement, Women's Sport and the Social Order During the Inter-War Period." *The International Journal of the History of Sport* 23 (7): 1112-1127.

Carlson, Alison. 1991. "When is a Woman not a Woman?" *Women's Sport and Fitness* 13 (2): 24-29.

Court of Arbitration of Sport. 2014. Dutee Chand v. Athletics Federation of India & The International Association of Athletics Federation. CAS 2014/A/3759. https://www.google.com/url?sa=t&rct=j&q=&esrc=s&source=web&cd=1&ved=0ahUKEwjkkaev6pHaAhUSVN8KHWyFAvkQFggnMAA&url=http%3A%2F%2Fwww.tascas.org%2Ffileadmin%2Fuser_upload%2FAWARD_3759__FINAL___REDACTED_FOR_PUBLICATION_.pdf&usg=AOvVaw2WBSevjiEc5t-Rf317XgWP.

Chapelle, Albert de la. 1982. Letter to de Alexandre de Mérode. August 17, 1982. Commission Medicale Correspondance, Avril 1983, Olympic Studies Centre Archives. Lausanne, Switzerland.

Clarey, Christopher: 2009. "Gender Test after a Gold-Medal Finish." *New York Times*, August 20, 2009, B13.

Clarey, Christopher, and Gina Kolata. 2009. "Gold is Awarded, but Dispute Over Runner's Sex Intensifies." *New York Times*, August 21, 2009, B9.

Cooky, Cheryl, and Shari L. Dworkin. 2013. "Policing the Boundaries of Sex: A Critical Examination of Gender Verification and the Caster Semenya Controversy." *Journal of Sex Research* 50 (2): 103-111.

Dreger, Alice Domurat. 1988. *Hermaphrodites and the Medical Invention of Sex.* Cambridge: Harvard University Press.

Epstein, David. 2014. *The Sports Gene: Inside the Science of Extraordinary Athletic Performance.* New York: Penguin Group.

Fénichel, Patrick, Françoise, Paris, Pascal Philibert, Sylvie Hiéronimus, Laura Gaspari, Jean-Yves Kurzenne, Patrick Chevallier, Stéphane Bermon, Nicolas Chevalier, and Charles Sultan. 2013. "Molecular Diagnosis of 5α-Reductase Deficiency in 4 Elite Young Female Athletes Through Hormonal Screening for Hyperandrogenismm." *Journal of Clinical Endocrinology & Metabolism* 98 (6): 1055-1059.

Ferguson-Smith, Malcolm Andrew. 1969. Letter to James R. Owen, November 6, 1969. Letter to Col. John Fraser, November 21, 1969. Correspondence Regarding the Buccal Smear Examination at the 1970 Edinburgh Commonwealth Games. Papers of Malcolm Andrew Ferguson-Smith. University of Glasgow, Scotland.

Ferguson-Smith, Malcolm Andrew, and Elizabeth A. Ferris. 1991. "Gender Verification in Sport: The Need for Change?" *British Journal of Sports Medicine* 25 (1): 17-20.

Fox, John S. (1993). "Gender Verification: What Purpose? What Price?" *British Journal of Sports Medicine* 27 (3): 48-149.

Franklin Simon, Ospina Bettancourt, Jonathan, and Silvia Camporesi. 2018. "What Statistical Data of Observational Performance Can Tell Us and They Cannot: The Case of *Dutee Chan*d *v. AFI & IAAF.*" *British Journal of Sports Medicine* 52 (7): 420-421.

Frost, Dennis. 2010. *Seeing Stars: Sports Celebrity, Identity, and Body Culture in Modern Japan.* Cambridge: Harvard University Press.

Guttmann, Allen. 1978. *From Ritual to Record: The Nature of Modern Sports.* New York: Columbia University Press.

Hanson, Sharon Kinney. 2004. *The Life of Helen Stephens: The Fulton Flash.* Carbondale: Southern Illinois University Press.

Hargreaves, Jennifer. 1994. *Sporting Females: Critical Issues in the History and Sociology of Women's Sports.* New York: Routledge.

Haper, Joanna, Lima Giscard, Kolliari-Turner, Alexander, Malinsky Fernanda Rossell, Wang, Guang, Martinez-Patino, Maria Jose, Angadi, Siddhartha S., Papadopoulou, Theodora, PIgozzi, Fabio, Seal, Leighton, Barrett, James, and Yannis P. Pitsiladis. 2018. "The Fluidity of Gender and Implications for the Biology of Inclusion for Transgender and Intersex Athletes." *International Federation of Sports Medicine* 17 (2): 467-472.

Hoberman, John. 1986. *The Olympic Crisis: Sport, Politics and the Moral Order.* New Rochelle: Caratzas Publishing Company.

International Association of Athletics Federation. 2011. "IAAF Regulations Governing Eligibility with Hyperandrogenism to Compete in Women's Competition." *International Association of Athletics Federation*, May 1, 2011. http://www.iaaf.org/about-iaaf/documents/medical.

International Olympic Committee. "IOC Regulations on Female Hyperandrogenism." International Olympic Committee, June 22, 2012. http://www.olympic.org/Documents/Commissions_PDFfiles/Medical_commission/2012-6-22-IOC-Regulations-on-FEmale-Hyperandrogenism-eng.pdf.

Kimmel, Michael. 1997. *Manhood in America: A Cultural History.* New York: The Free Press.

Lansbury, Jennifer H. 2014. *A Spectacular Leap: Black Women Athletes in Twentieth-Century America.* Fayetteville: University of Arkansas Press.

Littlefield, B. 2014. "Dutee Chand: A woman banned from women's sports." *Only a Game.* http://onlyagame.wbur.org/2014/10/11/dutee-chand-banned-iaaf.

Ljungqvist, Arne. 2011. *Doping's Nemesis.* Cheltenham: SportsBooks Limited.

Macur, Juliet. 2012. "I.O.C. Adopts Policy for Deciding Whether an Athlete can Compete as a Woman. *New York Times*, July 23, 2012. http://www.nytimes.com/2012/06/24/sports/

olympics/ioc-adopts-policy-for-deciding-whether-athletes-can-compete-as-women.html.
MacLaughlin, David T., and Patricia K. Donahoe. 2004. Sex determination and differentiation. *The New England Journal of Medicine* 350: 367-378.
Menier, Amanda. 2018. Use of Event-Specific Tertiles to Analyse the Relationship between Serum Androgens and Athletic Performance in Women. *British Journal of Sports Medicine* 52 (23), http://dx.doi.org/10.1136/bjsports-2017-098464.
"Mosaic in X & Y." 1967. *Time*, September 29, 1967.
Nyong'o, Tavia. 2010. "The Unforgiveable Transgression of Being Caster Semenya. *Women & Performance: A Journal of Feminist Theory* 20 (1): 95-100.
Patiño, María José Martínez. 2005. "Personal Account: A Woman Tried and Tested," *The Lancet* 366: S38.
Pieper, Lindsay Parks. 2016. *Sex Testing: Gender Policing in Women's Sports.* Urbana: University of Illinois Press.
"Polish Writer Calls Helen Stephens a 'Man.'" 1936. *Los Angeles Times*, August 6, 1936, A9.
Povich, Shirley. 1956. "This Morning," *Washington Post*, April 5, 1956, 53.
Putney, Clifford. 2003. *Muscular Christianity: Manhood and Sports in Protestant America, 1880-1920.* Cambridge: Harvard University Press.
"What Do You Think? Is This a Man or a Woman?" 1937. *Look,* February 1937, 37-40.
Reczek, Włodzimierz. 1967. Letter to Alexandre de Mérode, October 14, 1967. Commission Medicale Correspondance, 1960-1967, Olympic Studies Centre Archives. Lausanne, Switzerland.
Rice, Grantland. 1936. "Separate Olympics for Sexes in 1940 Planned." *Los Angeles Times*, August 12, 1936, A9.
Richardson, Sarah S. 2013. *Sex Itself: The Search for Male and Female in the Human Genome.* Chicago: University of Chicago Press.
Riess, Steven. 1999. *Touching Base: Professional Baseball and American Culture in the Progressive Era.* Urbana: University of Illinois.
Ritchie, Ian. 2003. Sex tgested, Gender Verified: Controlling Female Sexuality in the Age of Containment. *Sport History Review* 34(1): 80-98.
Rodda, John. 1967. "Klobukowska Misses Test for Misses." *Washington Post*, September 15, 1967, D1.
"Runner Caster Semenya has Heard the Gender Comments all Her Life." 2009. *Los Angeles Times*, August 21, 2009. http://articles.latimes.com/2009/aug/21/world/fg-south-africa-runner21
Sánchez, Francisco J., Patiño, María José Martínez, and Eric Vilain. 2013. "The New Policy on Hyperandrogenism in Elite Female Athletes is Not about 'Sex Testing.'" *Journal of Sex Research.* http://www.ncbi.nlm.nih.gov/pmc/articles/PMC3554857/.
Schultz, Jaime. 2014. *Qualifying Times: Points of Change in U.S. Women's Sport.* Urbana: University of Illinois Press.
Shapiro, Samantha. 2012. "Caught in the Middle." *ESPN The Magazine*, August 1, 2012.
Smith, Ben. 2015. "Caster Semenya: 'What I Dream of is to Become Olympic Champion.'" *BBC*, May 19, 2015. http://www.bbc.com/sport/0/athletics/32805695
Sönksen Peter H., Bavington L Dawn, Boehning Tan, Cowan David, Guha Nishan, Holt Richard, Karkazis Katrina, Ferguson-Smith Malcolm Andrew, Mircetic Jovan, and Dankmar Böhning. 2018. "Hyperandrogenism Controversy in Elite Women's Sport: An Examination and Critique of Recent Evidence. *British Journal of Sports Medicine* 52 (23) https://bjsm.bmj.com/content/early/2018/01/18/bjsports-2017-098446.
Thiebault, Jacques. 1968. Minutes of the Meeting of the Medical Commission, July 14-17, 1968. Box 89, IOC Meetings, 1968, IOC Meetings—67th Session Folder. Avery Brundage Collection. University of Illinois Archives, United States.
Todd, Janice. 1998. *Physical Culture and the Body Beautiful: Purposive Exercise in the Lives of American Women.* Macon, Mercer University Press.

Tullis, Matt. 2013. "Who Was Stella Walsh? The Story of an Intersex Olympian." *SB Nation*, June 27, 2003. http://www.sbnation.com/longform/2013/6/27/4466724/stella-walsh-profile-intersex-olympian.

Vertinsky, Patricia A. 1994. *The Eternally Wounded Woman: Women, Doctors, and Exercise in the Late Nineteenth Century*. Illini Books Edition.

CHAPTER 9

Sexual Harassment in Elite Sport

Terry Engelberg and Stephen Moston

In many countries, sport is officially recognized as having an important social function and as a powerful cultural force (e.g., Australian Sports Commission 2012). Through participation in sport people learn attitudes, behaviors and social norms, and while it is commonly assumed that such outcomes will be positive, there is an increasing body of evidence to suggest that sport exerts a negative influence. For example, a summary of the research evidence (Liston et al. 2017) shows that sporting environments are places where violence against women can occur directly, and also indirectly through the entrenching of violence-supportive attitudes and behaviors. Zeigler (2007) cautioned that the special status of sport as a force that positively impacts both individual development and societal cohesion is challenged by the logic of profit:

> ...competitive sport is structured by the nature of the society in which it occurs. This would appear to mean that overcommercialization, taking drugs, cheating, officials taking bribes, violence, and so on at all levels of sport are simply reflections of the culture in which we live. Where does that leave us today as we consider sport's presumed relationship with moral character development? (Zeigler 2007, 303).

In this chapter, we examine sexual harassment in elite sport. While this is a prevalent and serious issue, there has been relatively little research on the topic. For example, in 2002, Celia Brackenridge (Downes 2002) said:

> Everyone talks about the perils of doping, but if there were 100 drugs cases under investigation in football, or 60 in swimming, or 40 in tennis, there would be uproar. Yet that's the scale of the problem with sex abuse today.

Little has changed in the intervening period (Vertommen et al. 2016). Moreover, the lack of studies of sexual harassment in sport stands in stark contrast to the large volume of studies in settings such as the workplace (for a review, see Ilies et al. 2003) and academia (e.g., Rosenthal, Smidt, and Freyd 2016, Clear et al. 2014). This is curious as sport has many of the structural characteristics that are linked to the proliferation of sexual harassment (e.g., Fasting, Chroni, and Knorre 2014, Tomlinson and Yorganci 1997). These characteristics include skewed gender ratios (e.g., an absence of women in managerial positions), sexualized atmospheres (e.g., scantily clad cheerleaders) and organizational power (e.g., the power held by coaches), all of which have been found to influence the incidence of sexual harassment (Engelberg and Moston 2016). In fact, the problem of sexual harassment in sport is so profound that university students studying sporting disciplines are at a greater risk of experiencing sexual harassment than students from other disciplines (Fasting et al. 2011). It will be argued that there has been a longstanding failure of sporting authorities to recognize and confront this issue. Sexual harassment is so entrenched that it has effectively become a 'part of sport' (Australian Sports Commission 2001) leading to widespread inertia regarding the establishment of regulatory practices to address the issue.

DEFINING SEXUAL HARASSMENT

Despite several decades of legislation, there is still no clear consensus as to what sexual harassment is. Even though the term is widely used, interpretations of what is meant by 'sexual harassment' vary considerably. These issues are then compounded when attempts are made to measure incidence. We can illustrate this problem by reference to the situation in Australia, noting that the same basic problems appear to be universal.

In Australia, sexual harassment is defined under the Sex Discrimination Act 1984 (Australian Government 2016):

> A person sexually harasses another person if:
>
> (a) the person makes an unwelcome sexual advance, or an unwelcome request for sexual favours, to the person harassed, or
>
> (b) engages in other unwelcome conduct of a sexual nature in relation to the person harassed
>
> in circumstances in which a reasonable person, having regard to all the circumstances, would have anticipated the possibility that the person harassed would be offended, humiliated or intimidated. (37)

Some key points to bear in mind in understanding the types of harassment are that the behavior must be *unwelcome* and *sexual*, and that the offender (assuming them to be a *reasonable person*), should have anticipated that their actions would have been offensive, humiliating or intimidating. In 2018, the Australian Human Rights Commission conducted a major survey (featuring a large nationally representative sample) of sexual harassment. Prior to being asked about their experiences of sexual harassment behaviors, respondents were offered a simplified version of the definition, specifically:

> Sexual harassment is an unwelcome sexual advance, unwelcome request for sexual favours or other unwelcome conduct of a sexual nature which, in the circumstances, a reasonable person, aware of those circumstances, would anticipate the possibility that the person would feel offended, humiliated or intimidated. (Australian Human Rights Commission 2018, 23)

Survey respondents were then asked, "Have you ever personally experienced sexual harassment?" Given the complexities involved in the respondent's understanding of any such definition (e.g., interpreting the 'reasonable person' standard), attempts to measure the incidence of sexual harassment through 'Yes' and 'No' responses are problematic. In short, many respondents will deny having been sexually harassed, even though legally, they may well have experienced such behavior.

The respondents were next asked: "At any time or anywhere, have you ever experienced any of the following behaviours in a way that was unwelcome?" (Australian Human Rights Commission 2018, 109). Such behavioral definitions are an attempt to overcome the limitations of the earlier simplistic question. The list of behaviors included 16 items:

1. Unwelcome touching, hugging, cornering or kissing
2. Inappropriate staring or leering that made you feel intimidated
3. Sexual gestures, indecent exposure or inappropriate display of the body
4. Sexually suggestive comments or jokes that made you feel offended
5. Sexually explicit pictures, posters or gifts that made you feel offended
6. Repeated or inappropriate invitations to go out on dates
7. Intrusive questions about your private life or physical appearance that made you feel offended
8. Inappropriate physical contact
9. Being followed, watched or someone loitering nearby
10. Requests or pressure for sex or other sexual acts
11. Actual or attempted rape or sexual assault
12. Indecent phone calls, including someone leaving a sexually explicit message on voicemail or an answering machine.
13. Sexually explicit comments made in emails, SMS messages or on social media
14. Repeated or inappropriate advances on email, social networking websites or internet chat rooms
15. Sharing or threatening to share intimate images or film of you without your consent
16. Any other unwelcome conduct of a sexual nature that occurred online or via some form of technology.

The relationship between these behaviors and the earlier simplified definition is curious. Two of the items (1 & 16) reinforce that the behavior had to be 'unwelcome', the remainder did not. Three of the 16 items refer to the behavior as offensive (items 4, 5 & 7). None of the items use the words humiliate or intimidated, even though they were in the simplified definition. Instead, the word inappropriate, that was not part of the simplified definition (nor is it present in the legal definition), was used in four items (2, 3, 6 & 14). Furthermore, the words indecent (items 3 & 12) and intimate (item 15) may or may not be sexual.

It should also be noted that, as is often seen in surveys of sexual harassment, criminal offences such as sexual assault and rape (which have their own legal definitions) have been included (item 11). In surveys sexual harassment behaviors can thus range from intrusive questions through to rape.

If one ventures even further into the research, matters get only more complicated, with other surveys adopting their own idiosyncratic definitions that are invariably externally inconsistent (lack of correspondence with either the legal definition, or other surveys), and/or internally inconsistent (the survey items do not correspond to the chosen definition).

Asking "Have you been sexually harassed?" clearly hinges on how the term is defined. Many people have been sexually harassed but determining how many is problematic. In the last eight years in Australia a series of major surveys have put the incidence of sexual harassment (of women) within the range 20-85%, although it might be higher, or possibly lower.

Research efforts are further hindered by a lack of consistency in definitions across countries (see UN Women 2012), and also between organizations: behavior that is tolerated in one workplace, educational institution or sport setting may be unacceptable in another (see Engelberg and Moston 2016). This may be evident in several ways, such as differing policies between organizations in the same geographical region or the same type of industry. Even within a single organization, inconsistencies can be found. For example, language that is permitted on the sporting field, would not acceptable in the offices of management or the boardroom.

DEFINING SEXUAL HARASSMENT IN SPORT

Definitions of sexual harassment in sport are usually based on definitions in the workplace and these in turn are generally framed within sex discrimination policy and legislation. For example, in the U.S.A. the Women's Sport Foundation (2011) offers the following definition:

> Sexual harassment consists of unwelcome sexual advances, requests for sexual favors and other verbal or physical conduct of a sexual nature and can occur separately or be a part of abuse. Romantic and/or sexual relationships between coaches and athletes are regarded as an abuse of professional ethics, status and power.

Despite its implicit acknowledgement that sexual harassment can happen to both males and females and between those of equal organizational power, the Women's Sport Foundation highlights sexual harassment's effect on females and those of lower power (athletes). A similar but broader definition is provided by the Australian Womensport and Recreation Association (2009).

> Discrimination can take the following forms:
>
> a. Direct Discrimination—This means treating someone less favorably than you would treat others in the same circumstances.
>
> b. Indirect Discrimination—This occurs when a job requirement or condition is applied equally to all, which has a disproportionate and detrimental affect [sic.] on one sector of society, because fewer from that sector can comply with it and the requirement cannot be justified in relation to the job.
>
> c. When decisions are made about an individual, the only personal characteristics taken into account will be those which, as well as being consistent with relevant legislation, are necessary to the proper performance of the work involved.
>
> Harassment is described as inappropriate actions, behavior, comments or physical contact that is objectionable or causes offence to the recipient. It may be directed towards people because of their gender, appearance, race, ethnic origin, nationality, age, sexual preference, a disability or some other characteristic. AWRA is committed, to ensuring that its employees and volunteers are able to conduct their activities free from harassment or intimidation.

In these examples there are considerable overlaps between organizational and legislative definitions. Most definitions state that the behaviors must be 'unwanted', 'unsolicited' and 'of a sexual nature'. Some definitions contain a clause stating that 'a reasonable person' would consider the behavior to be sexual harassment. This means that, all matters considered, a reasonable person would find the behaviors objectionable or offensive. This is intended to prevent abuses of legislation on the part of the recipient.

Some definitions address the distinction (MacKinnon 1979) between *quid pro quo* (such as a coach making sexual demands of an athlete in return for privileges) and *hostile environment* harassment (such as a coach's crude behavior). Some organizations may adopt a more stringent policy than is required by law, as part of a wider policy workplace behaviors. For example, the Womensport Foundation (2009) definition addresses what appear to be consensual relationships between coaches and athletes as problematic: these relationships, which are not necessarily harassment, may involve an abuse of ethics, status and power.

Sexual Abuse in Sport

While some studies of sexual harassment include the behaviors of sexual abuse and rape, it is important to recognize that these offences are, strictly speaking, not examples of sexual harassment. Invariably, such offences are prosecuted under criminal rather than civil laws. One of the most widely reported forms of sexual abuse in sport is the sexual abuse of children, such as young gymnasts in the USA (United States Olympic Committee 2018, Hobson and Rich 2017), young basketball players in the USA (Willmsen and O'Hagan 2003), and young swimmers in Australia (Australian Associated Press 2015). Another widely reported problem is that of sexual assaults/rape of adults, such as numerous cases involving child and adult taekwondo athletes in the USA (Fuchs 2018).

Alexander, Stafford, and Lewis (2011) suggest that there is a "'grey zone' between sexual harassment and harm, to sexualised behaviour and sexual harm" (61). This issue was explicitly recognized by the International Olympic Committee (2007) in a Consensus Statement:

> Sexual harassment and abuse in sport stem from power relations and abuses of power. Sexual harassment refers to behaviour towards an individual or group that involves sexualised verbal, non-verbal or physical behaviour, whether intended or unintended, legal or illegal, that is based upon an abuse of power and trust and that is considered by the victim or a bystander to be unwanted or coerced. Sexual abuse involves any sexual activity where consent is not or cannot be given. In sport, it often involves manipulation and entrapment of the athlete. (3)

While the two problems are conceptually distinguishable, according to the same Consensus Statement, they are symptoms of the same failed organizational culture, one which facilitates such conduct.

HOW COMMON IS SEXUAL HARASSMENT IN SPORT?

Regardless of how it is defined and across differing contexts, sexual harassment has been found to be widespread. However, determining just how persistent and widespread is a challenging task. There are two key ways of assessing the prevalence of sexual harassment: through surveys and through archival data on reported cases. As discussed earlier, surveys invariably suffer from methodological concerns, and case data may be subject to problems such as under-reporting.

One further problem in attempting to determine the frequency of sexual harassment is that organizations may be reluctant to investigate this issue. If a study were to show a high incidence of sexual harassment, despite a commitment to eliminating the problem, bad publicity could still be generated for the organization concerned. Consequently, when organizations conduct in-house incidence studies, the results may not be made public.

In the context of sport, research into sexual harassment is very limited. Although sporting regulatory bodies provide guidelines (e.g., the Australian Sports Commission, UK Sport and others), there is both a paucity of systematic collection of incidence data and a lack of systematic academic research into both sexual harassment and other forms of sexual abuse in sport. This situation could be due to inertia in the sport and recreation industry regarding the establishment of regulatory practices for a problem that many are reluctant to acknowledge (Brackenridge 1997, Volkwein-Caplan et al. 2002).

Fasting et al (2014) report that prevalence rates of both sexual harassment and sexual abuse in sport settings fluctuate between 2 and 50 per cent. In part, this reflects the specificity of samples featured in studies (Fasting, Brackenridge, and Walseth 2007). For example, some studies have focused on male harassment of females, whilst others have been even more restrictive, such as harassment of female athletes by male coaches or female-female harassment (Volkwein-Caplan et al. 2002, Sand et al. 2011).

As with studies of sexual harassment in the workplace, studies of sexual harassment in sport have found strong differences in the perceptions of males and females. For example, the Australian Sports Commission (2001) surveyed the opinions and experiences of approximately 300 athletes and administrators. The study found that there was a dramatic difference in how males and females perceived harassment. In general, 20 per cent more males than females considered harassing behavior as 'part of sport'. One of the most dramatic differences between males and females was with respect to uninvited touching; 100 per cent of females considered this behavior as harassment, whilst only 22.5 per cent of males did. Further, nearly one in four males considered it acceptable to touch others (uninvited) and more than one in two males considered sexually explicit language as a normal part of sport. Another worrying finding was that one in ten female athletes perceived sexual propositions as part of sport and therefore 'acceptable', which lends support to the contention that females may be more accepting of such behaviors in a sport context.

Fasting, Brackenridge, and Sundgot-Borgen (2004) examined the prevalence of sexual harassment amongst 553 Norwegian female athletes by sport type. Their study included 56 different sport disciplines which were further subdivided into team and individual sports, whether revealing clothing was required for competition, gender structure and gender culture. They found that, although women in masculine environments were more likely to report experiencing sexual harassment, it is participation in sport itself that is more important than sport type. The authors concluded that gendered structural relations in sport persist and that these are connected to females' experience of sexual harassment.

In the USA Volkwein-Caplan et al. (2002) assessed the experience of sexual harassment of women in athletics, finding that about 20 per cent of athletes had been exposed to threatening behavior, such as sexist comments and physical advances.

Other sexual harassment research in sport settings has focused on sports science students (Fasting, Chroni, and Knorre 2014) and females in sports writing (Pedersen et al. 2009). Fasting, Chroni, and Knorre (2014) explored the experiences of sexual harassment of women in two settings (organized sport and education) in three countries: Czech Republic, Norway and Greece. Respondents in the Czech Republic and Greece were more likely to be recipients of sexual harassment than respondents in Norway. Overall however, sexual harassment (from male peers or supervisors/coaches) occurred more in education than in the sport setting. One possible interpretation of this finding was that women in sport were more 'accepting' of these behaviors, which is consistent with the Australian findings reported earlier.

Pedersen et al. examined the experiences of 112 females who were sport print media professionals. They found that 50.9 per cent had been recipients of sexual harassment (over the previous year) from a variety of individuals including supervisors, coaches, athletes and members of sports media with who they came into contact as part of their work. Although these women were negatively affected by such behaviors, they generally adopted a "you just grin and bear it" (349) approach to the problem and that "harassment in our own offices is often as bad as it is in the locker rooms…" (349). A similar feeling of acceptance of these behaviors as part of the job was amongst the findings of Hardin and Shain (2005) who found that women in sports media not only seem to accept discrimination and harassment as part of their jobs but also "see such treatment almost as 'routine'- not as deviant". (814).

The organizational characteristics of the setting where the harassment takes place may explain why women, in particular, may see these behaviors as normative. Dellinger and Williams (2002) note that organizational culture shapes people's meanings of sexual harassment and influences how they deal with sexualized behavior. These issues are reflected in how women athletes are portrayed in the media. For example, Fenton (2016) reports a content analysis of 2016 Olympic sport coverage, finding that women were consistently referred to as 'girls' or 'ladies', whilst men were far less likely to be referred to as 'boys' or 'gentlemen'. On a related theme, Hunt (2016) shows how women's sporting achievements would be linked to their male partners (effectively passing, or sharing the credit).

Failure to Act

One of the recurring issues in studies of both sexual harassment and abuse in sport is that sporting bodies have not been effective in dealing with such issues. For example, coaches who sexually harass or assault athletes often do not face any disciplinary action. Instead, the athletes may be asked to leave the team/organization. Other (relatively common) problems include:

- Sexualized training environments. For example, swim team bonding sessions involving pornography and strippers (Halloran 2014a)
- Use of models rather than athletes to promote women's sport. For example, when promoting the Colombian national football team uniforms, male players were recruited for the men's uniforms, female models were used for the women's uniform (de Menezes 2017)

- Failure to publicly identify alleged offenders. For example, names of alleged offenders in cycling were redacted in reports (Cary and Rumsby 2017, Ingle 2017)
- Failure to develop policies to address sexual abuse and harassment. For example, for over a decade the Queensland Academy of Sport (Australia) failed to develop relevant policies despite having previously hired coaches who had failed background checks (Australian Associated Press 2015).
- Failure to publicly identify convicted offenders. For example, names of confirmed offenders in swimming have been removed from lists of sanctioned swimming coaches (Seattle Times 2003, Le 2018)
- Inconsistent messaging. For example, sanctioned swimming coaches might be welcomed back into sporting environments (Halloran 2014b), or offered new employment opportunities (Australian Associated Press 2015).

Any solution must begin by first developing a coherent definition of sexual harassment. The current legal definitions incorporate terms that reflect decades of research and theoretical input, and while they have not been designed with survey research in mind, they must be our starting point. One of the first things to note is that most definitions do not include rape or sexual assault. Those offences have their own definitions and their inclusion in surveys as types of 'sexual harassment' is indefensible. In both data collection and reporting, these offences must be clearly distinguished from sexual harassment. The same restriction applies to bullying behaviors.

We can now focus on behaviors that clearly fall under most existing interpretations of sexual harassment. First, we have conduct that may involve sexual extortion (*quid pro quo*). Research tells us that there is a clear agreement that such behaviors are unequivocally categorized as sexual harassment (e.g., the views of males and females concur). The reasonable person standard is effective in such situations.

Second, we have 'unwelcome sexual conduct'. This includes the most pervasive forms of sexual harassment, sometimes referred to in the research literature as 'hostile environment'. The reasonable person standard is less effective in such situations, with clear differences between the views of men and women. Consequently, in survey research greater care is required in establishing that a behavior meets the legal standard of sexual harassment. For example, in Australia the person being harassed must view the conduct as *unwelcome* (a subjective assessment), and, with regard to the circumstances, a *reasonable person* would have anticipated that the behavior would be interpreted as (a) offensive, (b) humiliating, or (c) intimidating. Without at least one of those three conditions being met, a behavior might not merit the designation of sexual harassment (e.g., it may have been a misunderstanding).

The need to develop a measure of sexual harassment that is both valid and reliable has been an ongoing concern for several decades (e.g., Engelberg and Moston

1997, 2016). Unfortunately, many surveys adopt a ground zero approach, and offer up new definitions making comparisons across time, situation and populations, spurious. Sexual harassment is a serious problem and it is time for researchers to get serious about how to define and measure it.

Whilst acknowledging the inherent difficulty of such a move, we propose that the term sexual harassment be abandoned and replaced with a series of distinct offences or behaviors that will more closely align with both legal definitions and public perceptions. These are as follows:

- Rape and sexual assault
- Sexual extortion
- Sexual discrimination
- Bullying
- Unwanted romantic relationships

Adopting such categories would help to clarify survey construction and would help to eliminate the current confusion and trivialization of sexual harassment, whereby an explanation and single solution is sought for a widely diverse set of behaviors, ranging from unwanted romantic relationships to rape.

Conclusion

While sexual harassment serves many purposes (to its perpetrators at least), probably the most salient is to keep women out of sport. In many sporting clubs and organizations, the (predominantly) male coaches and managers engage in behaviors that reinforce their authority over their female athletes. For example, an independent inquiry into the conduct of coaches and administrators from Swimming Australia, showed that they had until as recently as 2009, engaged in "bonding nights" involving strippers and porn parties (Halloran 2014a). Regrettably, to many in sport, inquiry into sexual harassment is dismissed as an irrelevance that interferes with their core business: winning (Fasting and Brackenridge 2009). This position is highly prevalent and ultimately damaging to the integrity of sport.

References

Alexander, Kate, Anne Stafford, and Ruth Lewis. 2011. The experiences of children participating in organised sport in the UK. Edinburgh: University of Edinburgh/NSPCC Child Protection Research Centre.

Australian Associated Press. 2015. "Sport academy still not protecting youth a decade after Scott Volkers scandal—report." *The Guardian*, December 15. http://www.theguardian.com/sport/2015/dec/15/sport-academy-still-not-protecting-youth-a-decade-after-scott-volkers-scandal-report.

Australian Government. 2016. Sex Discrimination Act 1984. edited by Federal Register of Legislation. Canberra, Australia: Australian Government.

Australian Human Rights Commission. 2018. Everyone's business: Fourth national survey on sexual harassment in Australian workplaces. Australian Human Rights Commission,.

Australian Sports Commission. 2001. Australian research on harassment in sport. A snapshot In time: Athlete's perceptions of harassment. edited by Australian Sports Commission. Online: Australian Sports Commission.

———. 2012. The essence of Australian sport. edited by Australian Sports Commission. Canberra: Australian Government.

Australian Womensport and Recreation Association, AWRA. 2009. Australian Womensport and Recreation Association (AWRA) Equality Policy Melbourne: Australian Womensport and Recreation Association.

Brackenridge, Celia. 1997. "He owned me basically: women's experiences of sexual abuse in sport." *International Review for the Sociology of Sport* 32:115-130.

Cary, Tom, and Ben Rumsby. 2017. "Worst criticism dropped from independent report into British Cycling scandal." *The Telegraph*, June 13. https://www.telegraph.co.uk/cycling/2017/06/13/british-cycling-drops-worst-criticism-report-sexism-governing/.

Clear, Emily R., Ann L. Coker, Patricia G. Cook-Craig, Heather M. Bush, Lisandra S. Garcia, Corrine M. Williams, Alysha M. Lewis, and Bonnie S. Fisher. 2014. "Sexual Harassment Victimization and Perpetration Among High School Students." *Violence Against Women* 20 (10):1203-1219. doi: 10.1177/1077801214551287.

de Menezes, Jack. 2017. "Colombia Women's team furious after Adidas use former Miss Colombia model to unveil new kit." *The Independent*, November 10. https://www.independent.co.uk/sport/football/international/colombia-women-kit-launch-paulina-vega-dieppa-instagram-furious-model-james-rodriguez-a8047271.html.

Dellinger, Kirsten, and Christine L. Williams. 2002. "The locker room and the dorm room: Workplace norms and the boundaries of sexual harassment in magazine editing." *Social Problems* 49 (2):242-257.

Downes, Steven. 2002. "Every parent's nightmare." *The Guardian*, April 7. https://www.theguardian.com/observer/osm/story/0,6903,678189,00.html.

Engelberg, Terry, and Stephen Moston. 1997. *Sexual Harassment: The employer's guide to causes, consequences and remedies.* Sydney, Australia: Business & Professional Publishing.

———. 2016. "Hiding in plain sight: sexual harassment in sport." In *Research handbook of employment relations in sport*, edited by M. Barry, J. Skinner and T Engelberg, 295-309. Cheltenham, UK: Edward Elgar Press

Fasting, Kari and Celia Brackenridge. 2009. "Coaches, sexual harassment and education." *Sport, Education and Society* 14 (1):21-35.

Fasting, Kari, Stiliani Chroni, Stein E. Hervik, and N. Knorre. 2011. "Sexual harassment in sport toward females in three European countries." *International Review for the Sociology of Sport* 46 (1):76-89.

Fasting, Kari, S. Chroni, and Nada Knorre. 2014. "The experiences of sexual harassment in sport and education among European female sports science students." *Sport, Education and Society* 19 (2):115-130.

Fasting, Kari, Celia H. Brackenridge, and J. Sundgot-Borgen. 2004. "Prevalence of sexual harassment among Norwegian female elite athletes in relation to sport type." *International Review for the Sociology of Sport* 39:373-386.

Fasting, Kari, Celia Brackenridge, and Kristin Walseth. 2007. "Women athletes' personal responses to sexual harassment in sport." *Journal of Applied Sport Psychology* 19 (4):419-433.

Fenton, Siobhan. 2016. "Rio 2016: The charts which show how bad sexism is for female athletes." *The Independent*, August 19. http://www.independent.co.uk/sport/olympics/rio-2016-the-charts-which-show-how-sexism-affects-how-we-talk-about-female-and-female-athletes-a7197516.html.

Fuchs, Jeremy. 2018. "Fighting back." *Sports Illustrated*, September 10, 69-77. https://www.si.com/vault/issue/1018454/77.

Halloran, Jessica. 2014a. "Swimming Australia investigates coaches involved in a dirty pool of strippers and porn at bonding sessions in the Gold Coast " *Courier-Mail*, 13 September. https://www.couriermail.com.au/sport/more-sports/swimming-australia-investigates-coaches-involved-in-a-dirty-pool-of-strippers-and-porn-at-bonding-sessions-in-the-gold-coast/news-story/2673d786434c69cbcd294e9a0b0fce71.

———. 2014b. "VIP treatment for Australian swimming coach Barclay Nettlefold, caught in scandal of inappropriate behaviour towards female staff." *Courier-Mail*, September 14. https://www.couriermail.com.au/sport/more-sports/vip-treatment-for-australian-swimming-coach-barclay-nettlefold-caught-in-scandal-of-inappropriate-behaviour-towards-female-staff/news-story/a221213c964e0745e0e56d0158a1b8eb.

Hardin, Marie, and Stacie Shain. 2005. "Strength in Numbers? The experiences and attitudes of women in sports media careers." *Journalism and Mass Communication Quarterly* 82 (4):804-819.

Hobson, Will, and Steven Rich. 2017. "Every six weeks for more than 36 years: When will sex abuse in Olympic sports end?" *Washington Post*, November 17. https://www.washingtonpost.com/sports/every-six-weeks-for-more-than-36-years-when-will-sex-abuse-in-olympic-sports-end/2017/11/17/286ae804-c88d-11e7-8321-481fd63f174d_story.html.

Hunt, Elle. 2016. "Commentators take gloss off female Olympians' efforts and medals." *The Guardian*, August 9. https://www.theguardian.com/sport/2016/aug/09/rio-2016-commentators-take-gloss-off-female-olympians-medals.

Ilies, Remus, Nancy Hauserman, Susan Schwochau, and John Stibal. 2003. "Reported incidence rates of work-related sexual harassment in the united states: Using meta-analysis to explain reported rate disparities." *Personnel Psychology* 56 (3):607-631. doi: 10.1111/j.1744-6570.2003.tb00752.x.

Ingle, Sean. 2017. "British Cycling 'sexism' report delayed and names likely be redacted." *The Guardian*, February 8. https://www.theguardian.com/sport/2017/feb/07/british-cycling-report-sexism-bullying-allegations-shane-sutton.

International Olympic Committee. 2007. IOC adopts consensus statement on "sexual harassment & abuse in sport". Lausanne: International Olympic Committee.

Le, Phuong. 2018. "Olympian sues USA Swimming to allege sexual abuse cover-up." *The Gazette*, May 21. https://gazette.com/sports/olympian-sues-usa-swimming-to-allege-sexual-abuse-cover-up/article_816233cf-7037-5c2c-bbe2-87e41c2a37b4.html.

Liston, Ruth, Shaez Mortimer, Gemma Hamilton, and Robin Cameron. 2017. A team effort: Preventing violence against women through sport. Melbourne, Australia: Our Watch.

MacKinnon, Catherine. 1979. *Sexual harassment of working women*. New Haven, Connecticut: Yale University Press.

Pedersen, Paul M., Choong H. Lim, Barbara Osborne, and Warren Whisenant. 2009. "An examination of the perceptions of sexual harassment by sport print media professionals." *Journal of Sport Management* 23:335-360.

Rosenthal, Marina N., Alec M. Smidt, and Jennifer J. Freyd. 2016. "Still Second Class: Sexual Harassment of Graduate Students." *Psychology of Women Quarterly* 40 (3):364-377. doi: 10.1177/0361684316644838.

Sand, Trond S., Kari Fasting, Stiliani Chroni, and Nada Knorre. 2011. "Coaching behavior: Any consequences for the prevalence of sexual harassment?" *International Journal of Sports Science & Coaching* 6 (2):241-241.

Seattle Times. 2003. "Coaches who prey: The abuse of girls and the system that allows it." *Seattle Times*, December 14. http://old.seattletimes.com/news/local/coaches/.

Tomlinson, Alan, and Ilkay Yorganci. 1997. "Male coach/female athlete relations: Gender and power relations in competitive sport."*Journal of Sport and Social Issues* 21:134-155.

UN Women. 2012. "Sexual harassment in sport." http://www.endvawnow.org/en/articles/30-sexual-harassment-in-sport.html.

United States Olympic Committee. 2018. USOC statement regarding action to revoke USA Gymnastics' recognition as member national governing body

Vertommen, Tine, Nicolette Schipper-van Veldhoven, Kristien Wouters, Jarl K. Kampen, Celia Brackenridge, Daniel J.A. Rhind, Karel Neels, and Filip Van Den Eede. 2016. "Interpersonal violence against children in sport in the Netherlands and Belgium." *Child Abuse & Neglect* 51:223-236. doi: 10.1016/j.chiabu.2015.10.006.

Volkwein-Caplan, Karin, Frauke Schnell, Shannon Devlin, Michele Mitchell, and Jennifer Sutera. 2002. "Sexual harassment in athletics vs. academia." In *Sexual Harassment and Abuse in Sport - International Research and Policy Perspectives*, edited by Celia Brackenridge and Kari Fasting. London: Whiting & Birch.

Willmsen, Christine, and Maureen O'Hagan. 2003. "Coaches continue working for schools and private teams after being caught for sexual misconduct." *Seattle Times*, December 14. http://old.seattletimes.com/news/local/coaches/news/dayone.html.

Women's Sport Foundation. 2011. "Sexual Harassment and Sexual Relationships Between Coaches, Other Athletic Personnel and Athletes: The Foundation Position.", Women's Sport Foundation.

Zeigler, Earle F. 2007. "Sport management must show social concern as it develops tenable theory." *Journal of Sport Management* 21 (3):297-318.

Dark Sides of Sport

CHAPTER 10

In the Dark: The Construction of Sport and its Coaching Rhetoric

Susannah Stevens and Ian Culpan

INTRODUCTION

The social construct of sport is often viewed in an unproblematic light or alternatively, as a human practice fraught with destructive behaviours that inhibit human development. Although this highlights the different complexities that exist within the sporting realm, it subsequently fosters binaries. Our proposition promulgates that a broad cataloguing of binaries is not helpful in understanding the intricacies of sport and how this manifests within constructs such as the athlete-coach relationship. The assumption that binaries pervade sport, muddies the problematics associated with the epistemologies and ontologies of this human practice. The muddy-ness, we argue has it genesis, not in morality, or science, or economics, put rather in the adherence to a singular, outdated understanding of sport. We argue that this inhibiting singularity within sport and the athlete-coach relationship curtails evolutionary thinking and development around sport that is required to keep a pace with current times. This darkness of sport is eclipsing and inhibiting its future development as valued practice. Within the chapter, we use *sport* not *elite sport* purposively. We argue the problematics associated with epistemologies and ontologies do not discriminate between the two. So, to shine a little light on sport we must elucidate the many interpretations or various disputes of intent. Although this debate could devour a chapter in itself, our aim here is to merely provide context. Our argument focuses on the problematics associated with the apathy or even inertia associated with the evolution of thinking around what contemporary sport could mean and the benefits that accrue. This, we claim, is the 'dark side'.

ILLUMINATING SPORT

Traditional definitions regard sport as a physical activity that is competitive, requires skill, exertion and is governed by institutionalised views (Coakley, Hallinan, Jackson, and Mewett 2009). Sport is seen as "...institutionalised competitive activities that involve rigorous physical exertion or the use of relatively complex physical skills by participants motivated by internal and external rewards" (Coakley et al. 2009, 5).

Many definitions promulgate similar sporting ingredients (Collins and Jackson 2007). Woods similarly argues that sport must involve a physical component; be competitive; involve institutionalised games; and use specialised facilities and equipment (Woods 2007). Specifically, he articulates that sport is typically defined as "...institutionalised competitive activity that involves physical skill and specialised facilities or equipment and is conducted according to an accepted set of rules to determine the winner" (Woods 2007, 7). However, reducing sport to a rudimentary definition does little to expose the contention of sport sociologically, philosophically or paradigmatically as a human practice. So, whilst the majority of literature and praxis understands sport from this traditional modernist paradigm, it consequently habitually rejects the metaphysical and axiological questions necessary to understand the construct. Meier, on completion of a detailed analysis of the definitions of sport, concluded rather modestly that sport, in the proper environment and with the proper orientation, may indeed be most appropriately viewed as a form or subset of play (Meier 1981). This is because sport has been recognised as autotelic physical contests (played for their own sake) (Guttmann et al. nd.); and a social phenomenon. Sewart claims that "sport is a social phenomenon related to the intersubjective moral order. As opposed to the utilitarian and technical dimensions of life, sport has been identified as a moral, aesthetic, and dramatic phenomenon as well as a medium of individual self-fulfilment. As a moral phenomenon, sport is oriented to the dimension of interpersonal bonding" (Sewart 1987, 172).

Metaphysical and axiological examinations expose sports' cultural relativity, and Woods claims this could be originally seen thorough the different beliefs and attitudes regarding warfare, manhood, survival and honouring the gods (Woods 2007). Horne, Tomlinson and Whannel argue that by taking into account historical and social realms, sport does not have a fixed meaning. For example, the context of 'animal-sports' i.e. fighting, hunting, and shooting that hold different meaning across cultures, space and time (Horne, Tomlinson and Whannel 1999). Autopsy of Brohm's analyses of sport from a Marxist political position locates sport as a cultural counterpart for capitalism's economic domination. He explores the socio-political, technological, and institutional aspects of competitive sport and argues that the state uses sport as a means of subjugation and domination (Brohm 1978). Brohm contends that sport, through excessive competition, is characterised by a callous tyranny that fosters the development of simplistic, mechanistic sport androids that eventually become alienated from their bodies. Loy similarly, describes sport as an institutionalized construct, that demonstrates the athlete's physical prowess forcing him/her to do the majority of the work (Loy 1968). How quickly its pedestal falls, when sport is no longer religiously adulated as an unproblematic good. Irrefutably, sport can hold opportunities for flourishing, and many could be linked to social behaviour. Fair play, justice, conflict and dispute resolution, solidarity, or self-actualisation could be realised. However, it is negligible to abstain from philosophical debate that questions sports worth: "This idealized vision of sport is severely deficient insofar as it reduces sport to a separate reality whose meanings, metaphoric qualities, and regulating structures are disembodied from its material context" (Sewart 1987, 172).

Perhaps the one author who defines sport in light of this debate, is Peter Arnold. He considers sport indispensable to moral life, because without sport there is actually little need in everyday society for the extensive co-operation and personal qualities that sport commands (Arnold 1979, 1994, 1998). Arnold defines sport as an intrinsically valuable human practice and emphasises the connection between the educative value of sport and moral growth; assigning the following characteristics. (1) Is rule governed and practiced with traditions and customs; (2) Pursues its own intrinsic goal; (3) Is physically exertive; (4) Fosters social interaction, rivalry, contest and competition; and (5) Is practiced within a moral and ethical sense (Arnold 1979). Arnold contends that sport is best understood as a valued human practice, and sport as a form of moral education. Therefore, you will note his definition of sport includes *being practised within a moral and ethical sense.* This ideological assertion calls for an educative interpretation of sport, obligated to and practised in accordance with its ideals. Furthermore, he accentuates that unless the concept and practice of sport is comprehended from a social and moral paradigm, there is diminutive possibility of the end user (teachers, participants, officials, administrators or fans) developing appropriate attitudes, judgements and conduct towards it. McFee, in agreement, states that this is not inasmuch a product of rules themselves, rather the moral imperative of educated, human considerations on fairness and the spirit of the game (McFee 2004).

The discernible discomfort we have here, is that these definitions and understandings of sport are dated; significantly so. Given consideration to the rate of global change and paradigmatic debate within the academy can we really say that this work still holds contextual and cultural relevance? We would contend, that these definitions of sport are no longer suitable for contemporary times or contemporary youth. Moreover, we suggest that this outdated discourse, dogmatically embodied within the archetypal coach is slowly being rejected by the athlete. We argue that definitions and understandings of sport sit stagnant. They have been sidelined; and no ounce of anticipation, mental preparedness, training or guidance will see them played. Why would a coach put in a player whose position wasn't relevant or required? So, to ruminate this 'dark side' of sport, and in reflection on Kretchmar's (2005) philosophic inquiry, we have pondered three questions. Why do sport and its authorities seem to be paradigmatically incarcerated? Why is this embodied regulation being rejected? And where does the coach seem to fit within this process?

THE PARADIGMATIC INCARCERATION OF SPORT

From the analysis above, it would seem that sport understandings are imprisoned in the confines of modernity and as a consequence struggle to achieve relevancy with an increasing number of young people across the globe (International Council of Sport Science and Physical Education (ICSSPE) 2001). Modern rhetoric is characterised by extolling the virtues and benefits of sport where young people can benefit from a wide range of social, emotional, mental and physical attributes while at the same time controlling body weight and obesity issues. This rhetoric has powerful moral underpinnings that suggest young people should be involved, even coerced into physical activity particularly in education settings (United Nations Educational

Scientific and Cultural Organisation (UNESCO) 2013, 2017). However, there is an increasing body of evidence that is suggesting these confident claims need cautious treatment (Bailey et al. 2009). We suggest that such assured claims deliver the fallacy that the benefits of sport are conclusively established and there is little more to be said on the matter. Tinning warns, "we should be modest in the claims we make for the contributions of sport and physical education to active lifestyles" (Tinning 2005, 12). Bailey et al, in their academic review concluded that many of the educational benefits claimed for physical education and sport were dependent on contextual and pedagogical variables (Bailey et al. 2009). Contextual and pedagogical arrangements present a significant challenge and a need for further exploration particularly when sport by its very nature involves bodies and physical abilities that are highly visible exposing complex human vulnerabilities. Such vulnerabilities are situational and contextually unique requiring sophisticated and multiple understandings of contemporary youth culture. Particularly relevant in addressing vulnerabilities is the nature of power relations between a coach/teacher and the athlete/learner. Tomlinson and Yorganci suggest that the relations of power between the coach and the athlete is expressed in the spaces associated with training regimes, diet and weight control, inter-personal relations and strict codes of behaviour (Tomlinson and Yorganci 1997). These relations and spaces often render the athlete powerless and lead to a "normalcy of conditions conducive to harassment and abuse" (Tomlinson and Yorganci 1997, 152). The powerlessness is manifested, both for male and female athletes, by the deeply ingrained autocratic authoritarian leadership style that leads to a cycle of surveillance, bullying, control and dependency. Crosset (1986) conceptualised this as the master/servant relationship which he classifies as principally an abusive form of control where the athlete is denied any form of independence and any ability to make individual decisions. The net effect of this is the development of a false consciousness in the athlete. Here we highlight the inherent tension between contemporary youth, predisposed to actively seek independence and non-regulation, and the dominant dark side of sports culture embracing forms of domination, and control.

The work of Foucault becomes useful in identifying rationalities associated with the fundamental tension identified above. Here this tension has its genesis firstly, in the lack of evolutionary progress in the thinking about sport (see earlier) and secondly in the normative neo-liberal agenda and subsequent rationalities that pervade modern sport (Foucault 1980). It is this second focus, which is highlighted here. The central argument presented is that sport per se, across almost all Western democracies and Eastern bloc understandings of this democracy, has become captured by the global political economy. The consequence is that sport has become a mechanism of power in order to achieve governments' and the corporate world's economic agenda. This agenda setting is characterised by the establishment and monitoring of achievable targets, strict codes of behaviour, cogent training regimes, excessive competition, in depth performance reviews and strong auditing procedures. These mechanisms of power are strategies utilised by governments and corporates to govern people from a distance and in so doing create an illusion of freedom, self-control and self-regulation. It is called governmentality, which, put simply, means "governments create policies to guide, encourage, direct and even manipulate the population into certain ways of behaviour and particular forms of citizenship" (Foucault 1980). These mechanisms of power for sport are manifested in three dominant rationalities. One focused on the commodification of sport and the objectification of the athlete, the second on expert power and control by the coach over the athlete and the third is the creation of docile bodies. The next section will briefly outline what is meant by these three dominant rationalities.

Commodification

Free market political orientations, in the latter part of the 20th century, have dominated global economics with profound effects on all aspects of Western life. This orientation has created a deep and acute economic, social, political, cultural and behavioural upheaval in sport resulting in what Walsh and Giulianotti suggest is detrimental to the philosophy and practice of sport (Walsh and Giulianotti 2007). What these scholars have suggested is that the profound upheaval of sport is characterised by sport being governed by the ideology of the market place and there is little concern for its educative or intrinsic value. This commodification of sport, a dominant rationality, has seen the direct and uncontested quest for, and priority given to, profit. Sewart, for instance, argues that sport has become a trafficked commodity and that this market mentality has debauched and dehumanised its very essence (Sewart 1987). Walsh and Giulianotti suggest that all this is cause for moral concern and argue that this commodification "involves the violation of what we might take to be fundamental moral values that emerge from or through sporting activity be it at the elite or grassroots level" (Walsh and Guilianotti 2007, 10). Clearly, the market mentality has intruded on and had an intense effect in sport becoming commodified. Sewart evidences this pervasive rationality by identifying three areas of significance: (1) changes in rules, format and scheduling to accommodate the commercial interests of the electronic media. (2) the abandonment of the ethic of skill democracy whereby meritocratic principles of performance are ignored and the big-name players are given preference at sporting tournaments thereby ignoring previously agreed upon norms of sport that promote equality, justice and fairness. (3) the tendency for the spectacular and theatrical where attention and priority is given to the dramatic, the thrills and maximum entertainment with moments that essentially trivialise the inherent nature of the contest, the beauty of performance, joyfulness and the athleticism involved. Instead, what is presented is based on winning at all costs in order to maximise profits (For a full analysis, please see Sewart 1987).

Expert Knowledge and Control

The dominant rationality of expert power and control characterises sport per se none more so than the coach/athlete relations (Tomlinson and Yorganci 1997). It is evidenced in the domains associated with training regimes, excessive competition, performance monitoring, accountabilities, food and diet necessities, control of body weight and shape, sleep requirements, codes of behaviour and social relations. Essentially the coach assumes a measure of control over the athlete and exercises this power in a candid manner. This power relation, according to Tomlinson and Yorganci can create a dependency that runs the risk of unfolding into the abuse of the athlete irrespective whether they are male or female, and the seemingly total disregard for the growth and development of the athlete. Piggott labels this power abuse as paternalistic and in its gendered form is pervasive and "compounded by organisational sexuality that renders the female athlete potentially vulnerable to a variety of forms of discrimination and abuse" (Tomlinson and Yorganci 1997, 151). It is within this rigid and inhibiting rationality the authoritative position of the coach is unquestioned, occasioning the reproduction of knowledge, the establishment of an expert truth referenced to protect personal positions of power and the disregard for the humanness of the athlete.

Docile Bodies

As outlined earlier Foucault's governmentality assumes that through dominant rationalities people are governed through self-discipline, self-regulation and self-control. The resultant self-regulated behaviour creates what Foucault argues is a docile body. Foucault theorises that docile bodies are malleable disciplined objects that can be organised and arranged so that governing and dominant behaviours, or ways of doing things, are reproduced. This disciplined body becomes a receptive vehicle on which power manipulates, shapes, moulds and trains it. Bodies are subjugated and used but as Foucault argues, can be transformed and improved. Foucault calls this political anatomy which defines how bodies willingly operate uncritically with speed and efficiency determined by complex technologies of the self that are eager to subscribe to normalcy. In essence, docile bodies are about the act of controlling how bodies move, the manner in which they perform, interact and behave. This is the self-disciplining process created by personal and collective desires fashioned by powerful and dominant governing rationalities. In the sporting context clear and obvious links can be made in the creation of docile bodies. Mentioned above was the example of self-disciplining bodies through training regimes, excessive competition, performance monitoring and strict codes of behaviour relating to personal consumptions and social interactions. All of these mechanics of power Foucault labelled as bio-power. As Culpan suggests "the sporting body becomes the fundamental subjectivity in constituting what sport is" (Culpan 2017, 80).

YOUTH REJECTION OF REGULATION

The above three dominant rationalities of commodification, expert knowledge and docile bodies are manifestations of the neo-liberal political agenda. As Evans argues, neo-liberalism has become the social imaginary of globalisation (Evans 2014, 546) and we argue that it now underpins and is ubiquitous in sporting policies and practices across the globe. It is our thesis that this agenda is creating the dark side of sport for our young people. It creates the dark side by claiming to provide new freedoms, new opportunities to self-maximise. On analysis, it is simply providing new and extensive forms of regulation and control. The executive role of coach plays its traditional part, so versed in the reproduction of paradigmatic control of sport it no longer needs the play-book. However, we contend that youth are increasingly not wanting to do things by the book. Constructs in the sporting context, we argue, are being rejected by young people. In understanding youth culture, it is acknowledged that this construct must be very contextualised. However, from a New Zealand (NZ) perspective our young people, through a combination of societal change and their socio-critical physical education curriculum, are learning to critically analyse, de-construct and create new visions of the movement culture. As ubiquitous as the three dominant rationalities around sport are, we suggest that young people in NZ are beginning to reject the insidiousness of commodification and the expert knowledge. They are coming to realise that there are alternative truths and that the singular focus on performativity in sport is not necessarily a pathway they wish to pursue. In short, the neo-liberal imaginary for contemporary sport in NZ, arguably, is not going to determine young people's subjectivities. Youth are faced with global realities that require organisation. Not only of themselves, but as groups; and this capacity should not be scoffed at. Youth in NZ are consistently informed that they will have to solve and fix many worldly issues. When our future generations of graduates visit careers advisory services, they are not questioned for skills or talents, rather the problem they wish to solve. Has anyone given consideration to the possibility that youth simply do not have the time for sport? The cumulative growth of social entrepreneurship, interdisciplinary and inter-professional working paradigms, global economies, global citizenship, and urgent environmental social action as a response to climate change all demand new thought. Criticality and creativity of work and home life are not only becoming commonplace, they will soon be vital to survival as a species.

The resistance to an archaic sporting paradigm may be as a result of youth's changing, evolving worldly understandings of what it means to participate in this world. The notion of performativity and winning contemporarily, do not hold as much weight as well-being. The admiration of the winner was built upon a false adoration of strength from within a physical domain. The characteristics we appreciate, cheer for and strive to uphold are based on a genetic lottery (Tännsjö 2011). However, this notion of physicality, and physical skill as a singular definition of corporeal accomplishment are becoming increasingly irrelevant to youth. They learn in school that well-being comprises social, physical, mental and emotional and spiritual domains, and these need to be balanced to be well, to thrive. Yet the construction of sport continues to be built upon the performance of a body.

> "While they vary according to the particular nature of any one nation state's political structure, dominant cultural values, and civic or private bureaucratic structures, all systems share certain essential characteristics. World-class sport systems today include performance; the early identification; streaming and specialization of athletic talent; professional coaching; the use of professional nutritionists, biomechanicians, exercise physiologists, and sport psychologists; carefully organised training facilities with state-of-the-art equipment and instructional technologies; and financial rewards systems and incentives for athletes and sport associations. While the general public may

focus exclusively on performance results and the rewards of victory, high performance sport in the contemporary era is a complex whole with performance enhancement as one of its most central features." (Beamish and Ritchie 2006, 138)

The paradigm shift that occurred in the twentieth century still dominates sport, and is founded upon an international, scientific-succoured pursuit of "the linear record" (Beamish and Richie 2006, 141). Sport New Zealand recently conducted a nation-wide participation survey of over 6000 children and youth. They found the top nine sporting activities were: Running, jogging, informal play, playground play, informal games, trampolining, scootering, swimming, walking and biking. Approximately 97% of these sporting pursuits were non-competitive and only 3% were competitive. The tenth most popular was football or soccer, however interestingly only 30% had played competitively to 70% that played non-competitively (Sport New Zealand 2018). These insights suggest that organised, competitive sport at the population level, is no longer preferred when engaging in physical activity. Likewise, it provisions the argument for sport as *contest* not competition (Arnold 1998) as the majority of these activities are based upon intrinsic notions of challenge, not a formal competition against others. Trends like this, are mocking the evolution of sport with regards to rules, regulation, governance and competition. The barnacle-like devotion to hierarchies in the masquerade of tradition has seen sport repeatedly fail to acknowledge its power orders. For example, through the continual normalisation and marginalisation of people who fail to be normal "…who fail to display an intelligible sex and heterosexuality" (Larsson 2016, 8). It this type of archaic thinking is asphyxiating the evolution of the understanding of sport to keep pace with youth culture. Health Education classes now teach spectrums of gender alongside the difference between biological sex, sexual orientation, sexual preference, gender and address discriminative past-paradigms of binaries. The discussions for youth have progressed from the categorisation and labelling of human beings as *pink* or *blue* and needing one of each to participate in this world. Youth are not only rejecting racist regulation but are seeking opportunity to creatively socially oppose it. For example, Indigenous Māori in New Zealand, play the game of Ki-O-Rahi and undergo a process of 'Tatu' prior to each game or tournament. It is a respected part of the cultural element of the game. There is negation to which rules will be played, and normally the local tribe (iwi) facilitate this process. This not only takes into account the ontology of the human beings playing the game, but the land (whenua) in which it is played on. There is a spiritual connection (Brown 2016). Ki-O-Rahi is now not only played by Māori youth in NZ, it has become a mainstream context for learning. Perhaps youth are trying to tell us there is potential in this mutual agreement on what constitutes contest of sorts.

Youth are accepting that there is no need for a 'linear record' in all aspects of life. The dismissal of expert power is significant here, and an example of this is the notion of disruption.

"...the effects of disruption are beginning to extend far beyond the business world. For example, 'sharing economy' start-ups such as Uber and Airbnb are already disrupting regulatory frameworks. Meanwhile, some of the most disruptive technologies on the horizon (e.g., AI and robotics) will not only disrupt corporate business models, but also society as a whole — realigning income distribution, altering relationship between governments and citizens, and perhaps even calling into question fundamental aspects of the human experience...." (Ernst and Young Global Ltd 2017, 12).

The three primary disruptive forces are recognised as technology, globalisation and demographics. So, in a world that increasingly embraces disruption, failure, and creativity; a coach with an aim to counsel technical execution of a skill that possesses right, and wrong movements seems nonsensical. Moreover, this disruption, a predisposition towards actively seeking independence and non-regulation, comes with a sense of social justice. What to do with the complexity of a talented sporting child born to parents that underwent genetic modification? A second generation of genetically modified participants that didn't dope but are now exceptionally talented at sport (Miah 2005). The future of bio-technologies like gene therapy or gene doping may well shatter what we currently believe about non-discrimination of the athlete. Likewise, we need to acknowledge the shifting of the docile body towards the technological realm. It is here that we are reminded of the Deleuze and Guattarian approach of power, which connects technological evolution with an evolution of Foucault's panopticon (Basturk, 2017). For example, the Internet of Things (IoT) now exists to mobilise data exchange between a network of devices, home appliances, vehicles, and software. It goes beyond device connection of desktop, laptop and phone to enable the remote control of any object that can be wirelessly embedded. Ethical data sharing, consent and usage are all heightened with this broadened information access. The empowerment, or disempowerment, of youth through technology is unprecedented. This will not slow with the progression of virtual reality, AI, robotics, bionics—this list flourishes faster than a human being in sport ever could. There are new podiums in the guise of social media that can be claimed in a matter of minutes with little training, and fewer barriers, expenses and losses. These podiums can earn more money and prestige than a gold medal, in an eighth of the time and are not restricted by time, space or demographic. This accessibility, individualization and respect for the ontology difference of the consumer, accompanied by a mounting entrepreneurial demand of youth in their technological space and time is what will render sport and its coaches obsolete. Unless, sport looks to evolve in a similar way. The false consciousness rendered within the athlete (mentioned earlier in the chapter) continually wields opportunities for the coach to exert power when, where and how its suits (Martínková and Parry 2011). Yet, youth are grappling that pedagogical knowledge creates opportunity for learning and does not require *one* knowledge (Wright 2000). There is certainly an expectation of a coach to be a professional, if not an educator (McNamee 2011). However, we argue that if sport is to survive, or indeed thrive, then the archetypal professional coach must retire.

THE EVOLUTION OF THE DARK SIDE OF SPORT: DEALING WITH REJECTION

The authors agreed not to end in the dark. For one, it is not our style, moreover it would be hypocritical to critique a lack of evolution, without rumination on progressions ourselves. Given the scope of this chapter, we have chosen to focus on one area that could be developed—spirituality and embodiment in place of social. Definitions earlier in this chapter alluded to sport as a social phenomenon, obtaining a social element, and fostering social interaction. We argue, this notion of sport necessitating a social element is both limiting and outdated. Rather, the authors suggest that sport should include connection. To understand one of the pivotal characteristics of sport as connection, beseeches the comprehension of what constitutes an embodied relationship. The coach-athlete relationship is not the only relationship that occurs in a sporting world, and we must not separate emotion, social construction or eliminate discussion on discourse when it comes to human practice. Wetherell states that "human affect is inextricably linked...the semiotic (broadly defined) and the discursive...[and] the main things that an affective practice folds or composes together are bodies and meaning-making" (Wetherell 2012, 20). Sport is often identified as a meaning-making exercise, yet by isolating social, we raise a divisive barrier to an embodied understanding of connection within and through movement. Holism promised to revolutionize the way we think about people; how we educated them, treated them medically, promoted their spiritual growth, or helped them move—but it did not (Kretchmar 2000). Take surfing for example. To reduce a surfer's connection to a social sphere negates all spiritual connection they uphold and the relationship they have with the environment; the ocean. There is an incredibly complex interplay of sensory pleasure, spiritual meaning, anticipatory preparation and socio-political enculturation that shapes a sporting experience for a surfer (Stevens 2017). This embodied pleasure and movement meaning are built on ontological connections (Stevens 2017; Wellard 2013); but here connects and interacts with elements greater than other human beings. To reduce the sophistication of one's ability to connect within and through movement to social or to people suffocates ontological interpretations of one's relationships beyond an ego-centric position. Here spirituality is perceived, not necessarily of religious character, but rather of mindfulness (Scandurra 1999). This monist or holistic disposition includes one's spirit and is linked to understanding and valuing human existence, purpose and belief (Lodewyk, Chunlei, and Kentel 2009). Various conceptions over space and time acknowledge the importance of the educative potential for human flourishing; enlightenment or conscientisation (Freire 1970; Ruiz and Fernandez-Balboa 2005), existentialism (Arnold 1979), morality (Arnold 1999; Morgan 2006; Parry et al. 2007), the process of becoming or Nussbaum's capabilities (Nussbaum 2011).

Spirituality discourse is now saturating conversations on movement and sporting meaning (Hsu 2004; Lodewyk et al. 2009; McGuire, Cooper, and Park 2006; Parry et al. 2007). Whether it is for the greater spatial and temporal experiences and increased worldly understanding (Thorburn and Stolz 2015), one's enhanced awareness of self, or one's superior ability to reach and maintain a sense of peace, joy, purpose, desire, harmony or self-worth (Daly 2004); spirituality empowers holistic well-being, connection and growth. Subsequently, by not acknowledging that the experience holds emotional, social, spiritual and physical aspects of learning, human beings are disembodied (Halas and Kentel 2009; Kentel 2007; Sheets-Johnstone 1992, 1999). Lundvall and Maivorsdotter see embodiment as the moving body constantly engaging and connecting with the environment (Lundvall and Maivorsdotter 2010). Moreover, it excites creativity and difference: "When [music] passes through a body…there is no telling what that body might do—it might dance, fall asleep, become angry, tap a foot absentmindedly, or sing along" (Wissenger 2007, 257). It is these interactions that allow for youth to grow and their learning to be shaped by the complexities of the milieu, constructing a worldly view (Burkitt 1999). This is because bodily experience and understanding are always unfinished, as relationships and connections are formed continually through the transgression of boundaries of sense. For example, the toucher and the touched, the sound that is made and the sound that is heard (Merleau-Ponty 1968). These transgress human beings, body to body, but also transgress between subject and object. The noise of the whistle, the feel of the football boots, the smell of the wet grass, the taste of sweat. Sense is continually embodied to create a fleshly understanding of that experience. Prioritising youths embodied, spiritual connections could address the dire inflexibility of sports current state of regulation. The authors see the inclusion of embodiment and spirituality fundamental to evolution of understanding of what constitutes sport. This necessitates an acceptance that youth ontologically understand and participate in the sporting world as a whole being, in the context of other beings, and that the fleshly difference, not *sameness*, is what simultaneously cultivates, and is cultivated by, human flourishing.

The current boundary rope around the athlete is too restrictive, and the coaching regulation of bodies within sporting pursuits needs to declare. The scholarly and popular habituated body is one of a fixed nature that abides to the rules of biological science (Csordas 2003). Western human body dialogue traditionally viewed the body separately from the mind, which enabled it to be controlled and objectified (Bordo 1993; Kenny 1970). Considerable work has been done to reject this; The phenomenological rejection of dualism (Bourdieu 1984; Merleau-Ponty 1962), the docile body as a consequence of power (Foucault 1980) or the corporeal turn in feminism (Howson 2004, 2005) are all examples. Yet, we argue that this dark discourse is still emphatically being 'coached' and within the sporting realm, the body still remains something to work on (Armour 1999; Kirk 1992; Shilling 1991, 2004, 2010). Considerable thought needs to be given to evolving this motionless dissertation of sport. The athlete will reject this paradigm of performance within coaching situations, and they will do so because they will continue to progressively reject regulation and the absence and emphasis on connection. They will not wish for their bodily fluids are verified as drug-free or DNA apposite (Csordas 2003) or for their body to be hair-free (Dagkas and Quarmby 2012). They will no longer conform to the necessary sacrifice of their social, political, cultural or spiritual body to prejudice a scientific, biological one. The commodification of moving bodies for physical capital, and the normalisation of linear regulation projected by the embodied coach will struggle to market itself to the enlightened athlete. Walsh and Giulianotti suggests that such entrenched binary positions need adjudication if sport in the 21st century is to maintain its legitimacy beyond a restricted remit of a free market enterprise (Walsh and Giulianotti 2007). What Walsh and Giulianotti suggested was a mixed market economy where the free market neo-liberal agenda is kerbed and regulated by the State and global sporting organisations. Their suggestions involve: The State regulating markets by blocking detrimental practices, preventing and restricting unjust, excessive and corrupting behaviours; The reinvestment into young people's sport, via the State and global sporting bodies; Moral education about the underlying virtues, ideals and behaviour inherent in sport; and an expectation of the individual and/or collective to resist immoral behaviours and practices; and taking individual subsequent social action against the excesses of, and dominant rationalities identified above.

In essence, what Walsh and Giulianotti are suggesting is to diminish the "influence of money in sport, and reawakening in its practitioners a love for goals other than money" (Walsh and Giulianotti 2007, 131) What is of particular relevance in Walsh and Giulianotti's analysis is the suggestion of both a focus on young people and on education. Their proposal is to purpose the continued importance of sport in seeking human excellences while their work hints that sport, through the political economy, with State intervention and education, still has an important part to play in enhancing the human condition. So, we have a role, a responsibility, a call to action to address this dark side of sport. We contest, it is assisting youth with their cause; the resistance of regulation. We are charged with not requiring individuals to conform to the categorisation and binaries created by a sportified society. We are charged with assisting youth in their disruption of the paradigmatic incarceration of sport. Without a pedagogical disruption, sport will continue to reinforce the dominant discourse, fuel the void that is institutionalised and manipulate the body into moving in ways that conform to it (Stevens 2017). "We have been very willing to study the body as an object. We have been willing to advocate that we condition it, train it, but less willing or perhaps unwilling to simply celebrate our moving—to live the bodies we are" (Rintala 2009, 288). We need to acknowledge the role we play in perpetuating the dark side. We are not supporting youth to navigate a world of difference, with models and contexts fixed within a paradigm of sameness. Archaic expectations of 'empowering' youth with entrenched, normalising discourses in the hopes that youth will blindly accept this bodily fate, will not sustain. Our efforts to evolve sport lie in our abilities to educate, coach and empower youth with embodied awareness. A kinaesthetic intervention of sorts, one that allows coenaesthesis, and the feeling of creation connected with movement (Sheets-Johnstone 2014). A prioritisation of spiritual, somatic knowledge over the propositional, and an acceptance that sport's survival rests on the disruption of both *coach* and *athlete* altogether.

Conclusion

Sophisticated binaries and ideologies of performance continue to pervade and regulate sport. However, benching the plethora of well documented sociological problematics of gender relations, racial discrimination, class inequalities, performance enhancements, genetics modifications, power relations, political economies and the overabundant analysis of the 'isms' associated with sport does not sit well with youth. They are slowly rejecting the paradigmatic incarceration of sport. Accessibility of new knowledges from different paradigms, technological progression and worldly challenges demand creativity and promulgate ontological difference. At present sport and its coaching rhetoric do not. Disrupting monologues to progress new knowledge is vital to evolve the construct of sport, rethink empowerment and curtail dominating economic rationalities to avoid sitting in the dark.

REFERENCES

Armour, Kathleen M. 1999. "The Case for a Body Focus in Education and Physical Education." *Sport, Education and Society* 4, no. 1: 5-15.

Arnold, Peter. 1979. *Meaning in Movement, Sport and Physical Education*. London, England: Heinemann.

———. 1994. "Sport and Moral Education." *Journal of Moral Education* 23, no. 1: 75-89.

———. 1998. *Sports Ethics and Education*. London, England: Cassell.

———. 1999. "The Virtues, Moral Education and the Practice of Sport." *Quest* 51, no. 1: 39-53.

Bailey, Richard, Catherine Armour, David Kirk, Michael Jess, Ian Pickup, Rachel Sandford, and BERA Physical Education and Sport Pedagogy Special Interest Group. 2009. "The Educational Benefits Claimed for Physical Education and School Sport: An Academic Review." *Research Papers in Education* 24, no. 1: 1-27.

Basturk, Efe. 2017. A brief analyse on post panoptic surveillance: Deleuze&Guattarian approach. *International Journal of Social Sciences* VI, no. 2: 1-17.

Beamish, Rob, and Ian Ritchie. 2006. *Fastest, Higest, Strongest; a Critique of High-Performance Sport*. New York, New York: Routledge.

Bordo, Susan. 1993. *Unbearable Weight: Feminism, Western Culture and the Body*. Berkeley, CA: University of California Press.

Bourdieu, Pierre Felix. 1984. *Distinction: A Social Critique of the Judgement of Taste*. London, England: Routledge.

Brohm, Jean-Marie. 1978. *Sport a Prison of Measured Time: Essays by Jean-Marie Brohm*. Translated by Ian Fraser. London, England: Ian Links.

Brown, Harko. 2016. *Ngā Taonga Tākaro II: The Matrix*. Auckland, New Zealand: Wickliffe NZ Ltd.

Burkitt, Ian. 1999. *Bodies of Thought. Embodiment, Identity and Modernity*. London, England: Sage.

Coakley, Jay, Chris Hallinan, Steve Jackson, and Peter Mewett. 2009. *Sports in Society*. NSW, Australia: McGraw-Hill.

Collins, Chris, and Steve Jackson. 2007. *Sport in Aotearoa/New Zealand Society*. 2nd ed. Palmerston North, New Zealand: Dunmore Press.

Crosset, Todd. 1986. "Male-Coach-Female Athlete Relations." In *Norwegian Confederation of Sport Conference on Coaching Female Top-Level Athletes*. Sole, Norway.

Csordas, Thomas J, ed. 2003. *Embodiment and Experience: The Existential Ground of Culture and Self*. Cambridge, England: Cambridge University Press.

———. 2003. "Introduction: The Body as Representaion and Being-in-the-World." In *Embodiment and Experience: The Existential Ground of Culture and Self.*, edited by Thomas J Csordas. Cambridge, England: Cambridge University Press.

Culpan, Ian. 2017. "Olympism, Constructivism and Foucault's Technologies of Power: Governmentality at Work.". *Diagoras: International Academic Journal on Olympic Studies* 1, no. 75-94.

Dagkas, Symeon, and Thomas Quarmby. 2012. "Young People's Embodiment of Physical Activity: The Role of the 'Pedagogized' Family." *Sociology of Sport Journal* 29, no. 2: 210-26.

Daly, Mary Catherine. 2004. *Developing the Whole Child. The Importance of the Emotional, Social, Moral and Spiritual in Early Years Education and Care*. Queenston, England: Edwin Mellon Press.
Ernst and Young Global Limited. 2017. "The Upside of Disruption; Megatrends Shaping 2016 and Beyond." London, England: EYGM Ltd.
Evans, John. 2014. "Neoliberalism and the Future for a Socio-Educative Physical Education." *Physical Education and Sport Pedagogy* 19, no. 5: 545-58.
Foucault, Michel. 1980. *The History of Sexuality; Vol 1: An Introduction*. Translated by Robert Hurley. New York, NY: Pantheon.
———. 1980. "Powers and Strategies." In *Power/Knowledge: Selected Interviews and Other Writings by Michel Foucault*, edited by C. Gordon, 134-45. New York: Pantheon Books.
———. 1980. "Truth and Power." In *Power/Knowledge: Selected Interviews and Other Writings by Michel Foucault*, edited by C. Gordon, 78-108. New York, NY: Pantheon books.
Freire, Paulo. 1970. *Pedagogy of the Oppressed*. New York, NY: Herder and Herder.
Guttmamn, Allen, Joseph Maguire, Thompson William, and David Rowe. N.d. "Sports." In *Encyclopaedia Britannica*.
Halas, Joannie, and Jeanne Adele Kentel. 2009. "Giving the Body Its Due: Autobiographical Reflections and Utopian Imaginings." In *Why Do We Educate? Renewing the Conversation*, edited by D. Coulter and J. Wiens. Oxford, England: Blackwell Publishing Ltd.
Horne, John, Alan Tomlinson, and Gary Whannel. 1999. *Understanding Sport: An Introduction to the Sociological and Cultural Analysis of Sport*. London: Taylor and Francis Group.
Howson, Alexandra. 2005. *The Body in Society: An Introduction*. Illustrated ed. Cambridge, England: Polity Press, 2004.
———. 2005. *Embodying Gender*. London, England: Sage.
Hsu, Leo. 2004. "Moral Thinking, Sport Rules and Education." *Sport, Education and Society* 9, no. 1: 143-54.
International Council of Sport Science and Physical Education. 2001. "World Summit on Physical Education." Berlin, Germany: International Council of Sport Science and Physical Education.
Kenny, Anthony, ed. 1970. *Descartes: Philosophical Letters*. London, England: Clarendon Press.
Kentel, Jeanne Adele. 2007. "The Literate Mover: Strategies for Developing Movement Understanding in Learners." *Physical Education and Health Journal* 72, no. 4: 20-25.
Kentel, Jeanne Adele, and Teresa M Dobson. 2007. "Beyond Myopic Visions of Education: Revisiting Movement Literacy." *Physical Education and Sport Pedagogy* 12, no. 2: 145-62.
Kentel, Jeanne Adele, and Douglas Karrow. 2007. "Mystery and the Body: Provoking a Deep Ecology through the Situated Bodies of Teacher Candidates." *Complicity: An International Journal of Complexity and Education* 4, no. 1: 85-101.
Kirk, David. 1992. *Defining Physical Education: The Social Construction of a School Subject in Post-War Britain*. London, England: Falmer.
———. 1992. "Physical Education, Discourse and Ideology: Bringing the Hidden Curriculum into View." *Quest* 44, no. 1: 35-56.
Kretchmar, Scott. 2000. "Movement Subcultures: Sites for Meaning.". *Journal of Physical Education and Dance* 75, no. 5: 19-25.
———. 2005. *Practical Philosophy of Sport and Physical Activity*. 2nd ed. Champaign, IL: Human Kinetics.
Larsson, Hàkan. 2016. "Poststructualism and Embodiment in Sport." In *Researching Embodied Sport; Exploring Movement Cultures*, edited by I. Wellard, 8-20. New York, NY: Routledge.
Lodewyk, Ken, Lu Chunlei, and Jeanne Adele Kentel. 2009. "Enacting the Spiritual Dimension in Physical Education." *Physical Educator* 66, no. 4: 170-79.
Loy, John W. 1968. "The Nature of Sport: A Definitional Effort." *Quest* 10, no. 1: 1-15.

Lundvall, Suzanne, and Ninitha Maivorsdotter. 2010. "Aesthetic Aspects in Meaning Making—an Explorative Study of Dance Education in a Pete Programme." *Designs for Learning* 3, no. 1-2: 30-41.

Martínková, Irena, and Jim Parry. 2011. "Coaching and Performance Enhancement." In *The ethics of sports coaching,* edited by A. R. Hardman and C. Jones New York, NY: Routledge.

McFee, Graham. 2004. *Sport, Rules and Values: Philosophical Investigations into the Nature of Sport.* London, England: Routledge, Taylor and Francis Group.

McGuire, Brendon, William Cooper, and Michael Park. 2006. "Pastoral Care, Spirituality and Physical Education." *24* 4, no. 13-19.

McNamee, Michael. 2011. "Celebrating Trust: Virtues and Rules." In *The Ethics of Sports Coaching*, edited by A. R. Hardman and C. Jones. New York, NY: Routledge.

Meier, Kass. 1981. "On the Inadequacies of Sociological Definitions of Sport." *International Review for the Sociology of Sport* 16, no. 2: 79-102.

Merleau-Ponty, Maurice. 1962. *Phenomenology of Perception*. London, England Routledge.

———. 1968. *The Visable and the Invisable*. Evanstan, IL: Northwestern University Press.

Miah, Andrew. 2005. "Gene Doping: Shape of Things to Come." In *Genetic Technology and Sport*, edited by C. Tamburrini and T. Tännsjö. New York, NY: Routledge.

Morgan, Willam John. 2006. *Why Sports Morally Matter*. London, England: Routledge, Taylor and Francis Group.

Nussbaum, Martha. 2011. *Creating Capabilities: The Human Development Approach*. London, England The Belknap Press of Harvard University Press.

Parry, Jim. 2007. "The Religio Athletae, Olympism and Peace." In *Sport and Spirituality, an Introduction*, edited by J. Parry, E. Robinson, N. Watson and M. Nesti. London, England: Routledge.

Rintala, Jan. 2009. "It's All About the –Ing." *Quest* 61, no. 3: 279-88.

Roberts, Peter. 2000. *Education, Literacy and Humanization: Exploring the Work of Paulo Freire*. Westport, CT: Bergin and Garvey.

Ruiz, Beatiz Muros, and Juan-Miguel Fernández-Balboa. 2005. "Physical Education Teacher Educators' Personal Perspectives Regarding Their Practice of Critical Pedagogy." *Journal of Teaching in Physical Education* 24, no. 3: 243-64.

Scandurra, Anita, J. 1999. "Everyday Spirituality: A Core Unit in Health Education and Lifetime Wellness." *Journal of Health Education* 30, no. 2: 104 09.

Sewart, John. 1987. "The Commodification of Sport." *International Review for Sociology of Sport* 22, no. 3: 171-190.

Sheets-Johnstone, Maxine. 1992. *Giving the Body Its Due*. Albany, GA: State University of New York Press.

———. 1999. *The Primacy of Movement*. Amsterdam, Netherlands: John Benjamins Publishing Company.

———. 2014. *Putting Movement into Your Life: A Beyond Fitness Primer*. New York, NY: Amazon KDP.

Sport New Zealand. 2018 "Active Nz 2017 Participation Report." Wellington, New Zealand Sport New Zealand.

Stevens, Susannah. 2017. "The Joy of Movement in Physcial Education: The Enfleshed Body.", University of Canterbury.

Tännsjö, Torbjörn. 2011. "Genetic Engineering and Elitism." In *Genetic Technology and Sport*, edited by C. Tamburrini and T. Tännsjö. New York, NY: Routledge.

Thorburn, Malcolm, and Steven Stolz. 2015. "Embodied Learning and School-Based Physical Culture: Implications for Professionalism and Practice in Physical Education." *Sport, Education and Society* 22, no. 6: 721-31.

Tinning, Richard. 2005. "Active Lifestyles and the Paradoxical Impact of Education and Sport." In *Association Internationale des Ecoles Superievres d'Education Physique Congress*. Lisbon, Portugal.

Tomlinson, Alan, and Ilkay Yorganci. 1997. "Male Coach/ Female Athlete Relations: Gender and Power Relations in Competitive Sport." *Journal of Sport and Social Issues* 1, no. 2: 134-55.

United Nations Educational Scientific and Cultural Organisation (UNESCO). 2013. "Berlin Declaration. Fifth International Conference of Ministers and Senior Government Officials Responsible for Physical Education and Sport (Mineps V)." Berlin, Germany.

———. 2017. "The Ministers Meeting at the Sixth International Conference of Ministers and Senior Officials Responsible for Physical Education and Sport (Mineps Vi)." Kazan, Russia.

Walsh, Adrian J, and Richard Giulianotti. 2017. *Ethics, Money and Sport: This Sporting Mammon*. London, England: Routledge.

Wellard, Ian. 2013. *Sport, Fun and Enjoyment*. London England: Routledge.

Wetherell, Margaret. 2012. *Affect and Emotion: A New Social Science Understanding*. London, England: Sage.

Wissenger, Elizabeth. 2007. "Always on Display: Affective Production in the Modelling Industry." In *The Affective Turn: Theorizing the Social*, edited by Patricia Ticineto Clough and Jean Halley. Durham, NC: Duke University Press.

Woods, Ron. 2007. *Social Issues in Sport*. Champaign, Illinois: Human Kinetics.

Wright, Jan. 2000. "Bodies, Meanings and Movement: A Comparison of the Language of a Physical Education Lesson and a Feldenkrais Movement Class." *Sport, Education and Society* 5, no. 1: 35-49.

CHAPTER 11

Sport and Global Culture Industry: The Olympic Games, Modernity, and Dialectic of Enlightenment

Jung Woo Lee

INTRODUCTION

Essentially, the Olympic Games are an international sporting competition. Yet, the implications of this global sports mega-event are not just limited to the domain of sport. In fact, the Olympic Games are often interlinked with social, economic and political issues. The history of the Olympic Movement includes many occasions wherein the sporting contest turned into a political game (Cha 2009, Rowe and Lee 2018, Senn 1999). In addition, the Olympic Games, especially their mediated version, are often considered a cultural ritual in which various social identities such as national, racial, and gender identities are displayed and contested (Collins 2011, Hargreaves 2000). Moreover, a project of hosting the Olympic Games often entails urban or local redevelopment which requires huge economic and environmental cost (Choi and Heo 2013, Preuss 2008). These suggest that the action on the sporting ground alone cannot fully explain the nature of the Olympic Games.

From the viewpoint of critical sociology, this chapter examines the development of the Olympic Games. It should be noted that the modus operandi of the global sports mega-event frequently mirrors wider social and political circumstances in which each Olympics is held (Horne and Whannel 2016). This sporting festival is also reflexive of the historical and material conditions of the society within which the event unfolds (Roche 2000). In this light, this essay looks at the characteristic of the Olympic Games with a specific reference to the notion of modernity and global culture industry. To do so, the Frankfurt School's critical theory offers a useful theoretical framework for this investigation into the evolution of the Olympic Games. This theoretical perspective, which points out the contradictory elements in social change towards modernity and the ideology embedded in culture industry (Horkheimer 1947/ 2004, Marcuse 1964/ 2002), is particularly relevant to the critical reading of this international sporting competition. The working mechanism for the contemporary Olympics appears so much commercialised that the fundamental principles of the event which pursue the realisation of universal humanism on the sporting ground tend to be largely overlooked. This is surely a sign of the Olympic Movement being degenerated which cast a shadow over the future of the sports mega-event. The critical theory aptly points out this negative shift.

This chapter is mainly concerned with the broader developmental process of the Olympic Movement. Understandably, this essay aims at providing a theoretical review of the way in which this global event unfolds. A specific Olympic example is being mentioned only when it is relevant to this theoretical consideration. In this respect, it may be useful to introduce the key concepts within Frankfurt School's critical theory at some length before discussing a sociological aspect of the Olympic evolution. In the following two sections I will outline the major features of modernity and its consequences in relation to the dialectic of enlightenment. Then, I will consider how the logic of modernity is demonstrated through the Olympic Games. The next section provides the critical reading of commercialised and rationalised Olympic Games with reference to the global culture industry. After this, I will critically evaluate the fundamental principles of the Olympism. This chapter finally concludes that the degenerative effect of the dialectic of enlightenment becomes more evident in the Olympic Games in the late modern global society.

MODERNITY AND SOCIAL DEVELOPMENT

The notions of modernity and modernisation are perceived as a significant social paradigm and process which initially developed in Europe in the eighteenth century and subsequently spread to other parts of the world (Hobsbawm 1962). The formation of modernity comprises, as Held (1995) notes, "deeply structured processes of changes taking place over long periods" which eventually resulted in the restructuring of almost every social relation that every individual encountered. Modernity is the concept that is of paramount sociological importance because the process of modernisation triggered arguably the most comprehensive transformation of the society in history. Especially, such changes occurred in the four distinguishable but interrelated dimensions: the social, the cultural, the economic and the political (Hall 1995).

First, the social and cultural dimensions of modernity are closely related to the spirit of the enlightenment which emphasised critical rationalism and empiricism in the eighteenth century Europe (Smith 1998). The proponents of the enlightenment movement paved the way for the cultivation and dissemination of modern social thoughts to the wider society. With the increasing amount of empirical knowledge produced through scientific experiments and experiences, reason and rationality eventually replaced religious doctrine as the ways of organising and establishing social order (Hamilton 1995). It should be noted that religious belief permeated nearly every social relation during the pre-modern period. Religion provided an important source of communal identity and the church wielded authority to regulate and even repress the freedom of thoughts and the behaviour of individuals in the mediaeval times (Durkheim 1897/ 2006).

The secularisation led to the situation where the influence of the church on society gradually weakened (Weber 1948/ 1991). The liberation from religious constraints resulted in the production and accumulation of knowledge that mainly focused on humanism whose main purpose was to increase the gratification and welfare of people (Hamilton 1995). Also, the use of scientific technology dramatically improved a productive capacity which allowed people to enjoy material abundance. In effect, materialism and compulsive consumption came to be dominant features of the emerging secular culture. In addition, people began to seek their identity through an individualistic lifestyle which reflected the secularised social values (Hamilton 1995). Furthermore, scientific research helped people to overcome the environmental condition that had restricted the development of society in the pre-modern time (Giddens 1990). Based on systematic observation and calculation, people began to control and exploit the surrounding environment in an attempt to build better living and working conditions. This suggests that critical reason and rationality, which provided philosophical underpinnings for the humanist worldview and scientific innovation, strengthened their position as one of the major social currents that determined the nature of society. This change made the improvement and advancement of humanity a major goal of social development.

Second, modernity gave rise to the industrial revolution and the subsequent growth of the capitalist economy. In the pre-modern period, agriculture was the dominant form of industry and manufacturing production still remained labour and skill intensive (Porter 1990). Also, this handcraft industry largely took place within the work unit of the household, and the most goods produced in this industrial setting were largely consumed for the personal purpose (Brown 1995). The technological advance in the nineteenth century considerably changed the industrial and economic landscape of Britain and eventually that of western European countries. The most notable feature of the economic shift in this period was probably the establishment of factories and the reorganisation of labour forces (Hobsbawm 1962). The use of a machine diminished the role of skilled labourers in the production process. Also, this change created a clear demarcation between homes as a place to rest and factories as a place to work. In addition, lands which had been mainly used for the cultivation of agricultural products underwent the process of the enclosure for the industrial purpose (Royle 1997). This meant that a large number of peasants came to be factory workers who had to sell their unskilled labour on daily basis.

This industrial shift engendered a situation in which the growth in manufacturing products was far greater than that in agricultural output (Jackson 1990). Also, this mechanisation of the manufacturing process meaningfully enhanced the efficiency of each production unit in the factories. As noted earlier, this was the working condition that contributed to material prosperity in society. Importantly, in the factories, most items began to be produced as a form of commodities which meant that goods were made to be sold in the market. This change to some extent boosted consumerism in society (McKendrick, Brewe and Plumb 1982). This was the prelude of the emerging capitalist market economy. The advance in transportation technology is another important characteristic of industrialisation that facilitated the establishment of the capitalist market system. Building a transportation infrastructure such as railways and canal networks was a crucial element for the burgeoning trade routes between rapidly growing cities (Brown 1995). Through this, a large portion of locally produced goods was sold to be consumed in other parts of the country. Consequently, the commercially oriented nationwide economic relations started to emerge.

Third, modernity led to the development of the nation-state as a supreme political unit and the subsequent rise of nationalism as a dominant form of political ideology (Held 1995, Hobsbawm 1962). In fact, this political development was closely tied to the industrialisation of society and the establishment of the capitalist market economy. During the initial stage of industrialisation, a government needed to mobilise the mass population in order to propel its developmental initiative. Given that empirical science, which offered a theoretical orientation towards the industrialisation, was a relatively new idea, the authority needed to educate its people a minimum level of literacy and technological competency so as to foster modern individuals (Gellner 2006). The introduction of public education fulfilled this role and it was through this school system that people began to learn a new sense of belongingness and of responsible citizenship (Royle 1997). As the capitalist economy advanced further, the containment of domestic trade and commercial exchanges within a specific boundary was required in order for the government to control and regulate economic activities including effective taxation (Gellner 2006). Under this condition of secular capitalism, the construction of national identity was a useful political project because this helped the administrative integration of the state. Nationalism as a political ideology that binds the members of an 'imagined' national community together also appeared in this historical context to meet these economic needs (Anderson 2006).

So far, I discussed the major features of modernity and social changes facilitated by them. These include 1) the reason and critical rationalism as a dominant philosophical underpinning of the society, 2) the reduction in church's authority and the eventual secularisation, 3) the industrialisation and subsequent establishment of the capitalist economy, and 4) the formation of nation-states as a legitimate political unit and the rise of nationalism. Modernisation at its initial stage was closely tied to positive social values such as the growth, the improvement and the advancement of humanity. As will be examined later in this chapter, these social conditions also built circumstances wherein a modern form of sporting activities were developed and institutionalised which eventually led to the commencement of the first Olympic Games in 1896 (Horne, Tomlinson, et al. 2013, Roche 2000). Before moving on to the analysis of the modern Olympics, however, it is necessary to identify some degenerative social changes taken place in the later stage of modernisation which was in contradiction to the optimistic worldview that the early modern society had engendered.

DIALECTIC OF ENLIGHTENMENT

Broadly speaking, it is true that the idea of modernity and modernisation contributed to the betterment of the social and economic conditions of humanity. Yet, history does not always unfold in a linear pattern moving forwards to the advancement. In fact, it is not unusual to see that historical development often faces a reactionary social current which flows against it (Horn 2013). Similarly, the enlightenment project that had initially propelled the progressive social movement in opposition to the traditional authority gradually turned into another type of a constraint that restricted the freedom of individuals. In other words, a means of individual liberation deteriorated into a vehicle for social oppression. In relation to this, the writings of the Frankfurt School's critical theorists, particularly Horkheimer and Adorno's 'Dialectic of Enlightenment' (1947/ 2002) and Adorno's 'One-Dimensional Man' (1964/ 2002), provide valuable theoretical models for investigating this historical shift occurred in the late modern society.

First, the logic of critical reason and rationality which had questioned the social order and authority underpinned by religious doctrine was replaced by the notion of instrumental reason and rationalism which mainly emphases utility value and efficiency of social actions (Horkheimer and Adorno 1947/ 2002). This suggests that the nature of social organisation became increasingly goal-oriented and that every social institution was simply considered as a utilitarian tool for realising the aim of society. Understandably, this gave rise to the situation which permitted the objectification of human beings and the exploitation of their interaction in so far as such a social control met the needs of society (Craib 1992). This produced social conditions that justified the manipulation of other human beings by social institutions in the name of the advancement. In contrast to the critical reason in the earlier period, the instrumental reason operated as a vehicle for social repression that limited the ability to cultivate an individual's potential for developing oneself into an independent and autonomous human being at the expense of maximisation of utility and rationalisation of society as a whole (Horkheimer 1947/ 2004). As a consequence, humanitarian concepts such as dignity and integrity were no longer regarded as important moral principles. The development of humanity entered the phase of regression after all.

Moreover, such development reveals the ideological nature of instrumental reason which works as a means of social domination (Craib 1992). Once a new social order was established after the enlightenment movement and modernisation, those who had led the reformative actions gradually became a member of an emerging dominant class. When they held a powerful position in society, the dominant groups eventually tended to protect their political and economic interest by solidifying the new social structure and institutions which largely served for them. In this respect, any political projects that helped to sustain the existing social system could be defensible by the logic of instrumental rationalism (Horkheimer and Adorno 1947/ 2002). At the same time, any attempts to challenge the current social order was stigmatised as irrational dissents which were interrupting the status quo. This is ironical because the idea of reason and rationally at this stage of modernisation functioned as an iron cage that inhibited further advancement of humanity (Weber 1948/ 1991). In this paradigm, social actions which appeared to be liberating were, in fact, repressive at the same time, and it was surely a paradox of the historical development.

The second negative dialectic that the Frankfurt School academics point out is the permeation of the logic of market capitalism and of consumerism into the realm of culture (Adorno 1991, Horkheimer and Adorno 1947/ 2002, Marcuse 1964/ 2002). Before the emergence of industrial capitalism, there existed two separated forms of culture: the intellectual and the material (Marcuse 1964/ 2002). Material culture largely comprises practical knowledge for livelihoods such as technical skills and the actual pattern of living such as the division of labour within the family. By contrast, intellectual culture includes creative activities that conceptualise higher moral standards and idealism. The examples of this form of culture include music, painting, literature and philosophical writing. In this respect, Adorno (1991) notes that the domain of intellectual culture remained independent from and autonomous to political and economic circumstances prior to the consolidation of the capitalist market system. This situation enabled those who involved in the domain of creative culture to circulate critical reading and interpretation of the existing social structure and to illuminate a more idealistic and alternative vision of society. In so doing, these intellectuals eventually gave a direction to realise the utopian principles through their work. In relation to this, it is important to note that without this relatively autonomous intellectual culture, the enlightenment movement which challenged and ultimately overturned the traditional authority could not have been formed.

However, during the later stage of industrialisation in which the logic of commercial relations penetrated into many aspects of social life, the relative autonomy that the intellectual culture had enjoyed vanished almost completely (Horkheimer and Adorno 1947/ 2002). Such a shift was closely related to the domination of instrumental reason and rationality which denigrates an idealistic imagination with little practical implications although it is an essential element of artistic expression (Held 1980). Within this paradigm, there is little space where artistic objects displaying an idealistic worldview with a critical undertone can flourish. By contrast, this social system primarily promotes a mass culture which sustains the logic of market capitalism and consumerism. As a result, the realm of culture which used to have multiple facets finally changes to the one-dimensional entertainment industry where few critical sensitivity can be found, and thereby marginalising the role of the intellectual culture in society (Marcuse 1964/ 2002).

One notable consequence of such a paradigm shift is that culture gradually merged into an ideological tool because their contents mainly portray the dominant social order underpinned by industrial capitalism and consumerism (Craib 1992). In this respect, it is not surprising that the dominant class actively engages in promoting the consumable popular culture industry as a form of legitimate leisure activity (Marcuse 1964/ 2002). With the advancement of production and communication technologies, such an ideological cultural commodity can be even more effectively circulated within the society (Craib 1992). In that sense, a cultural product is seen as narcotic of the people that continually fosters a one-dimensional man lacking critical reason who is almost entirely subordinated to the dominant social system (Marcuse 1964/ 2002). Therefore, mass culture comes to be what Althusser (1971) calls an ideological state apparatus that functions to sustain the existing social structure in the late modern period.

MODERNITY AND THE FORMATIVE STAGE OF THE OLYMPIC GAMES

Sporting competitions, especially international contests, are by no means value neutral. They often reflect and reinforce a dominant form of socio-cultural values and political ideologies (Cha 2009, Horne, Tomlinson, et al. 2013). In this respect, this section will consider how the Olympic Games in the late nineteenth and the early twentieth centuries mirrored the notion of modernity and modernisation mentioned earlier. In order to comprehend the connection between the Olympics and modernity more clearly, it is necessary to look at the nature of modern sports which is closely tied to the process of modernisation.

At this point, it is worth paying brief attention to Guttmann (2004) seven characteristics of modern sport: secularism, equality, bureaucratisation, specialisation, rationalisation, quantification, and the obsession with records. It should be noted that in the pre-modern time, a large number of sporting competitions took place as part of religious rituals and festivals. As society became more secularised, the link between church and sport weakened, and sport was gradually established as a secular leisure activity. The concept of equality is related to humanism which is one of the major moral values of modernity. This ethos highlights equality between every human being, and fair play and an equal opportunity are, at least in theory, fundamental organising principles of modern sport. In terms of bureaucratisation, modern sport is institutionalised and governed by national and international sport governing bodies. The bureaucratisation also entails standardisation and codification of sport which indicated the influence of industrialisation. The division of labour is another characteristic of the modern industrial society, and the specialisation of roles and playing positions in sport reflects this trend. With regards to rationalisation, athletes train in a more effective regime with the frequent use of sports science technology in order to enhance their performance more effectively. As to quantification, from a goal in football to umpire's decision in gymnastics, most records in sport are kept in numbers, and statistics offers a useful reference to understanding sport. The introduction of numerical values to sports may not unrelated to scientific thinking that the enlightenment movement promoted. Finally, setting a new record is one of the main purposes of modern sport, and this desire to improve human potential symbolically represents the progress and advancement of humanity.

In consideration of Guttman's seven characteristics, it is now clear that modern sporting practice emerged as a part of the transition to modern society. In this light, it is by no means a coincidence that the idea of hosting the first modern Olympics was conceived in the late nineteenth century. This was the time when the process of modernisation gained its momentum at least in the West (Roche 2000). This was also a period when long-haul travel became more convenient due to the advancement of transportation technology at that time (Robertson 1992). As an international multi-sport competition, the Olympic Games offered a world stage where the individual's sporting talent was displayed and celebrated. In effect, the Olympic Games in this formative stage symbolically represented the notion of individuality and human progress.

In addition to the modernist values embedded in sport, the early modern Olympic Games also reflected wider social development being made which were primarily initiated by modernity. These include nationalism, internationalism, capitalism and humanism. First, the rise of nationalism and looming internationalism were the major political development in the West in the late nineteenth century (Held,

McGrew, et al. 1999). This political circumstance allowed the organisation of different international movements, and the foundation of the International Olympic Committee (IOC) in 1894 and the revival of the Olympic Games in 1896 were not unrelated to this current (Roche 2000). Baron Pierre de Coubertin, the founder of the modern Olympic Movement, originally imported the English physical education system to French schools in order to foster muscular and patriotic youths amidst the surge of nationalist politics in Europe (Horne and Whannel 2016). At the same time, the Baron also saw the potential of the gentlemanly sporting spirit that could enhance a mutual understanding between the nation-states (Young 1996). This amalgamation of nationalism and internationalism motivated Coubertin to conceive the idea of restoring the Hellenic tradition of the Olympic Games in modern time (Spaaij 2012). It should be noted that the nationalist politics and the internationalist movement contradict to each other. The Olympic Games that embraced these incompatible ideas is the development of the double-edged sword as a result: the ethos of Olympism that promotes peace and international fraternity and the principle of competition that provokes the rivalry between the nations.

Second, the Olympic Games are closely connected to metropolitan culture. The urbanisation was one of the major consequences of the industrialisation, and this development made a city the focal point of politics, economy and culture (Hobsbawm 1962). The fact that the Olympic Games were awarded to a city, not a country, despite being an international sporting contest implies the growing significance of the urban areas in the political and economic geography at that time. The inaugural modern Olympics took place in Athens in recognition of the Hellenic Olympiad which had been held during the period of Classical Greece. Paris, St. Louis, and London hosted the next three Olympic Games respectively. These locations were some of the most industrialised metropolitans in the late nineteenth and early twentieth centuries (Horne and Whannel 2016). An institutionalised competitive sport was considered an important aspect of urban life as a form of rationalised recreation (Holt 1989, 1991). Thus, it was rather sensible for the IOC to choose the three major cities as a host. Additionally, these early modern Olympic Games were staged together with the international exhibitions where modern technological innovations and a diverse range of industrial products were on display (Roche 2000). The visibility of the sporting competition was obscured by the much larger scale industrial fair when both events took place simultaneously. Nonetheless, these occurrences indicate a connection between the nature of the public occasions which epitomised a modernist worldview and the culture of modern industrial cities that welcomed such international events.

Third, the Olympic Games embraced elements of a cultural ritual that celebrated the advancement of humanity from the outset. Drawing on the Hellenic philosophical notion of body, mind, and spirit, the founding members of the IOC envisioned the sporting contest to be an occasion where modern individualism based on humanism was displayed (Goldblatt 2016). The Olympic motto, the Olympic flag and the Olympic flame are arguably the three most distinctive symbols that demonstrate the humanistic values. When the IOC was founded in 1894, it adopted "faster, higher, and stronger" as the official motto of the Olympic Games. Such a slogan clearly represents the mindset of modern human beings who are in pursuit of continuous development and progress. The five Olympic rings and the Olympic flag which portrays the five interlocking rings were designed and introduced to the event in 1912. Initially, the colours depicting the Olympic flag symbolised the five founding member states of the IOC (Toohey and Veal 2000). Yet, from the Olympic Games in 1920 onwards, the five rings were used to signify the five continents so that the Olympic symbol represented the union of the world under the banner of universal humanism (Guttmann 1994). The Olympic flame was first lit at the Amsterdam Games in 1928. This fire on the cauldron in the stadium embodied the spirit of the Olympic Movement including progressivism and universal humanism, and therefore the flame was considered one of the sacred symbols of the sporting competition (Guttmann 1994). In that sense, the Olympic flame symbolically encapsulated modernity mirrored through the Olympic Games.

GLOBAL CULTURE INDUSTRY AND THE ONE-DIMENSIONAL OLYMPICS

The formative stage of the Olympic Games reflected the nature of modernity and embraced humanistic idealism as a working principle. Yet, as market capitalism developed into the dominant economic system, the logic of commercialisation was gradually permeating into the Olympic Movement (Boykoff 2014). While an element of entrepreneurship can be found in every Olympic Games including the inaugural event, it is from the 1960s that the fusion of state and corporate interests in the Olympics began to increase (Toohey and Veal 2000). As the scale and scope of the event kept expanding, the cost of hosting the Olympics also grew. At the same time, with the development of media and communication technology, the popularity of the international sporting competition was rapidly on the rise at a global scale (Smart 2018). This provided a business opportunity for the IOC to sell Olympic related products including broadcasting rights in order to finance the Olympic Movement (Horne and Whannel 2016). This means that the Olympic Games were transforming from a modern ritual to a global spectacle.

Such a change led to the first privately funded Olympic Games in Los Angeles in 1984. By being a sponsor of the event, commercial companies such as *Coca Cola* actively promoted both their products and the Olympics globally, and the live television broadcasting of the Games also attracted billions viewers' attention from the world. This occasion opened a new era of the Olympics as the Los Angeles Games created an immense economic profit for the first time in the history of the IOC (Dyreson 2015). After witnessing the commercial viability of the event, the sport governing body introduced an exclusive Olympic sponsorship programme, namely, the Olympic Partners (Toohey and Veal 2000). With the increasing global impact of the sporting competition, a number of transnational corporations were eager to be associated with the Olympics. As this new sponsorship programme required a long-term contract, the sport governing body was able to secure a sustainable income. In addition, the IOC also began to charge major media companies a huge amount of money for securing exclusive broadcasting rights. Because the televised Olympic Games never fail to attract a huge number of audiences, the media company's demands on the Olympic contents are always high (Horne and Whannel 2016).

Understandably, the media rights are the most expensive product that the IOC sell, and its price continuously increases whenever the contract is due (Smart 2018). Through the commodification, the IOC can enjoy economic surplus.

As the commercialisation of the Olympic Games develops further, the IOC's dependency on major sponsors and media companies also deepens. This creates a window through which the logic of the logic of market capitalism enters the Olympic industry without much friction, and eventually, promotional culture and consumerism dominate the operational mechanism for the sports mega-event (Maguire, Butler, et al. 2008, Smart 2018). The five-ring logo and Olympic athletes frequently appear in numerous branding and advertising campaigns during the period of the Olympic Games, and many commercial booths are installed inside the Olympic venue to promote sponsors' brand (Boykoff 2014). In this manner, consumerism is celebrated in the guise of Olympism (Maguire, Barnard, et al. 2008). Moreover, in order to protect the rights of the official sponsors, the use of signs implying the event by non-Olympic partners are legally prohibited regardless the size of the business including small street vendors (Kennelly 2016). This prevalent of the marketing logic inside the Olympic movement indicates the modern project is turning into a one-dimensional culture industry.

Additionally, as a way to enhance the marketability of the global sporting event, some competitions are scheduled to take place in either the early morning or the late night, especially when the Olympic Games are held outside North America and Europe. This is because the live actions from the Olympic stadium can be transmitted during the prime time in the West where the most profitable media consumption happens (Billings 2008). This shift of playing time exemplifies that the principle of commercialism outweighs the performance condition of athletes. In other words, for the sake of the profit, some Olympic athletes are alienated from their field because they have no choice but to accept this odd schedule. This development may hint that the instrumental rationalism geared to market capitalism is at work at the Olympic Games today. This is also a clear example of commodification of the Olympic symbols and of Olympic experiences. In this respect, a number of researchers claim that the Olympic five rings which used to symbolise universal humanism now simply function as yet another commodity sign (Boykoff 2014, Maguire 2011, VanWynsberghe and Ritchie 1998)

In order to comprehend the Olympic Games as part of the global culture industry, I find the notion of Disneyization suggested by Bryman (1999, 2004) particularly useful. He argues that the nature of cultural production in a late modern society where neo-liberal consumerism is predominant becomes similar to that of the Walt Disney business. More specifically Bryman (2004) identifies four dimensions of this process, which include theming, hybrid consumption, merchandising, and emotional labour. As the recent Olympic Games increasingly display carnivalesque and festive characteristics, the process of Disneyization can be applicable to the Olympic industry (Horne and Whannel 2016, Tomlinson 2004). Theming refers to the division of the event venues and the ascription of a particular meaning or narrative to each location. The Olympic complex often consists of a number of sporting clusters, and the site also contains themed and branded non-sporting zones where diverse cultural and commercial activities take place (Horne and Whannel 2016). Hybrid consumption indicates the widespread of crossly promoted commodities by different institutions in many different places. An Olympic themed souvenir shop can be seen in different locations in the host city, and a number of branded goods and services can be experienced and purchased at the Olympic sites. Merchandising means the promotion of goods with a particular logo and sign. Each Olympic Games produce a range of merchandising products from key holders to fashion items. Emotional labour requires its staff to be cheerful and friendly at the point of a consumer transaction. The delivery of the Olympic Games also relies on emotional labour in the sense that Olympic staff, especially volunteers, are expected to be approachable and welcoming to foreign visitors and athletes.

Put simply, the Disneyization is the rationalisation of the culture industry. With the increasing influence of transnational corporations and major media company on the Olympics, the IOC has to stage a commercially lucrative and media-friendly event (Dyreson 2015). While the fundamental principles of the Olympism clearly demonstrate universal humanism and advancement of humankind, such idealistic social values are often neglected in reality (Maguire 2011). Rather, it is consumerism that the Olympic industry truly celebrates (Boykoff 2014). Intensive multi-media promotional activities for the Olympic sponsors and the Olympic Games itself during the two week period of the event prove this trend (Smart 2018). This may be a sign that the instrumental reason prevails over the critical reason at the Olympic venue where the maximisation of profits and the reinforcement of consumer capitalism are the two main modes of operation. This logic also justifies the exploitation of Olympic staff and the alienation of Olympic athletes. The Disneyization of the Olympic Games clearly reflects such a tendency. In effect, the Olympic Games are now being incorporated into culture industry in Adorno's sense (1991). As the global capitalism has been replacing the spirit of Olympism, the nature of the Olympic Games is likely to become one-dimensional also.

The Modern Olympic Myth

At this juncture, it is worth considering the fundamental principles of Olympism and critically evaluating the impact of the late modernity on the Olympic idealism. In this section, particular attention is paid to two issues: the ethics of sport participation and peace promotion. The first principle of the Olympic Movement states that "Olympism seeks to create a way of life based on the joy of effort, the educational value of good example, social responsibility and respect for universal fundamental ethical principles" (International Olympic Committee 2015). This is a clear reflection of humanitarian social values that the early modern principle highlighted. Yet, in the late modern Olympic Games, it appears that such an idealistic notion becomes less important for some Olympians. The unlawful use of a performance-enhancing drug by elite athletes exemplifies this. Doping clearly violates the first principle of the Olympism which includes "the joy of effort", "the educational value of good example", and "social responsibility". While the IOCs implemented strict regulations to eliminate this practice, those so-called unclean athletes continue to enter the sport competition. In fact, this problem is closely related to the logic of late modernity. In the Olympic Games today, professionalism which glorifies winning a match is much more valued than amateurism which praises the love of sport. This circumstance reflects the liberal capitalist worldview within which the winner-take-it-all approach is prevalent (McDonald 2009). Additionally, the Olympic Games now display the nature of the global culture industry where almost every component of the event turns into a commodity including athletes (Andrews 2004). Because an athlete gains more economic value when he or she wins Olympic medals, the culture of winning at all costs including the use of drug easily permeates to the Olympic industry. In that sense, the unlawful, unhealthy and unethical practice is ipso facto a rational action (Beamish 2010). This demonstrates the operation of the instrumental reason and rationality in sport within the paradigm of the late modern consumer capitalism.

With regard to peace promotion, the second fundamental principle writes that "the goal of Olympism is to place sport at the service of the harmonious development of humankind, with a view to promoting a peaceful society". This is another type of Olympic idealism that mirrors internationalism. In relation to this, in 1992, the IOC reinvented the tradition of Olympic truce that the Ancient Greek society had observed. Importantly, the United Nations also formally endorsed this peace-making mission of the IOC in 1993 (Spaaij 2012). Nevertheless, the Olympic Truce, which asks to cease any international conflict or warfare during the sport competition, is difficult to be materialised in the contemporary social and political climate. First, sporting prowess at the Olympics is seen as a barometer to measure the power of competing nations in peacetime (Bairner 2005). This nationalistic emotion attached to sport often creates tensions between countries. Given the recent rise of populist nationalism in the world (Fukuyama 2018), the Olympic Games potentially function as a cause of conflict. Secondly, the classical Hellenic society observed the truce because of religious meaning attached to the ancient Olympia. It should be noted that the Olympic Games were part of a religious ritual which worshipped Zeus, the most powerful god in Greek mythology (Toohey and Veal 2000). Given that religion was the most important aspect of social life in the ancient society, making war during religious festivals including the Olympic Games was seen as an unholy gesture (Golden 1998). By contrast, the power of religion is relativity weak in the modern secular society. As a result, it is difficult to expect the Olympics to act as a war deterrent today.

CONCLUSION

Thus far, this chapter looked at the nature of (late) modernity with reference to Frankfurt School's critical theory. The socio-political dimensions of the Olympic Games have been critically examined in relation to the early modern and late modern developments. This study shows that the revival and unfolding Olympic Games did not happen in a social vacuum. Instead, they clearly reflected a broader social and political atmosphere surrounding the sporting event. Thus, it is necessary to consider these non-sporting factors systematically in order to draw a more accurate picture of the Olympic Games.

During the formative stage (1894-1932) the Olympic Movement largely functioned to promote the modernist world view which emphasised the advancement of humanity. Yet, in the late modern Olympics (1964 to Present) the logic of consumer capitalism dominates the way in which the sports mega-event is organised and delivered. This demonstrates the transformation of the Olympics from the modern enlightenment project to the global culture industry.

Once modern social institutions, which acted as agents for social reforms, are established, they tend to operate as a social structure that controls and regulates the behaviour of people in an attempt to reinforce the dominant social order of the time. The Frankfurt School's critical theory offers an explanation for this paradox with the notions of the dialectic of Enlightenment and of one-dimensional culture (Adorno 1991, Horkheimer and Adorno 1947/ 2002, Marcuse 1964/ 2002). The Olympic Games, which used to be a cultural occasion that disseminated universal humanism and internationalism in the past, now primarily work as global culture industry through which market capitalism and consumerism are continually reinforced and reproduced (Boykoff 2014, Maguire 2011, Smart 2018).

However, I do not mean that the spirit of the Olympic idealism is now dead and buried due to the prevalent of commercialism. As the participation of the Refugee Olympic team in the 2016 Olympics in Rio de Janeiro and the sporting union between North and South Korea at the 2018 PyeongChang Winter Olympics show, there is still a chance that the Olympic movement can be a positive force in our society (Rowe and Lee 2018). At the same time, there is a danger that the unchecked hyper-commodification of the Olympics can lead to the annihilation of the Olympic ideals. This prophecy of the one dimensional dark-age Olympics must be avoided. Therefore, it is important to keep our eye on and, if necessary, to protest against the practice of the IOC and the Olympic Partners which spreads neo-liberal consumerist ideology lest the Olympic Games be totally subordinated to the capitalist market system.

REFERENCES

Adorno, Theodore W. 1991. *The culture industry.* London: Routledge.
Althusser, Louis. 1971. *Lenin and philosophy and other essays.* London: New Left Books.
Anderson, Benedict. 2006. *The imagined community.* 2nd. London: Verso.
Andrews, David L. 2004. "Sport in the late capitalist moment." In *The commercialisation of sport*, edited by Trevor Slack, 2-28. Abingdon: Routledge.
Bairner, Alan. 2005. "Sport and the nation in the global era." In *The global politics of sport: The role of global institutions in sport*, edited by Lincoln Allison, 87-100. Abingdon: Routledge.
Beamish, Robert. 2010. "Toward s sport ethic: Science, politics, and Weber's sociology." In *Sociology of sport and social theory*, edited by Earl Smith, 3-14. Champaign, IL: Human kinetics.
Billings, Andrew C. 2008. *Olympic Media: Inside the biggest show on television.* Abingdon: Routledge.
Boykoff, Jules. 2014. *Celebration capitalism and the Olympic Games.* Abingdon: Routledge.
Brown, Vivienne. 1995. "The emergence of the economy." In *Modernity: An introduction to modern societies*, 90-121. Cambridge, England: Polity.
Bryman, Alan. 2004. *The Disneyization of society.* London: Sage.
———.. 1999. "The Disneyization of society." *The Sociological Review* 47 (1): 25-47.
Cha, Victor D. 2009. *Beyond the final score:The politics o sport in Asia.* New York, New York: Columbia University Press.

Choi, Cheong R, and Chul M Heo. 2013. "Economic changes resulting from Seoul 1988: Implications for London 2012 and future Games." *The International Journal of the History of Sport* 30: 1854-1866.

Collins, Sandra. 2011. "East Asian Olympic desires: Identity on the global stage in the 1964 Tokyo, 1988 Seoul and 2008 Beijing games." *The International Journal of the History of Sport* 28 (16): 2240-2260.

Craib, Ian. 1992. *Modern social theory: From Parsons to Harbermas.* 2nd. New York, New York: St. Martin's Press.

Durkheim, Emile. 1897/ 2006. *On suicide.* London: Penguin.

Dyreson, Mark. 2015. "Global television and the transformation of the Olympics: The 1984 Los Angeles Games." *The International Journal of the History of Sport* 32 (1): 172-184.

Fukuyama, Francis. 2018. *Identity.* London: Profile Books.

Gellner, Ernest. 2006. *Nation and nationalism.* 2nd. Oxford: Blackwell.

Giddens, Anthony. 1990. *The consequences of modernity.* Cambridge, England: Polity.

Goldblatt, David. 2016. *The Games: A global history of the Olympics.* London: Macmillan.

Golden, Mark. 1998. *Sport and society in Ancient Greece.* Cambridge: Cambridge University Press.

Guttmann, Allen. 2004. *From ritual to record: the nature of modern sports.* 2nd. New York, New York: Columbia University Press.

———.. 1994. *Games and empires: Modern sport and cultural imperialism.* New York, New York: Columbia University Press.

Hall, Stuart. 1995. "Introduction." In *Modernity: An introduction to modern societies*, edited by Stuart Hall, David Held, Don Hubert and Kenneth Thompson, 3-18. Cambridge: Polity.

Hamilton, Peter. 1995. "The Enlightenment and the birth of social science." In *Modernity: An introduction to modern societies*, edited by Stuart Hall, David Held, Don Hubert and Kenneth Thompson, 19-54. Cambridge, England: Polity.

Hargreaves, John. 2000. *Freedom for Catalonia? : Catalan nationalism, Spanish identity, and the Barcelona Olympic Games.* Cambridge: Cambridge University Press.

Held, David. 1980. *Introduction to critical theory: Horkheimer to Habermas.* Cambridge: Polity.

———. 1995. "The development of the modern state." In *Modernity: An introduction to modern societies*, edited by Stuart Hall, David Held, Don Hubert and Kenneth Thompson, 55-89. Cambridge: Polity.

Held, David, Anthony McGrew, David Goldblatt, and Jonathan Perraton. 1999. *Global transformations: Politics, economics and culture.* Cambridge: Polity.

Hobsbawm, Eric. 1962. *The age of revolution: 1789-1848.* London, England: Abacus.

Holt, Richard. 1989. *Sport and the British: A modern history.* Oxford, England: Oxford University Press.

———. 1991. "Women, men and sport in France, c. 1879-1914: An introductory survey." *Journal of Sport History* 18: 121-134.

Horkheimer, Max. 1947/ 2004. *Eclipse of reason.* London: Continuum Publishing Company.

Horkheimer, Max, and Theodor W Adorno. 1947/ 2002. *Dialectic of enlightenment: Philosophical fragments.* Stanford, California: Stanford University Press.

Horn, A. J. 2013. "Marx's historical dialectic." *Critique* 41 (4): 495-513.

Horne, John, Alan Tomlinson, Garry Whannel, and Kath Woodward. 2013. *Understanding sport: Socio-cultural analysis.* 2nd. London, England: Routledge.

Horne, John, and Garry Whannel. 2016. *Understanding the Olympics.* 2nd. Abingdon: Routledge.

International Olympic Committee. 2015. *The Olympic Charter.* Lausanne: International Olympic Committee.

Jackson, R. V. 1990. "Government expenditure and British economic growth in the eighteenth century: Some problems of measurement." *Economic History Review* 43: 217-245.

Kennelly, Jacqueline. 2016. *Olympic exclusions: Youth, poverty and social legacies.* Abingdon: Routledge.

Maguire, Joseph. 2011. "Branding and consumption in the IOC's 'Celebrate Humanity' campaign." *Sport in Society* 14 (7-8): 1056-1068.

Maguire, Joseph, Katie Butler, Sarah Barnard, and Golding Peter. 2008. "Olympism and consumption: An analysis of advertising in the British media coverage of the 2004 Athens Olympic Games." *Sociology of Sport Journal* 25: 167-186.

———. 2008. "'Celebrate humanity' or 'consumers?': A critical evaluation of a brand in motion." *Social Identities* 14 (1): 63-76.

Marcuse, Herbert. 1964/ 2002. *One-dimensional man*. London: Routledge.

McDonald, Ian. 2009. "One-dimensional sport: Revolutionary Marxism and the critique of sport." In *Marxism, cultural studies and sport*, edited by Ben Carrington and Ian McDonald, 32-47. Abingdon: Routledge.

McKendrick, Neil, John Brewe, and John H. Plumb. 1982. *The birth of a consumer society: The commercialization of eighteenth-century England*. London, England: Europa.

Porter, Roy. 1990. *English society in the Eighteen century*. 2nd. London, England: Penguin.

Preuss, Holger. 2008. "The Olympic Games: Winner and Losers." In *Sport and society: A student introduction*, edited by Barrie Houlihan, 415-438. London: Sage.

Robertson, Roland. 1992. *Globalization: Social theory and global culture*. London: Sage.

Roche, Maurice. 2000. *Mega-events and modernity*. London: Routledge.

Rowe, David, and Jung W Lee. 2018. "The Winter Olympics and the two Koreas: how sport diplomacy could save the world." *The Conversation*. January 10. Accessed January 15, 2019. https://theconversation.com/the-winter-olympics-and-the-two-koreas-how-sport-diplomacy-could-save-the-world-89769.

Royle, Edward. 1997. *Modern Britain: A social history 1750-1997*. 2nd. London: Arnold.

Senn, Alfred E. 1999. *Power, politcs, and the Olympic Games: A history of power brokers, events, and controversies that shaped the Games*. Champaign, Illinois: Human Kinetics.

Smart, Barry. 2018. "Consuming Olympism: Consumer culture, sport star sponsorship and the commercialisation of the Olympics." *Journal of Consumer Culture* 18 (2): 241-260.

Smith, Mark J. 1998. *Social science in question*. London: Sage.

Spaaij, Ramon. 2012. "Olympic rings of peace? The Olympic Movement, peacemaking and intercultural understanding." *Sport in Society* 15: 761-774.

Tomlinson, Alan. 2004. "The Disneyfication of the Olympics?: Theme parks and freak-show of the body." In *Post-Olympism?: Questioning sport in the twenty-first century*, by 2004, edited by John Bale and Mette K Christensen, 147-163. Oxford: Berg.

Toohey, Kristine, and A J Veal. 2000. *The Olympic Games: A social science perspective*. Wallingford: CABI.

VanWynsberghe, Rob, and Ian Ritchie. 1998. "(Ir)Relevant ring: The symbolic consumption of the Olympic logo in post modern media culture." In *Sport and postmodern times*, edited by Genevieve Rail, 367-384. Albany, New York: State University of New York Press.

Waddington, Ivan. 2000. *Sport, health and drugs: a critical sociological perspective*. London: Spon Press.

Weber, Max. 1948/ 1991. *From Max Weber: Essays in sociology*. London, England: Routledge.

Young, David C. 1996. *The Modern Olympics: A strrugle for revival*. Baltimore: Johns Hopkins University Press.

CHAPTER 12

Racism in Elite Sport: A Re-examination of the Historical Case of South African Football

Gustav Venter

INTRODUCTION

Recent events during the 2018/19 season of Italy's top football league, the Serie A, saw the Senegalese international, Kalidou Koulibaly (currently playing for Napoli), suffer racial abuse at the hands of Internazionale supporters during a fixture played at the San Siro in Milan (Baldini 2018). This served as a stark reminder of the darker side of elite sport which continues to lurk beneath the surface, particularly in the case of Italian football where incidents such as these, coupled with violent clashed between supporters, have continued to blight the league's reputation in recent years (Baldini 2018). This essay considers this darker side of elite football, but shifts the analytical lens across both time and geography to the historical case of South African football.

It constitutes an analysis of a hitherto underexplored domestic football tournament played in 1977, known as the Mainstay League Cup, and argues that this event should be viewed as a confluence of several significant political, economic and social forces prevalent in South African football at the time. Given the fact that professional football was a product of the segregated society under which it was being played in 1977, this essay traces the complex process of partial integration attempted by football officials for varying reasons during a turbulent time in the country's political history. To some degree the Mainstay League Cup was a product of these attempts, and ultimately represented a microcosm of various challenges facing South African football specifically—and broader society generally—at the time. The analysis concludes with a reflection on the present-day situation, one which is drastically different from 1977, but which continues to present a new set of challenges to both footballing and societal progress in South Africa.

SOUTH AFRICAN FOOTBALL IN 1977

The contours of professional football in South Africa in 1977 reflected the labyrinthine nature of apartheid legislation at the time. Three professional leagues under three different controlling bodies—two of which were racially defined—operated concurrently on the domestic scene. It was a period of great complexity, change and uncertainty within football. In order to contextualize this state of affairs, it is necessary to first take a step back to clarify how this came to pass. Professional football only arrived in South Africa in 1959 with the formation of the whites-only National Football League (NFL). Prior to this the game had been played on an amateur basis since the British colonial period dating back to the late 1800s, with the first regional football association having been established in 1882 (Venter 2018, 424). The segregated nature of colonial society also meant that the game developed separately among South Africa's different racial groups, which in turn led to separate controlling bodies being created over time (Venter 2018, 424).

The advent of apartheid in 1948 brought a far more rigid form of segregation as compared to the colonial period, and this permeated all forms of South African society, including sport. Despite this, South Africa was able to rejoin as a FIFA member in 1952, having earlier left the organization in 1926 when it decided to affiliate to the English Football Association instead (Bolsmann 2010, 31). But the white South African Football Association (SAFA)'s right to claim full control of domestic football through affiliation with FIFA was challenged over the ensuing decade by the non-racial South African Soccer Federation (SASF), formed in 1951 as a merger between three separate controlling bodies previously defined along racial lines and operating outside white sport (Bolsmann 2010, 36). These efforts finally paid off as South Africa was suspended from FIFA in 1961 as a result of pressure applied against the racial policies prevalent within South African sport at the time (Bolsmann 2010, 39). Apart from a brief period in 1963-4 during which the suspension was temporarily lifted, it remained in effect until FIFA's 1976 Congress in Montreal, at which point South Africa was completely expelled from the world governing body.

Despite South African football's international isolation, the NFL enjoyed a period of significant growth during the 1960s as the professional game proved popular domestically. Attendances peaked at just over the two million mark in 1969 (Venter 2015, 267). By the end of the decade two other professional leagues were also operating in the country, namely the National Professional Soccer League (NPSL)— formed in 1967, but which was re-organized into a league for Africans only from 1971 onwards—and the non-racial Federation Professional League (FPL), formed outside government structures in 1969 (Venter 2018, 432–3). The FPL maintained an anti-apartheid stance and was open to all South Africans willing to challenge apartheid legislation in terms of the sharing of facilities for example, although in practice the majority of the league's members were colored and Indian players playing for clubs along South Africa's coastal belt.[1]

The 1970s brought about drastic changes in domestic football, partly as a result of economic and social forces, but mostly due to political changes occurring at both a national and sporting level. A key development was South Africa's expulsion from

---

[1] The Population Registration Act of 1950 classified South African citizens into four racial groups, namely African, colored, Indian and white. The term 'black' is used to denote 'African' in this chapter. The term 'colored' refers to the descendants of mixed relations between European settlers and the original inhabitants of the southern tip of Africa. It also includes citizens of mixed parentage. South African Indians are the descendants of indentured workers brought from India to the Natal Colony beginning in 1860.

the International Olympic Committee (IOC) in 1970—an important indicator of the rising international pressure being applied against apartheid sport in the context of the post-colonial period. The South African government's response was the introduction of the "multinational" sports policy in 1971—one that allowed very limited contact between racially-defined teams under certain conditions. The central objective was to portray a limited form of sporting integration internationally, while still adhering to the central tenets of the apartheid system, most notably the "separate development" of South Africa's different race groups (Venter 2017).

A central objective of white football administrators in South Africa was to have the country's FIFA suspension lifted. Multinationalism provided a platform from which to push for integration in football (with government approval) by arranging a number of tournaments between different racially defined teams during the 1970s. The multinational policy also evolved over time, slowly allowing a greater degree of contact between teams at different levels. However, these experiments were ultimately unsuccessful in gaining re-entry into FIFA as South Africa was expelled from the organization in July 1976 in a climate of extreme hostility. The events during the Soweto uprising on 16 June 1976—which further vaulted South Africa into the international spotlight for all the wrong reasons—represented the final blow to any hope of finding favor at FIFA. At the same time the white NFL was far removed from its heyday in the late 1960s and was feeling the economic effects of declining attendances (Venter 2015). Sponsors were also increasingly attracted to the NPSL on account of the league's large black consumer base (Alegi & Bolsmann 2010). The South African football landscape was changing at a rapid rate by the time 1977 arrived, and it was this uncertain milieu within which the Mainstay League Cup competition was spawned.

CREATING THE 1977 MAINSTAY LEAGUE CUP

An important development in the wake of South Africa's expulsion from FIFA was the formation of the Football Council of South Africa in November 1976 (Bolsmann 2010, 41). This replaced a previous entity known as the Top Level Committee that had acted as an umbrella body for the various racially defined controlling bodies within domestic football. The premise behind this committee was to create a single controlling authority for the game (while adhering to apartheid legislation) that would be responsible for expanding multinational football as part of a broader attempt to gain re-entry into FIFA. A fundamental challenge to this objective was the fact that the non-racial South African Soccer Federation refused to take part in any of the multinational experiments and to join the Top Level Committee, and as such the committee could never claim full control over all football structures in the country.

A significant marker of the footballing trade winds prevalent at the time was the fact that George Thabe, head of the (black) South African National Football Association (SANFA), was elected as president of the Football Council. Thabe became arguably the most powerful football official during this period given the struggles experienced by the white NFL, as well as the fact that SANFA's professional league, the NPSL, was attracting larger sponsorships from white-owned South African companies eager to market their products in the black townships.

The stated objective of the Football Council was the "normalizing" (i.e. integration with government approval) of football in South Africa. In this regard a key project undertaken by the council was the introduction of a competition that included clubs from its constituent (racially-based) organizations in 1977 (Football Council of South Africa, Press Statement 1976). This took the form of the Mainstay League Cup and the significance of this move lay in the fact that a limited number of individual players from different racial groups were permitted to move between competing clubs on a "loan" basis for the purposes of this competition. As such black players could (and did), for example, turn out for white NFL clubs in some of these fixtures (and *vice versa*). The competition provided a glimpse of club-level integration—something which eventually arrived the following year in 1978—but also served to illustrate some of the potential challenges that lay ahead. Alegi and Bolsmann allude to some of these aspects that emerged during the Mainstay tournament—the likes of which included high travel costs, spectator violence and constrained movement of fans as a result of segregation laws (Alegi & Bolsmann 2010, 8–9). These and other elements will be expanded upon below.

A close examination of the Mainstay competition's outcome reveals the multilayered context in which it was played. The implementation of the player loan system had to be done within the framework of the National Party's modified sports policy as announced on 23 September 1976—a significant development coming in the wake of the Soweto riots and "a renewed international campaign [against South African sport] led by African states" (Booth 1998, 104). The new policy, consisting of eight points, essentially entailed the extension of the multinational concept down to club level. Previously such encounters were only permitted at a quasi "national" level for teams representing South Africa's different racial groups. The most noteworthy points contained within the updated policy of September 1976 were the following:

1. That the sportsmen and sportswomen of the Whites, Coloreds, Indians and Black peoples *belong to their own clubs and control, arrange and manage their own sports matters.*

4. That in the case of team sports, the boards or committees of every population group arrange their own leagues or rosters *within their own national context.*

5. That where it has been mutually agreed upon, boards or committees, in consultation with the Minister of Sport and Recreation, *may also arrange leagues or matches in which teams of different population groups play against each other* (SACOS, Sport Policy as Announced on 23 September 1976).

Points 1 and 4 above illustrate the fact that the policy was still built on the concept of multinationalism with each racial group responsible for its own sporting affairs.

However, it did contain a new dimension in point 5 regarding competition at club level. The latter was now more readily permissible in consultation with the minister of sport, Piet Koornhof. In the case of football this meant that the Football Council could move forward with a single competition containing clubs from different racial groups. Such a competition could also take place over an extended period of time. This was different to the situation in 1975 when FASA had to obtain special permission for the Chevrolet Champion of Champions club tournament—a previous multinational experiment—to take place. The latter was played over a short period of time and could be justified in terms of the previous policy since it included only the "best" teams from each racial group. However, whereas the modified September 1976 policy paved the way for more regular contact between clubs from different race groups, it did not entail movement of individual players from different race groups between these clubs. In other words, it did not yet represent full integration.

In this regard the Football Council had to negotiate carefully with Koornhof to allow limited movement of players on a loan basis during the Mainstay competition. However, prior to that discussion the council's own position appears to have been uneven on this issue. One of George Thabe's fears related to the potential purchase of black players by NFL clubs since, from his point of view, white clubs possessed more financial clout. This was true in some sense, but at the same time it can be argued—with the benefit of hindsight—that he overestimated the financial resources of NFL clubs during this period. He made his concerns known in a confidential memorandum sent to Koornhof in January 1977. The memorandum informed the latter of the recent formation of the Football Council, and proceeded to analyze proposals received from SANFA (Thabe's own organization) and FASA (the white controlling body) regarding the proposed "normalization" of football in South Africa. Thabe then essentially promoted the SANFA proposal and directed a request to Koornhof for the suggestions to "be considered as confidential" (Thabe, Memorandum to Piet Koornhof 1977).

Thabe's analysis provides telling insight into the background power dynamics prevalent at the time. He stated that the Football Council was forced to accept FASA's proposal for normalization since, had that not been the case, "the Whites on the committee would have attacked us [the black officials] in the Press and we would have been accused of being 'verkrampt' [ultra-conservative]" (Thabe, Memorandum to Piet Koornhof 1977). FASA's proposal entailed the formation of a competition in 1977 containing clubs from all council-affiliated bodies as well as the non-racial SASF. It further stated that "the Government should be approached to authorize the selection of mixed teams. It is suggested that two or three players could be interchangeable in each team, irrespective of color" (Thabe, Memorandum to Piet Koornhof 1977). According to Thabe, the council accepted the proposal with the provision that "only a limited number of champion clubs of the various leagues would participate", but that this had since become unacceptable to the NFL which wanted all its clubs to participate (Thabe, Memorandum to Piet Koornhof 1977). This was undoubtedly the result of the economic predicament facing the NFL at the time as clubs were battling for financial survival—hence the desire to include all these clubs in a new competition offering additional sponsorship and revenue possibilities.

Thabe further argued against the FASA proposal by stating that—should such a competition be successfully completed—"some members would bring pressure to bear for the establishment of a multiracial club league immediately". According to him the NPSL (under the auspices of SANFA) was also of the opinion that

> such a league would lead to the disappearance of the NPSL which was built into the most popular sports organization in South Africa and the pride of every Black. The NPSL clubs had misgivings about the establishment of a multiracial club league at this stage since it seems to threaten their identities…It is felt that friction may arise if white teams, playing in a mixed league, should buy Black players from Black clubs. It is appreciated that wealthy white clubs would be able to pay exorbitant [sic] fees to the top Black players to the chagrin of the Black clubs who will be reduced to acting as training ground for Black players. This could lead to animosity with dire results (Thabe, Memorandum to Piet Koornhof 1977).

This exchange serves as further confirmation that Thabe was greatly concerned about the potential dominance of white clubs (in terms of buying power) within a multiracial context. Consequently a situation arose whereby the most powerful football official at the time, who happened to be black, was supporting the government's idea of multinationalism in order to protect the identity of the league and professional clubs under his auspices. In this regard the white football officials—particularly from within the professional ranks—were the ones who opposed pure multinationalism and pushed the boundaries towards establishing integration at club level as a form of self-preservation. This stands out as a notable irony within the broader context of South African football's power struggle during the 1970s. It is also difficult to dismiss Thabe's stance on multinationalism as merely another instance where blacks were being co-opted into the system at the hands of dominant white officials who provided proverbial crumbs off the master's table (in the form of access to facilities, for example). The desire by black clubs to protect their identities is a notable phenomenon within the milieu of apartheid-era sport which was of course constructed on the idea of separate identities.

Thabe's views also appear to have been mirrored among some sections of black football supporters. During this volatile period the football publication, *Sharpshoot Soccer*, canvassed the views of black soccer followers regarding the potential for multiracial football:

> We feel that our readers represent a sizeable section of informed Black opinion, and therefore we asked in our December [1976] issue for YOU, the reader, to write in, and tell us whether YOU were in favor of mixed football or not. The response has shaken us. We have not had ONE SINGLE positive reply. Every fan who has written to us has been dead against the idea…But we should like more letters from our readers…So whether…you feel that mixed football would be the death of Black soccer, or whether you feel that

> this might be the salvation of the game in South Africa, write in and give us your views (Lyon, "We want your views" 1977).[2]

This is by no means a reliable barometer of black opinion but still serves to indicate that Thabe was not alone in fearing the arrival of multiracial football. As a result he suggested to Koornhof that SANFA's proposal for a mixed league would be a better fit within the framework of multinationalism. This represented a far more cautious approach to mixed play than what was being proposed by FASA and the NFL. SANFA conceded that previous multinational tournaments (where large amounts of prize money were involved) led to dangerous and volatile situations, and consequently suggested that future multinational encounters between clubs should be done purely on a friendly basis with no prize money at stake. These matches would then be used as trials for the selection of mixed provincial sides on merit, with the latter then competing in a mixed provincial league where "club pride and what it generates...will be absent" (Thabe, Memorandum to Piet Koornhof 1977). From SANFA's point of view this would have represented a method for implementing mixed play at a higher level while simultaneously protecting the identity of black clubs at the lower level. Thabe concluded by stating that:

> ...we are under considerable pressure from various sides to reject Government policy and to play multiracial soccer immediately. Whites have played an important and often determining role in this...We shall be glad if our proposals are considered without delay in order that all concerned could be informed of the decision (Thabe, Memorandum to Piet Koornhof 1977).

The memorandum essentially constituted a tactic on the part of Thabe to circumvent the constraints that he was operating within on the Football Council—i.e. having to incorporate the demands of white officials for faster integration. By arguing that SANFA's proposal would be a more optimal course of action within the framework of multinationalism he attempted to obtain direct support from Koornhof for SANFA's desired route forward. In this regard the secretary of the Department of Sport and Recreation, Beyers Hoek, concurred with Thabe's analysis and recommended to Koornhof that permission be given to the Football Council for a provincial merit league to be instituted with teams selected on merit (Hoek, Memo aan Minister: Meriete Sokkerliga 1977). Such a multiracial provincial competition was eventually announced in April 1978, but during the intervening period the idea of a professional multiracial club league was still on the table.

At a Football Council meeting on 16 January 1977 it was decided to pursue a recommended league plan that closely resembled FASA's proposed structure—namely a mixed club league with "free interchange" of players. The NFL also

---

[2] Emphasis as contained in original article. The same publication then contains further letters decrying multiracial football. Readers opined that black players would not be able to express themselves at white clubs (in terms of playing style) and that black clubs would become inferior (and even bankrupt) if white clubs were permitted to buy star players.

obtained its wish of having all thirteen of its first division clubs present in the competition (Football Council of South Africa, Minutes of Executive Committee Meeting, January 16, 1977). The influence of Michael Rapp, chairman of the NFL, was clear in this regard since he was the convener of the ad hoc committee tasked by the council to "work out the details of the league" (Football Council of South Africa, Press Statement 1977). The council adopted this proposed structure despite Thabe again stating that SANFA's view on the matter was that only the top clubs from each association should participate in the competition (Football Council of South Africa, Minutes of Executive Committee Meeting, January 16, 1977).

From that point, negotiations with Koornhof were entered into in terms of bringing the competition to fruition. Thabe and Rapp subsequently met with the minister and emphasized that the Football Council had decided to conduct a competition containing approximately 30 teams from the different football associations in 1977, and that this would be run on an experimental basis. Individual leagues of the different associations would continue as per normal. The main point of contention was the suggestion by the council representatives that "movement of players from one club to the other would be on an unrestricted basis" (Football Council of South Africa, Minutes of Executive Committee Meeting, February 8, 1977). Koornhof apparently balked at this suggestion, indicating that "such a league would not be in conformity with the government's sports policy...[since the policy stated that] merit or integrated sport would be allowed at the levels of provincial and international selected teams. This is excluded at the levels of clubs" (Football Council of South Africa, Minutes of Executive Committee Meeting, February 8, 1977). This argument was in line with the policy allowing the mixture of clubs from different (racial) associations into single competitions, but not yet the mixture of individual players (from different race groups) into single teams at that level. The latter was still only permissible at provincial or national level.

According to Thabe and Rapp, they underlined the importance of allowing some movement of individual players and argued that if this was not permitted they would not be able to control club officials who would likely take matters into their own hands and implement integration anyway. Ironically they cited the case of the non-racial SASF which had for years played mixed (non-racial) football, and according to Thabe and Rapp they "were not aware that the government was acting" against this and as a result they failed "to understand why the Council should be treated differently". As a compromise they suggested to Koornhof that "movement of [at least] three players from one race group to join another should be permitted" (Football Council of South Africa, Minutes of Executive Committee Meeting, February 8, 1977). They also emphasized that the Football Council "would not play multinational football under any circumstances". In reply Koornhof indicated that he would give the government's response to this suggested framework within due course (Football Council of South Africa, Minutes of Executive Committee Meeting, February 8, 1977). These delicate negotiations continued and a further meeting was held with Koornhof on 10 February 1977. At this point Thabe and Rapp again suggested that players be allowed to move purely on a loan basis between clubs during the competition. The loan scheme was ultimately accepted and as a result the 1977

Mainstay League Cup represented a significant development within South African football since this was the first competition played within the framework of government policy where (limited) racial integration took place at club level.

CONTROVERSIES ON AND OFF THE FIELD

The Mainstay League Cup began on a firm financial footing, with the Football Council having acquired the largest football-related sponsorship (R70,000) for a single competition in South Africa up to that point. Alegi and Bolsmann (2010, 10–12) have pointed to the important role played by large corporate sponsors such as South African Breweries (SAB), the United Tobacco Company (UTC, today British American Tobacco) and Stellenbosch Farmers' Winery (SFW, owners of the Mainstay cane spirit brand) in shaping professional football during this period. In this regard the Mainstay competition was a further manifestation of this trend.

From the Football Council's perspective, the 1977 Mainstay League Cup competition represented an important experiment in terms of potentially replacing the individual professional leagues and becoming a so-called "Super League" from 1978 onwards. This would subsequently prove to be a contentious point, but for the 1977 Mainstay tournament the format saw the 32 competing teams divided into four sections containing eight teams each (Zagnoev, "Mainstay League Cup Logs as at 31 October 1977" 1977). The NPSL and NFL leagues proceeded as per normal during the year, while Mainstay fixtures represented a new addition to the calendar, taking place along a sectional basis on weekdays with each team playing the seven other members within its section once. At the conclusion of the league phase the leading team in each section advanced to the semi-finals, played over one leg, followed by the final played on the same basis.

However, as indicated earlier, the Mainstay competition was plagued by controversy virtually from the outset. The first issue related to venue allocation and in this regard *World* lamented the fact that the initial fixture list did not include any matches between (white) NFL and (black) NPSL teams at black grounds (such as Orlando Stadium). All such encounters were in fact allocated to NFL grounds and the reason purported by Michael Rapp in the media related to the Department of Bantu Administration and Development's refusal to grant the necessary permits required by whites to enter black areas ("Taking the first step backwards" 1977). The initial indication from Thabe and other officials was that matches would be played "irrespective of the condition of the ground". However, once it became clear that black teams would essentially need to play away from home against NFL teams, *World* accused sport officials of "mixing sport with politics", pointing out that these same officials had often decried such interference on previous occasions ("Taking the first step backwards" 1977).

Despite these off-the-field complications the initial reception to the matches themselves was positive. In this regard *Sharpshoot Soccer* reported that the competition was "running smoothly" during its first month and opined that "everyone connected with [the] Mainstay League deserves some early and hopeful congratulations for an excellent start to a difficult programme". However, simultaneously it did warn that "the steeper slopes [were] still to come" (Lyon, "Mainstay league is running smoothly" 1977). This remark proved to be prophetic as crowd trouble erupted at an afternoon match between the NFL's Highlands Park and the NPSL's Moroka Swallows Limited at the Rand Stadium on Saturday 5 June 1977. *Sharpshoot Soccer* pointed out that each team had "its own brand of vociferous and dedicated supporters", and that this was the first high profile fixture between black and white sides based in Johannesburg. Given these factors it regarded a riot as inevitable:

> The game itself...was a good and exciting match, and if the spectators overstepped the mark, then this was only to be expected. We have warned in these very columns of the dangers of playing White against Black, but if it is a necessary step on the road to fully integrated soccer, then let us all hold our breaths and keep swimming (Lyon, "Cancellations not the major problem" 1977).

As had previously been the case during multinational matches it was the off-side law that sparked the trouble. In a high-scoring encounter Swallows came from 2–0 behind to draw level at 2–2, thereby creating much excitement among the team's supporters since a win over one of the NFL's top teams was seemingly within their grasp. But Highlands regained the lead with a third goal which "looked suspiciously off-side", leading to a Swallows player being booked for arguing with the referee. The same player was then later sent off for a second bookable offense, at which point the Swallows supporters "really boiled over". Some invaded the pitch which led to the match being abandoned—although it was restarted (and completed) as a friendly encounter some 20 minutes later, with the scoreboard reset to 2–2 no less ("Great clash at the Rand" 1977).

The crowd trouble experienced during the above encounter did not represent an isolated incident during the competition, but rather one of many instances of uncontrollable crowds at various Mainstay matches. This much was reported in the media ("Mainstay's League Cup broke new ground" 1977), and led to administrative headaches for the Football Council. For example, the latter was held responsible for damages caused to security fencing at the Jan Smuts Stadium in Pietermaritzburg on 28 October 1977. This occurred when "violence erupted and spectators rushed onto the field" during a match between the NFL's Durban City and the NPSL's Leeds United (Pietermaritzburg City Treasurer's Office, 1977). The cause of this particular incident again related to the interpretation of the off-side law. The *Rand Daily Mail* described the chain of events as follows:

> Last night's trouble flared when [Durban] City's Brian Balfour netted the third goal and Leeds goalkeeper, Bernard Mbhele, refused to part with the ball. He claimed that Balfour was off-side and several of his teammates lent support. This was the signal for dozens of black fans to invade the pitch throwing bottles, cans and stones at the referee, linesmen and policemen who tried to restore order (Lerman, "Mainstay game abandoned in chaos" 1977).

Crowd violence was also reported at three separate Mainstay matches played over the same weekend, including a referee being stabbed in the head (O'Flaherty, "Soccer officials injured by fans" 1977). These problematic incidents did not constitute the only point of criticism directed towards the competition. It was also condemned in some quarters as far as achieving its stated objective was concerned. In this regard—despite the introduction of the loan system during the competition—it still bore a close resemblance to previous multinational tournaments. Football writer Derrick Thema consequently criticized the competition's credibility and blamed George Thabe as well as some reluctant teams for turning the Mainstay League Cup into "another multinational league" (Thema, "More clubs must follow Arcadia" 1977). Thabe was purported to have played a significant role behind the scenes in terms of the breakdown of various negotiations between clubs regarding the potential loaning of players. This would have been in line with his stance on player movement, as highlighted previously. Within this milieu there were few notable player moves between clubs, thereby eroding the tournament's believability as an integrated multiracial competition.

Whereas the aforementioned troubles were certainly significant, they were dwarfed by events that followed in August 1977. Early that month the Mainstay League Cup was plunged into a full scale crisis when fixtures were halted as a result of seven "rebel" NPSL clubs refusing to complete the schedule. The clubs in question also refused to take part in the following season's proposed Mainstay "Super League" and much of the controversy centered on prevailing issues within SANFA and the NPSL. The professional clubs demanded a greater degree of autonomy in their dealings with Thabe's SANFA, with the latter eventually caving in to these demands. Mainstay fixtures recommenced on 16 September 1977 with a match between Cape Town City and Moroka Swallows Limited (Zagnoev, "Mainstay League Cup—1977 Attendances: September" 1977). This left the competition with a fixture backlog that had to be cleared in a short space of time before the end of the 1977 season, which resulted in a flurry of fixtures during the month of October.

STUMBLING TO THE FINISH LINE

The temporary suspension of Mainstay fixtures is perhaps the reason why Alegi and Bolsmann incorrectly assert that the competition was never completed (Alegi & Bolsmann 2010). The semi-finals and final were in fact contested early in November 1977 between four NFL sides—each of which finished at the top of their respective sections (Zagnoev, "Mainstay League Cup Paid Attendances—Semi Finals and Final" 1977). With NPSL teams having been eliminated by that point it cleared the way for top black players to play as loaned "guests" for the semi-finalists. Lucas "Masterpieces" Moripe (of the NPSL's Pretoria Callies) turned out for Arcadia Shepherds (alongside Vincent Julius, a colored player who was a permanent fixture for Shepherds that season as the club flaunted government policy regarding his inclusion in the white NFL) in their semi-final against Wits University, with the latter fielding Patrick "Ace" Ntsoelengoe of Kaizer Chiefs ("Arcadia broke the red tape" 1977).

However, even this much-needed additional dimension would not have materialized had the competing teams not agreed (and obtained permission from administrators) to waive the tournament rule regarding cup-tied players. This rule—which is a standard feature of major football competitions to this day—dictates that once a player has appeared a certain number of times (sometimes this need only be one occasion) for a team in a specific competition, then he is not permitted to appear for a different club in the same competition during that season. In this regard Wits, who wanted to acquire Ntsoelengoe on loan, floated the idea to Arcadia and proposed that the Pretoria club obtain Moripe on a similar basis as compensation (Lerman, "Wits, Arcs agree to bend Cup rules" 1977). This was cleared by the relevant authorities, and the prolific Julius scored the only goal of the encounter, sending Arcadia Shepherds into the final. There they faced Cape Town City, who had defeated Durban City in the other semi-final.

The final was played at Arcadia's home ground, the Caledonian Stadium, in Pretoria on 12 November 1977. It was notable for the fact that Julius and Moripe were joined by another star guest player, Ephraim "Jomo" Sono, who turned out for Cape Town City. In a clear indication that they were eager to retain Moripe's star power in their lineup, Arcadia opted to play him despite the fact that he was involved in a cup match for his parent club, Pretoria Callies, earlier that same day (Lerman, "Day-night Master" 1977). The decision proved to be the right one as Arcadia prevailed in a one-sided encounter, winning by a 5–1 margin in front of a reported paid attendance of just over 9,000 spectators. Having finally drawn to a close the competition was described as a success in some quarters of the media, particularly in light of the fact that it did represent a tentative (if largely clumsy) move towards partial integration (Lerman, "Mainstay League was a success" 1977). However, as a whole the venture experienced numerous challenges both on and off the field, and *Sharpshoot Soccer* summarized this dimension appropriately in the competition's aftermath:

> Halfway through, the competition was halted by internal wrangles between the [black] NPSL and SANFA. Later the games restarted but many staggered to chaos and ended up in riots when white referees came under fire from the black sector of the spectators. Quite a few games were abandoned because of misunderstandings of the rules of the game. Many rules and decisions (which are never applied by Black referees in black associations, through inexperience or negligence) sounded foreign to black fans when correctly put into practice by white referees ("Mainstay's League Cup broke new ground" 1977).

The controversy over refereeing decisions clearly mirrored developments during the multinational experiments from preceding years. This again underlined the complexity and volatility present within the process of moving towards football integration. Another challenge faced by organizers related to the financial aspect of the competition. In this regard the vast travel distances logged by clubs resulted in high travel costs which led to notable losses against the competition's travel fund.[3]

Given the fact that the Mainstay League Cup was marketed by administrators as a significant step towards "normalizing" South African football, the final analysis left the tournament well short of this and other objectives. Even the match report of the final itself—despite being positive—was placed without a photo on the inside back page of the following Monday's *Rand Daily Mail* (Lerman, "Mainstay League was a success" 1977). This was largely symbolic of the way the tournament was received within football circles. The lack of interest in its concluding matches can also be attributed to the fact that the four semi-finalists were all from the NFL, which meant that there was very little novelty factor during the knock-out stage of the competition (other than the black guest players).

Conclusion

In many ways the 1977 Mainstay League Cup constituted a microcosm of South African football at the time. It was dressed up as an integrated multiracial competition, but bore a much closer resemblance to previous multinational tournaments since the proposed movement of players between black and white clubs only materialized on a small scale. As had been the case during preceding years the non-racial SASF and its professional league, the FPL, also rejected it as mere multinationalism and refused to participate in the venture, thereby maintaining the ideological rift within professional football. Furthermore, the Mainstay competition was also affected by the boardroom politics prevalent within this milieu and the complicated apartheid legislation pertaining to sport.

When placed in its proper historical context it serves as an important reminder of the darker side of elite sport, particularly as far as the case of South African football was concerned. While the Mainstay competition itself was an attempt—for varying reasons—to mitigate the racialized nature of South African football, it was shaped by the most significant historical forces of the day. As such it represented a nexus of issues pertaining to race, politics, economics and sport. Subsequently the competition was never repeated in the same format since sanctioned football integration arrived the following season after the collapse of the white NFL at the end of 1977, leaving its teams to join the two other professional leagues in the country, namely the NPSL and FPL (Bolsmann 2013). Government-sanctioned integration therefore arrived by default in football—more than a decade before the eventual abolition of apartheid no less.

Today, the South African football landscape is notably different as a result of the sweeping changes that have occurred in the country since the early 1990s. After the arrival of football unity in 1991—i.e. the formation of a single controlling body for the game, namely the South African Football Association (SAFA)—South Africa was

---

[3] The travel fund was accumulated by pooling 15% of the gate takings from each match in the competition. This meant that teams drawing large attendances would subsidize the travel of those with low attendances.

quickly welcomed back into the international football community. After the country's first democratic elections in 1994 sport was regarded as an important vehicle, at least symbolically, through which to forge a new inclusive South African identity. International sporting successes, most notably winning the 1995 Rugby World Cup and the 1996 African Cup of Nations football tournament, were celebrated widely by South Africans from all walks of life. These developments were seen as encapsulating the inherent potential of the young democracy under Nelson Mandela's presidency.

At the same time structural challenges remained. From a societal perspective the country continues to grapple with the issue of bringing about redress for the legacy of apartheid in a way that would allow all South Africans to stride confidently into the future. Many of the debates relating to the work place, such as demographic representation at various levels, have been mirrored in the sporting arena. In this regard the issue of team selection at national and regional level has been a significant point of contention since the late 1990s. While apartheid itself was dismantled over a quarter of a century ago, the continued racialized nature of the sporting (and public) discourse indicates that its ghosts remain. Football has, however, been notably absent from debates over the demographic composition of teams. This is largely because the game is dominated by black players at all levels. Instead the codes of cricket and rugby, traditionally dominated by whites, have been the most prominent targets of post-apartheid selection controversies. In this regard progress towards establishing more representative teams has been regarded as too slow in many quarters, leading to more aggressive legislation mandating teams and federations to select a suitable number of black players at all levels.

Analyzing the structural dynamics relating to player development in cricket and rugby lies beyond the scope of this chapter, but it is fair to postulate that this is a highly complex domain being impacted by multiple forces. The picture is further complicated when introducing the desire for political expediency as an additional variable. While football itself falls outside of this debate, the game continues to face a different dark side not related to race, but rather to aspects of corruption and maladministration. In this regard the legacy of South Africa's hosting of the 2010 FIFA World Cup has since been tainted by allegations of bribery (Hartley 2016). The domestic game has also been blighted by issues of match fixing and crowd safety, while the disappointing performances of the men's national team over the past ten years has, at least temporarily, removed football from any positive sporting discourse around nation building (Venter 2018). While South African football has come a long way since the 1977 Mainstay League Cup, the reality is that not all the gains have been positive and that a darker side continues to lurk in different shades beneath the surface.

REFERENCES

Alegi, Peter and Bolsmann, Chris. 2010. "From Apartheid to Unity: White Capital and Black Power in the Racial Integration of South African Football, 1976–1992." *African Historical Review* 42, 1:1–18.

"Arcadia broke the red tape." *Sharpshoot Soccer,* November, 1977.

Baldini, P. 2018. "One death alleged racist abuse and a Boxing Day of shame in Serie A." *Guardian*, December 27, 2018. https://www.theguardian.com/football/blog /2018/dec/27/one-death-alleged-racist-abuse-and-a-boxing-day-of-shame-in-serie-a.
Bolsmann, Chris. 2010. "White football in South Africa: empire, apartheid and change, 1892–1977." *Soccer & Society* 1–2:29–45.
———. 2013. "Professional Football in Apartheid South Africa: Leisure, Consumption and Identity in the National Football League, 1959–1977." *The International Journal of the History of Sport* 30, 16:1947–1961.
Booth, Douglas. 1998. *The Race Game: Sport and Politics in South Africa*. London, Frank Cass.
Football Council of South Africa. Minutes of Executive Committee Meeting. January 16, 1977. Football Association of South Africa Papers 1892–1992, Historical Papers Research Archive, University of the Witwatersrand, South Africa.
———. Minutes of Executive Committee Meeting. February 8, 1977. Football Association of South Africa Papers 1892–1992, Historical Papers Research Archive, University of the Witwatersrand, South Africa.
———. November 22, 1976. Football Association of South Africa Papers 1892–1992, Historical Papers Research Archive, University of the Witwatersrand, South Africa.
"Great clash at Rand," *Sharpshoot Soccer,* July, 1977.
Hartley, Ray. 2016. *The Big Fix: How South Africa Stole the 2010 World Cup*. Johannesburg, Jonathan Ball.
Hoek, Beyers. "Memo aan Minister: Meriete Sokkerliga [Memo to Minister: Merit Soccer League]." January 17, 1977. PV476/1/34/21/2, Piet Koornhof Private Documents, Archive for Contemporary Affairs, University of the Free State, South Africa.. Translated from Afrikaans.
Lerman, Sy. "Day-night Master." *Rand Daily Mail,* November 10, 1977.
———. "Mainstay game abandoned in chaos." *Rand Daily Mail,* October 29, 1977.
———. "Mainstay League was a success." *Rand Daily Mail,* November 14, 1977.
———. "Wits, Arcs agree to bend Cup rules." *Rand Daily Mail,* November 2, 1977.
Lyon, Richard. "Cancellations, not the major problems." Sharpshoot Soccer, July, 1977.
———. "Mainstay league is running smoothly." *Sharpshoot Soccer,* May, 1977.
———. "We want your views." *Sharpshoot Soccer,* February, 1977.
"Mainstay's League Cup broke new ground." *Sharpshoot Soccer,* November, 1977.
O'Flaherty, Brian. "Soccer officials injured by fans." *Rand Daily Mail,* October 31, 1977.
Pietermaritzburg City Treasurer's Office, Letter to Football Council of South Africa, November 17, 1977, Football Association of South Africa Papers 1892–1992, Historical Papers Research Archive, University of the Witwatersrand, South Africa.
SACOS. "Sport Policy as Announced on 23 September 1976." SACOS Minute Book. Francois Cleophas Private Collection.
"Taking the first step backwards." *World,* April 6, 1977.
Thabe, George. "Memorandum to Piet Koornhof." January 7, 1977. PV476/1/34/21/2, Piet Koornhof Private Documents, Archive for Contemporary Affairs, University of the Free State, South Africa.
Thema, Derrick. "More clubs must follow Arcadia," *Sharpshoot Soccer,* May, 1977.
Venter, Gustav. 2015. "Long Balls in the Dying Moments: Exploring the Decline of South Africa's National Football League, 1970–1977." *The International Journal of the History of Sport* 32, 2:265–285.
———. 2017. "Slippery Under Foot: The Shifting Political Dynamics within South African Football, 1973–1976." *South African Historical Journal* 69, 2:265–287.
———. 2018. "South Africa." In *The Palgrave International Handbook of Football and Politics*, edited by Jean-Michel de Waele, Suzan Gibril, Ekaterina Gloriozova and Ramón Spaaij, 423–445. Springer.

Zagnoev, Dudley. "Mainstay League Cup—1977 Attendances: September," Document. Football Association of South Africa Papers 1892–1992, Historical Papers Research Archive, University of the Witwatersrand, South Africa.
———. "Mainstay League Cup Logs as at 31 October 1977." Document. Football Association of South Africa Papers 1892–1992, Historical Papers Research Archive, University of the Witwatersrand, South Africa.
———. "Mainstay League Cup Paid Attendances—Semi Finals and Final," Document. Football Association of South Africa Papers 1892–1992, Historical Papers Research Archive, University of the Witwatersrand, South Africa.

CHAPTER 13

The Fortress and the Cave Dwellers: A Story from Bosnian-Herzegovinian Football

Gary Armstrong and Massimiliano Maidano

INTRODUCTION

The Bosnian-Herzegovinian (BiH) town of Široki Brijeg (SB) (Broad Hills) is renown in Balkan political circles for its defense of Croatian and Catholic identity against peoples whom its citizens argue have long attempted to erase the town's culture and name from the maps of Europe. The town has experienced centuries of political and military strife via the Ottomans, the Habsburgs, Fascism and Communism. In contemporary times the town's sense of resistance lies in the face of the imposition of a democratic political milieu that followed the end of the Yugoslav Conflict of 1991-1995 fought between the peoples known as Croats, Serbs and Bosniaks (Bosnian Muslims). This conflict which cost the lives of an estimated 200,000 civilians and military, brought the term "ethnic cleansing" into common parlance in European political debate and, following the Serb-led massacre of 8000 Bosniak men and boys at Srebrenica, produced convoluted legal debates around the ownership of genocide. Host to some 29,000 residents contemporary SB is the administrative center of the West Herzegovinian Canton of BiH an entity with a 98% Herzegovinian-Croat demographic. For those who live in its boundaries the town is metaphorically a fortress; a siege mentality is integral to its citizen's sense of being. One of the core features of this lived resistance identity is the town's football club Široki Brijeg NK (SBNK). Its hard core fan group who declare themselves as *ultras* gather under the name of the *Škripari* (*Cave-dwellers*) a nomenclature derived from a local drawn militia who supported the Croatian Fascists *Ustaša* (uprising) who allied with the Axis during World War II. In the latter conflict the *Škripari* made incursions on the Communist Partisans enemy from their hide-outs in the caves in the hills above SB (Redžić, et.al 2005). Today, the contemporary *Škripari* celebrate the civic and the sporting for the expressions of their Croat nationalist narratives of resistance against the central BiH Government based in Sarajevo and its perceived Bosniak hegemony. They are ready to defend their town, football club, and Croatian identity from any ethno-political invader that challenge that they perceive as theirs. For some onlookers this fan gathering is a dark force in the assumed enlightened world that is sport and implicitly acts a hindrance to the establishment of a post-conflict civil society. We consider the matter more complex and suggest analysis must consider variously a sense of people, place and participation and the metaphor of light shining upon darkness. In what follows, the analysis seeks to address the issue of football-related disorder challenging both the categorical notions that such disorder has provoked while also seeking to locate these behaviors in wider socio-historical contexts.

SIEGE AND RESISTANCE

Historical antecedents make the citizens of SB consider themselves as the quintessential Croats. This is collectively defined via celebrations of Catholicism and ethno-political nationalism and by the more individualized celebration of being considered capable and self-sufficient. Catholicism was awarded to the Croats in 925 under the Papacy of John X who conferred the title of King on the Croat Tomislav. The political project of generations of Croats is an independent nation inclusive of the various Croat demographics in the Balkans. Believing they are a people derived from modern-day Poland who migrated to the Adriatic coast and merged with the Illyrians, the Croats are in their own estimation Slavs but Westernized Catholic ones with the Latin Gaj alphabet and different from Orthodox Serbs and their Eastern Cyrillic alphabet. Some historical processes have sought to make them both. Consequently Croat populations have long evidenced resistance before the town Siroki Brijeg's foundation. Following their arrival in the 15th century the Ottomans attempted to convert the locals to Islam usually with violence but also utilizing economic sanctions via tax on farms and restrictions on property ownership. Some Croat-Catholics revolted with weapons, others preferred peaceful disobedience. By the end of the Ottoman epoch which lasted from the 15th to the 19th century most inhabitants of the region had retained their Catholic faith (Anscombe 2014). Such resistance was accelerated in 1846 when members of the Franciscan Order placed the first stone for the construction of the town's monastery. Since this epoch the town has become an important regional center for the Catholic Church and a site of pilgrimage for Catholics worldwide.

In the late 19th century the town fell under the administration of the Habsburgs Austro-Hungarian Empire. This regime helped promote the building of churches and other infrastructures. Despite this and in order to combat insurrections of Croat nationalists, the Empire tried in various ways to convince the Croats that they were part of a broad provincial Slavic—*bošnjaštvo*—identity (Bougarel 2017). The pursuit of ethnic homogeneity was attempted in part by the organization of cultural events funded by Vienna. However, these only resulted in an accentuation of Croat traditions around food, clothing, language, music and religious practices. Nothing changed the Croats. The early 20th century saw a progressive increase in the sense of Croatian nationalism and the aspiration of many was to include SB in the borders of a Croatian Independent State with Zagreb as the capital of the Croatian people. Further political turmoil saw the collapse of the Hapsburgs Empire in 1918. As a result, SB came under the Kingdom of Serbs, Croats and Slovenes. In 1939 the Croats attained some independence with the autonomous Banovina of Croatia. In 1941 the Independent State of Croatia appeared (a *de facto* puppet state of the Nazis). It was in this time that the original *Skiripari* came to prominence.

TWENTIETH CENTURY CONTESTS

During World War II, SB was actively involved in pursuing the centuries-long dream of becoming part of Croatia. The *Škripari* guerilla militia fought alongside the *Ustaše* forces and collectively massacred more than 500,000 Serbs amongst other ethnic minorities (Ramet and Listhaug 2011). The *Škripari* also fought with Axis forces to resist the Red Army of Marshal Tito, and to confuse matter fought both with and later against the *Cetnik* forces of the Serbs. After the defeat of the *Ustaše* and the Axis forces, Croatia became the sixth republic to join the newly founded Socialist Federal Republic of Yugoslavia. Trouble followed. The Croats from Herzegovina "paid" for the *Ustaše* atrocities more than Croats from elsewhere. In 1946, when the Red Army arrived in SB, some 12% of its citizens were murdered by firing squads including 12 Franciscan Friars who refused to deny their faith. During the times of Yugoslavia the town received little infrastructural funding from the communist regime and was renamed *Lištica* after the name of the river that flows through the town. The name SB hinted too much of the towns Croat-Catholic origins in the eyes of the Communists.

Following the fall of communism in Croatia in 1991, the town was once again involved in the fight to be part of a Croatian nation. The Croatian Republic of Herzegovina which existed from 1991 until 1995 was an unrecognized geo-political entity and proto-state which including the territories of the Croatian demographic majority in BiH (mostly Herzegovina and some Central parts of BiH). The years of the Yugoslav conflict accentuated the Croatian and SB sense of self. In those years SB was not a direct site of military confrontation, but did suffer the deaths of some 80 of its citizens and a Serb aerial bombing in April 1992. The center-right political party HDZ (Croatian Democratic Union) for Croatians in BiH was begun in 1990 and in 1992 funded the establishment of the Croatian Defense Council (HVO). This military unit consisting exclusively of Croats defending Croat peoples and the lands conquered in the war years originally from Serbian forces and later from the Bosniak. Many SB citizens enlisted in its ranks and saw front-line military action. The citizens believe their men were amongst the bravest of the Croatian defenders.

The General Framework of the Dayton Peace Accord agreed in November 1995 brought the Yugoslav conflict to a close. Two Entities were formed; the Serb Republika Srpska wherein Serbs exist in a demographic majority and the BiH Federation which sees an uneasy existence between the Bosniak majority and Croat minority. The Federation is divided into ten cantons, generally of one ethnicity. Government structures at national level are weak, ensuring that smaller regional Headquarters are disproportionately influential. Although elections in BiH are generally considered to be free and fair, politicians campaign on a basis of protecting "national" interests which reinforces ethno-nationalist sentiment and clan loyalties. Perceiving themselves to be discriminated against and outnumbered by Bosniaks in government (and sports) institutions the permanent sense of grievance the town of SB carries did not prevent the same town evidencing rapid economic growth in post-war BiH due to variously; industrial and commercial developments, Croats diaspora remittances, and the entrepreneurial capabilities of its citizens. This combination of local pride and a belief in business acumen and a general pride in citizenship is integral to the fortress mentality of SB which underlines the wish for their own military, taxation system and local administration (Gold and Revill 2014).

The desire to be in charge of their own destiny also had a footballing profile. Croatia was admitted to FIFA in 1992 and into UEFA the following year. Finishing third in the France 1998 World Cup finals saw the symbiosis of nation and football like never before. This nation of 4.1 million and just seven years old was revealed to the tournament as having the most fanatical fans and with the team checker-board shirts the most blatant statement of national colors and sporting bodies. Meanwhile in 2013 Croatia became the 28th member of the European Union. Despite the population electing to join a pan-European identity many persist in defining their neighbor of different ethnicities as "Others" and in some cases enemies (Wingfield 2003). And thus whilst happy to belong to a supra-political entity run from Western Europe the SB citizens argue for the possibility of three domestic change: one seeks to make Western Herzegovina an independent state, another suggests the creation of a third Croat-led political entity in BiH, the final one argues the town should-somehow- seek to rejoin the administration contemporary Croatia. Such sentiments are manifested and amplified by the contemporary *Škripari* who with their banners, images and chants in the defense of ethno-political borders. Football thus includes by celebrating its exclusivity. The Janus-face nature of the game is not recent.

NAMING RIGHTS: PATRIOTS AND COMRADES

The history of SBNK narrates the story of the region and the development of the town. Football began in SB in 1946 via the Borak gymnastic club. Two years later the football club became an independent entity with a Board drawn from the traditional professions, alongside those from politics and finance. The white and blue club colors were, oral narratives reveal, a product of garments left behind by the militia fighting for the independent state of Croatia. The colors remained even if the clubs name changed. In 1949 the Club was renamed Boksit after the bauxite mine that was the town's main employer, and played its matches in the outer city location of Tnn in proximity to the bauxite and aluminum factories that were the town's main employers. Politics was soon to interfere with football. In 1950 the Club was forced by the Communists to change its name to Lištica which then again in 1953 to FC Mladost (Youth), a common name for many football teams during Communism. The clubs blue and white badge with a ball in the center was forced under Communism to display a Red Star symbol. In 1952, having moved to the Pecara district of the town a stadium capable of holding 10,000 spectators was built with state funds. The club remains at this location the stadium albeit considerably up-graded in post-communist years via private funding.

Long considered a dark era for both town and club the Communist regime oppressed SB citizens and Herzegovinian-Croats in general. Expressions of Croat identity be they linguistic, artistic, or religious was forbidden. Under Tito the club had a mediocre playing profile mostly in the lower regional leagues of Yugoslavia. Any singing of Croat songs or displays of Croat or anti-communist sentiment at such fixtures were forbidden, those who disobeyed faced jail sentences. To add to the insult, SB citizens were forced to pay taxes that part- funded the FK Velež club from Mostar (located some 30 kilometers way) instead of their own club. Ironically such impositions are considered to have strengthened both the Croat identity and the pride—or maybe cussedness—of SB citizens and their wish for an independent state.

Communism ended *de facto* in late 1980s. The fall of Communism in 1990 saw the explosion of the hitherto subtly re-emerging ethno- nationalist political sentiments. Football was a very obvious vehicle for those in the 1980s post-communist milieu to use as the metaphorical vehicle for calls for independence of the Herzegovinian region. In 1991 the then Mladost NK added the sponsors name of Dubint (a local coal and marble company) to raise the club publicity. The club thus came to represent the re-birth of a suppressed ethno-political identity and celebrated concomitantly the anti-communist and capitalistic soul of the town. This continued throughout the conflict years wherein a regional football league programme was sustained. It was somewhat inevitable in the immediate post-conflict year of 1996 the club would be renamed Široki Brijeg NK. The Croatian checker-board (*sahovnica*) design representing the two ancient states of red (Southern) and white (Western) Croatia was incorporated in the club crest and the red star removed.

The clubs players reflected the socio-political situation. Historically, the club signed only Croat-Roman Catholics players to the complete exclusion of those from Serbian Eastern Orthodox or Bosniak Muslim background. Selection of players elsewhere is similarly subtle in that any player with the necessary abilities can play for Sarajevo FK but restrictions may be applied to Croats and Serbs who promote the dismantling of the current political structure of BiH or who have been known to have expressed anti-Islamic sentiments. Such a policy at SBNK was primarily an attempt by the various boards of directors to defend symbolically the purity of the club's Croat-Catholic identity. As the club grew in the post-conflict years and achieved regional and national victories that got them into Europe-wide competitions the selection policy changed. Policy was top-down and came with political baggage. In the 1990s Zlatan Milo Jelic held the position of Club President. The policy of this former General of the Croatian Defense Force was to recruit only Croats. This was rationalized as a way of making SBNK a Croat club and inspiring and encouraging Croat youth to play for "their" club. There were thus no Serb or Bosniak players wearing the team shirt in the post-war. A few years ago Jelic was indicted by the BiH authorities on behalf of the International Court of Justice in The Hague for persecution of Bosniaks, ethnic cleansing and promoting forced labor. The townsfolk attribute to him as the man behind the great success the club experienced on the pitch in the past 20 years. Authoritarian and uncompromising he was best remembered for having got things done. Since Jelic stood down players from South America, Africa and even Albania have been welcome. In 2018 Club President Miro Kraljevic (also a former HVO General) eased the exclusionist policy and have employed Russian and Macedonian nationals, some of whom may well be Orthodox in their religious beliefs.

Those on the terraces meanwhile reflect the playing staff in being nearly exclusively Croat including Croats living elsewhere in BiH. To such visitors the club acts a sacred center, providing those with a sense of comfort that someone with greater proximity than them to the perceived "Other", is keeping the flame of Croatian identity alive. This same ethos attracts visitors with no local connection. Croat migrants living in Germany seeking to maintain their social ties with the people follow SBNK both online and via periodic visits. Catholic Scottish and Irish football enthusiasts see in the club and its followers a similarity to the ethno-nationalist struggles in their respective nations. The club, whilst having Presidents who are also members of the dominant HDZ political party, does not overtly represent the same Croatian political entity but instead promotes a general Croat cultural identity via this most public of spectacles that proclaims that Croats will not disappear or be silenced by contemporary BiH political arrangements. Its loudest voices in such defiance are the *Škripari*.

THE CATHOLIC CAVE MEN

The *Škripari* are the town's most public male sub-culture. Founded in the immediate post-conflict situation of 1996, they identified with the *ultra* culture of Italian football in terms of choreography and display and the hooligan culture of British football with its penchant for violent confrontation. The *Škripari* consider themselves the 21st century knight Croat patriot defenders of the town. Composed almost exclusively of male members between the ages of 18-50 they are collectively located in the north stands of their home stadium. They display pyrotechnics inside the stadium and carry banners that proclaim the club's name and history and the portraits of Croatian national heroes. Others display sacred Christian symbol alongside the flags of Croatia and the Croatian Republic of Herzegovina. In their club house is a giant painting depicting nine armed *Škripari* from the World War II years holding a banner with a motto reading "Under this Holy flag until Victory". A 2008 a UEFA Championship qualifying match between Široki NK and Beşiktaş JK Istanbul (1-2) saw the *Škripari* display a depiction of a Medieval Croat knight (implicitly a reminder to the visitors of the Crusades), and a banner proclaiming *Antemurale Christianitatis (Bulwark of Christendom)* in honor of a document awarded by the Christian authorities (usually the Pope) to nations who defended Europe from Islam particularly during the Middle-Ages and Renaissance. The *Škripari* thus praise God and celebrate His existence and sustenance.

At the same time, the *Škripari* celebrate their independence from any forces of Mammon. Some vote for the HDZ party, which has controlled the town since the first multi-party elections took place in late 1990. The key players in the *Škripari* never accept any political representative telling them how to act or who to vote for. Similar to other *ultras* attitudes across Europe, the *Škripari* at times display hostility to official political representatives—and to the officials of their club. That said the relations between the *Škripari* and club representatives and politicians is generally good albeit disagreement have occurred over player transfers, the direction of the club and the policing of supporters conduct.

The *Škripari* boast that they do "politics" their way. In the immediate post-war years football was a way for some to continue the hostilities that had sustained massacres in the previous years. The *Škripari* at the time consisted of some 40% veterans who had seen front line action and were very capable in hand to hand combat.

The rest of their numbers consisted of the youths too young for the war years but who sought to do their bit for the Croats' cause and enjoy the recreational fighting and ritualized conflict that football fixtures provided. In these years the *Škripari* attained a reputation in BiH football circles for being both a group that consisted of capable fighters and one that sought out football-related conflict. Visiting SB was something visiting supporters did with some trepidation.

A decade later the *Škripari* declared they only defended themselves and no longer did they seek confrontation; things had changed. The group was never quasi-military in structure. Whilst it had named positions and a sense of hierarchy any policy was hard to enforce. Over the past decade internal tensions have been evident within the group as one would expect from an entity that began in the immediate post-conflict milieu. In recent years most proclaim that they support the club to promote Croat identity and fight only when the group is under attack. Others—lesser in number— seek to return to the older founding policy of the group namely one that celebrated the articulation of ethnic insults and celebrated assaults on rival supporters for both the enjoyment of transgression and as an expression of their assumed superior ethno-nationalist masculinity. The contemporary *Škripari* support the club through singing patriotic songs but generally avoid ethnic or political insults. Exceptions always exist and those are usually ostracized by being dragged out of the stadium or "invited" to leave. Control of miscreants is easier in the stadium than in streets and towns. Rogue elements can enter their proceedings. Such supporters are not seen regularly amongst the *Škripari*. During some high profile matches "mercenary" supporters are present. Some believe these mercenaries were sent by Machiavellian politicians with the objective of creating ethno-political tension. This occurred at the ever contentious Široki Brijeg NK vs. Sarajevo FK fixture (a *de facto* contest between Croat and Bosniaks). In the 2010 fixture two fans who had not hitherto been seen on the terraces brought with them a swastika flag. Most of the regular *ultras* did not support such a display. To other non-Croat onlookers, this only reinforced the past-fascist affiliation of SB and stimulated the potential for further disorders and hatreds. This potential was realized in 2009.

FORTRESS FOOTBALL

Both SBNK and Sarajevo FK have for some 20 years attracted some of the most skilled players and capable coaches in the BiH Premier League. Both clubs carry long-standing ethno-political baggage which the respective fans utilize in displays that are variously; accusatory, insulting and carnivalesque. The fixture however goes beyond a contest of tactics and skills; it is emblematic of the post-conflict relations between the Croatian and Bosniaks communities. The FK Sarajevo *ultras* gather under the name of *Horde Zla* (Hordes of Evil). When playing against Croatian teams their fans articulate insults against Croat nationalists and invoke the killings of the *Ustaše* as a reminder of Croat barbarity. The Sarajevo *ultras* furthermore consider the *Škripari* and implicitly their football club as representative of variously; the HVO, fascism and a long-standing antipathy to Islam. The dark red jersey of Sarajevo FK in the eyes of SB supporters celebrates the (similar) colors of the Turkish national team and the one time Ottoman invader.

Flowers and shapes play a role. The *Horde Zla* express their Bosniak nationalism through the waving of the "fleuer-de-lis". This symbol of *Lilium bosniacum* (a native Bosnian-Herzegovinian flower) was displayed found on uniforms and flags of the Bosnian Army composed almost exclusively by Bosniaks soldiers. Post-War Bosniaks see the flower as "theirs". The same fans at times wave the crescent moons symbol of European Muslim Identity begun at the time of the Ottoman Dynasty of Osman 1 and displayed on the flags of the Turkish military. The fixtures between the two sides provide occasions for rivals to enact feats of invasion and transgression. Such behaviors are always collective in practice but extremes of behavior in such contests can be attributed to individual propensities. Intentions and insults can reach beyond the verbal. Fixtures are often marred with violence and on one occasion death.

On October 4, 2009, some 500 "hard-core" Sarajevo FK *Horde Zla* followers travelled to Široki Brijeg for the clubs fixture against their rivals in a fleet of coaches and some private vehicles. They arrived in SB to challenge the fearsome fighting reputation of the *Škripari*. Some 90 minutes before kick-off the town center streets witnessed running street fights. In origin the disorder involved the *Horde Zla* and concerned and annoyed local (male) SB residents. Once alerted to events the *Škripari* moved all together from their gathering some 400 meters distance away to fight the invaders. The subsequent altercation featuring hand to hand combat with anything moveable thrown across the faction and became one of the largest public disorders in BiH since the war years.

The few dozen uniformed officers present struggled to restore order. Vehicles and shop windows were damaged. Both non-combatant civilians and hardcore fans sustained injuries. A police car was set on fire. Gunshots were fired by both factions. One man fired seven bullets, killing a 24-year old Sarajevo FK supporter named Vedran Puljic (a student by occupation and a religious hybrid by virtue of a Catholic father and a Muslim mother). The autopsy revealed that the bullets were fired from a gun belonging to a police officer on duty that day. The police officer had not fired the shots. The exact circumstances concerning how the officer's gun ended up in the hands of citizen are still unknown. The death of a football fan in the post-conflict milieu was unheard of. The event shocked the Balkan region (Reuters 2009).

The man accused of the murder was Oliver Knezović an ethnic Croat who grew up in Sarajevo. He had once belonged to the Croatian Defense Force paramilitary group named *Kažnjenička Bojna (Punishment Troop)*, a militia noted for their sadism against captured Bosniaks. Arrested and placed in custody, he escaped hours later despite the presence of eight police officers. Knezović made it to neighboring Croatia where he lay low for weeks before eventually turning himself in to the Croatian authorities. Knezović declared to the press that he had indeed taken a police gun from an officer but had long returned the weapon to the owner before the murder. Like many BiH Croats, the suspect held dual Croatian and BiH passports. Since there are no extradition agreements between BiH and Croatia, nine years after the murder the accused remains at liberty.

Culpability stalked the debates. Some believed the bullets could have come from a member of the *Horde Zla* who stole the gun or been fired by a police officer affected by Post-Traumatic Stress Disorder (PTSD). Some police officers on duty faced accusations of being accomplice to the murder; some police remain suspended from duty on charges of negligence and remain under investigation. The disorder and death strengthened the ethnic prejudices. The politicians were fearful that the disorders would escalate and see a return of armed hostilities. The hatred-thankfully- was confined to the articulations of football club representatives and nationalist politicians on sport and news TV programs who predictably accused the "ethnic other" of initiating the violence. Meanwhile there were reputations to defend. The *Škripari* alongside fellow citizens organized a demonstration to both claim their innocence and stress their status as legitimate defenders against unprovoked violence. A march was similarly organized in Sarajevo by the *Horde Zla* denouncing the violence of the Croats and seeking justice for Vedran Puljic. Their accusations stated that the *Škripari* were a modern version of the HVO and they evidenced behavior incompatible with both sporting environments and the post-conflict milieus. The fixture which had been abandoned because of the murder was finally played in November 2009 without visiting fans who were barred from travelling by the Football Association of Bosnia-Herzegovina (Savez) a declaration enforce by the State Civil Forces. The evening fixture ended in a 2-0 victory for the home team and attracted a crowd of some 2,000 who sang Croatian nationalist songs throughout.

OLD WOUNDS, NEW WOUNDS

BiH is far from a healed society and football carries and perpetuates many societal fault-lines. That said, some found a use for the game. In the immediate post-war years various projects to the sum of eight million Euros by the Fédération Internationale de Football Association (FIFA) and the Union of European Football Associations (UEFA) was given Savez to build grassroots football schemes aimed to develop teams and intra-ethnic tournaments to help create a sense of normality. The efficacy of such efforts is forever considered in Sport for Development and Peace debates (Collison et al. 2018). Football might be forever providing a "cruel optimism" (Berlant 2000) but, we would argue, does have a role to play in the post-conflict context. Its stadiums in our analysis provide the outlets to purge emotions, fixtures facilitate antagonisms, obnoxious impulses are conducted under the scrutiny of the state authorities; this realization may contain greater potential violence and indeed might be functional in reducing ethno-political insult and violence in the wider society. When such behaviors occur the state has to respond. Legal debates often ensue, political get involved and all those involved are reminded that words and actions have consequences. A sense of citizenship and notions of civil society are implicit in such controversies.

Various offices have sought to promote civil society through football. Some football-related progress was evidenced with the constitution of on intra-ethnic football league in the 21st century. In 1992, when Savez was begun each "constituent people" (a term to indicate the three major ethnic group of the country Bosniaks, Serbs, Croats) had their own ethnic-league. In 2002, BiH politicians and FIFA members advanced concerns about the possible negative consequences of such an arrangement in terms of it sustaining inter-ethnic tensions and ethnic violence (Sterchele 2012). These concerns were not unfounded. When a national league was created Football did indeed put teams and fans from different ethnic backgrounds in contact. The same league however gave room for physical and verbal violence (Sterchele 2012). UEFA agreed that Savez would be allowed to have a tripartite system similar to the state system of the country, with a rotating presidency; each of the three presidents would represent one ethnic group. This model was also an attempt to encourage the country to by-pass nationalist elites and to invite the country to reform, however, UEFA undermined the notion of power-sharing (Lijphart 1969 in Cooley and Mujanovi 2015) when it warned that this was a temporary scenario and in 2011 FIFA and UEFA handed BiH a suspension from all international football activities with the aim of forcing Savez to have just one permanent president and therefore ease bureaucratic relations between Savez and UEFA and FIFA. Football-related progress is thus complicated, but worth a try. The problem we suspect lies in people not processes.

For all its peace-building rhetoric, Savez was hardly a role model for the much sought civic society Monies given to the organization have been frequently unaccounted for. Corruption in the domestic football contexts is rife; the leagues mired in allegations of match-fixing (Hugson and Skillen 2014; Sterchele 2012). A "normalization committee" in 2011 composed of former BiH football players believed to be good in both negotiation and diplomacy was formed by Savez in an attempt to accommodate FIFA requests. The same year a single president was elected and a 15 member executive board constituted. While the new situation is portrayed as a success for football's governance some football coaches and club officials complain that the solution masks internal ethnic divisions. Furthermore the Bosnia-Herzegovinian national team which supposedly should represent the three constituent people, seen mostly by Croats as a Bosniak concern. Croatian and Serbian players at times have expressed publicly that they were left out at the first participation of BiH at a World Cup in 2014. Some players indeed have claimed to have played all the qualifications matches then omitted from the World Cup squad. These dynamics contribute to the fact that the vast majority of Croats and Serbs support respectively the Croatian and Serbian national team instead of Bosnian-Herzegovinian. People fall back on the familiar.

LIVING IN THE DARK?

In contemporary BiH, all adults can vote in elections that offer the opportunity for representation and implicitly a sense of checks and balance in the political process. But representation is not the issue at large, rather it is the sense of security too easily found in ethno-political nationalism combined with the comfort ever evident in a sense of Place. These primal sentiments see SB as a state within a state wherein its many antagonisms celebrate occasions of collective experiences be they religious or civil; football is such an arena. Recent history makes this so. Croatians have a double-bind to any sense of post-conflict normality. The end of Communism led just two years later to civil war. This double-displacement of social hierarchies has since seen the Croats seeking a sense of who they and who they were (Mouffe 2018). This forces us to ask what *leitmotifs* can or might people live by (Edgerton 2018). A variety of details thus play a role in that question; food, words, alphabets and even melodies provide for ways of being and ways of seeing and celebrating the Croatia of the imagination, a belief inseparable from military contexts and ever drawing comfort and security on the notion of a Merciful Christian God. The eulogized characters of antiquity remain unknowable but function as background chatter periodically resurrected sometimes by politicians trading the cynical manipulation of ethno-political fears for votes (Kripke 1972).

Contemporary SB sees lives shaped by institutions both secular and religious. What we see in SB is the occasional fevered attention to political processes combined with an on-going political disillusionment. In such a context a shared sense of history provides a comfort—and the sense of suffering-become very significant when allied with ethnicity. Believing they constitute a race but live in a nation which both past and present is ever-willing to rebut their sense of "people" their politics react to the unpredictable and are confrontational; they seek to seize political initiatives before their adversaries take advantage. The town acts as a *cordon sanitaire* against those who would seek to harm it and them. In the absence of militia those living in the fortress defend, actually and metaphorically, the ancestral from the ethnic Other, be they the invading hordes of rival football fans or more recently the lawyer, the accountant and the bureaucrat representing that perceived as the hostile state.

The notion of the good citizen is pertinent in all of this. Is it best manifest as a permanent liminality to the current political situation existing as a hostage to ancestral history? How central we might ask must the juxtaposition of cultures be to the everyday process of "getting on" with life? Answers don't come easy, real life is messy; cultures and people drift—class, age and gender play their part. As the post-conflict years add up memory is not as collective as it once was. The youth of the town allow space for the abstract over the portrait and can see their looking glass self-informed by greater realizations provided by global social media. A willingness of the SB entrepreneurial to do business with the ethnic other sees some Croatians going against ethnic exclusivity might even see the ton acting in defiance of the theory of the "Big Sort" (Bishop 2008) evident in the USA.

In all of this, the *Škripari* provide for avenues of negotiation as to what is right and wrong. They are auto-referential but also reflexive on both self and society. They present narratives as to what they stand for and what they oppose. As non-state actors they have carved out an important position for themselves in the post-conflict milieu. Their focus is football and they offer a mainly pleasurable de-personalized narrative appreciative of athletic performance. For today´s *Škripari* the Serb is the ethnic "Other" but not an enemy and whilst some *Škripari* will not socialize in any way with Bosniaks, others have business relations. Like their forefathers they are Croatian nationalists and some exhibit right-wing views but amongst them will be liberals and anarchists. They thus tolerate political antagonism for the sake of the celebration of the same football club and town. Whilst few would ever admit to seeking a multi-ethnic political setting they do not racially abuse African-born footballers and in recent times are condemnatory towards those in their midst articulating racist opinions. The *Škripari* by virtue of their existence force debate around what is appropriate and permissible.

FOOTBALL AS BEACON?

The death of the *Horde Zla* visitor on the street of SB some nine years ago remains unsolved. The accused was trialed in Split, Croatia in 2017. He admitted taking the gun from a police officer and firing 10 bullets towards the *Horde Zla*. There was no evidence however that he fired the bullet that killed. A recent interview with the brother of the deceased saw him claim to know the identity of the killer. He refused to reveal a name claiming that even if he did justice would not follow. The *Škripari* meanwhile argue that the accused was not a SB citizen and his motivation was a product of his Sarajevo upbringing. No further inter-ethnic deaths around football have occurred since that day albeit one fan of Sarajevo was shot dead at a match over a dispute involving control of illegal drug markets in what was an intra-Bosniak issue. On a lighter note SB citizens were out in their thousands to celebrate the successes of the Croatian national team at the 2018 World Cup. Despite being losing finalists the subsequent carnival of celebrations allowed some the opportunity to celebrate the Croatian sense of self as well as articulate political frustrations. The words and songs that praised the Croats intermingled with chants against the state of BiH. Such an event helped the impetus and disgruntled taunt the despised state but in a situation infinitely preferable to the perpetuation of private violence against random Bosniaks citizens. Football was and remains instrumental in making nationalism banal (Billig 1995).

Football can facilitate and at times control raw emotion. It can by its proxy role minimize political antagonism and offer avenues for the diplomat. The club and the stadium permits the performances of the celebration of self, the affirmation of meaning and draws upon and provides for variously; limited and partial inclusiveness, resistance towards the ethnic other and commemorations with the deceased—the stadium being the one public theatre where the dead are celebrated with noise. The game appeals to the everyday citizen and provides a metaphor for a functioning, organic society that is inclusive of all shapes, sizes and mentalities. Football narrates ideas of class, nation, citizenship, gender, commerce, facilitates networks and conviviality and establishes a sense of *communitas* (Turner 2018). It is at national level a membership criteria to Modernity. It invites inquiry as to how a society presents and interprets itself and carries no end of potential for both peaceful co-existence and antagonism. It is also available some for 40 weeks a year. It is never innocent of political machinations but provides a zone in which formal political system cannot easily permeate. It provides a way of coping with tensions permitting celebrations of the past and an arena to negotiate the future. Leaders of nations cannot ignore it.

The post-conflict provides a complex base-line from which to build a new civil society; peace-builders are well aware that what it is we share and what are the biggest differences we live by are crucial to processes of Trust. The notion of political performance is pertinent; if people are cynical about national elites, local ethno-political informal elites become entrenched- who beyond them can citizens trust? (Runciman 2018). Because football is what BiH shares, it carries many seductions, but to put faith in it is risky. Who is policing the masculine hegemony the game produces? In the time of armed conflict and terror where were the masculine censures addressing all forms of violation? If they were not evident then why do we assume they will be in the post-conflict? We might, following Rieff (2016), ask whether in the post-conflict there is a need for less memory. When a people's history is haunting, acts and places provide the texture and interiors for the sense of the eternal return. Can bygones ever be bygones? Forgetting is not forgiving and should not be equated with healing (Ibid.). Crucial to such a notion is the contexts of meaning and memory and when they bring with them a sense of duty.

Football can facilitate dark forces; the game is never entirely rational. Wisdom and arbitration is needed in so many of its contests. And, pertinent to the *Škripari* history teaches us that whilst some enter caves for shelter and protection from enemies, others enter such places seeking wisdom and visions (Hunt 2019). The *Škripari* are not in themselves a dark force, they are however part of the walls and weapons that feature as much in the realities of the earth today as they did in medieval times. We might best see them as the *Agora* of the town, a forum willing to be introspective about themselves as much as accusatory towards the ethnic "Other". Meanwhile there are other dark forces to be negotiated in BiH some of which have wider geo-political resonance. In June 2018 Britain sent 40 military personnel to BiH to join a 600 strong joint NATO and EU "specialist surveillance and intelligence task force" named Operation Althea to assist in the prevention of Russian meddling in the BiH Presidential elections scheduled for October. We might conclude thus that football as a most public arena of social life and indeed civil society can make things seem darker because the light is ever on it.

Acknowledgements

The authors are indebted to the people of Siroki Brijeg and those employed in various capacities in BiH football for their time and reflections.

References

Anscombe, Frederick. 2014. *State, Faith, and Nation in Ottoman and Post-Ottoman Lands*. Cambridge: Cambridge University Press.
Berlant, Lauren. 2011. *Cruel Optimism*. Durham NC: Duke University Press.
Billig, Michael. 1995. *Banal Nationalism*. London: Sage.
Bougarel, Xavier. 2017. *Islam and Nationhood in Bosnia-Herzegovina: Surviving Empires*. Bloomsbury: London.
Bishop, Bill, and Robert Cushing. 2008. *The Big Sort: Why the Cluster of Like Minded Americans is Tearing Us Apart*. Boston, MA: Houghton and Mifflin.
Collison, Holly, Simon Darnell, Richard Giulianotti and David Howe. 2018. *Routledge Handbook of Sports for Development and Peace*. London: Routledge.

Cooley, Laurence and Jasmin Mujanovic. 2015. "Changing the Rules of the Game: Comparing FIFA/UEFA and EU Attempts to Promote Reform of Power-Sharing Institutions in Bosnia-Herzegovina." *Global Society* 29(1)1: 42-63.

Edgerton, David. 2018. *The Rise and Fall of the British Nation: A Twentieth Century History.* London: Allen Lane.

Gold, John, and George Revill. 2014. "Landscapes of Defence." *Political Science* 29(3): 229-239.

Hayden, Robert. 2012. *From Yugoslavia to the Western Balkans: Studies of a European Disunion, 1991-2011.* Leiden and Boston: BRILL.

Hugson. John, and Fiona Skillen. 2014. *Football in South Eastern Europe. Form Ethnic Homogenization to Reconciliation.* London: Routledge.

Hunt, Will. 2019. *Underground. A Human History of the Worlds Beneath our Feet.* London: Simon and Schuster.

Keil, Soeren, and Valerie Perry. 2015. *State Building and Democratization in Bosnia and Herzegovina. South Eastern Studies.* London: Routledge.

Kripke, Saul. 1972. *Naming and Necessity.* Cambridge, MA: Harvard University Press.

Lijphart, Arend. 1969. "Consociational Democracy." *World Politics* 21(2): 207-225.

Mouffe, Chantal. 2018. *For a Left Populism.* London: Verso.

Ramet, Sabina, and Ola Listhuag .2011. *Serbia and the Serbs in World War Two.* Basingstoke: Palgrave Macmillan.

Redžić, Enver, and Robert Donia. 2005. *Bosnia and Herzegovina in the Second World War.* London: Cass Military Studies.

Reuters. 2009. 'Soccer-Violence in Bosnia leaves one dead, 22 injured'. *Reuters World Football*, October 4.

Rieff, David. 2016. *In Praise of Forgetting: Historical Memories and Its Ironies.* New Haven: Yale University Press.

Runciman, David. 2018. *How Democracy Ends.* London: Profile.

Sterchele, David. 2012. "Fertile Land or Mined field? Peace-Building and Ethnic Tensions in Post-war Bosnian Football." *Sport and Society* 16(8): 973-992.

Turner, Keith. 2018. *Communitas: The Anthropology of Collective Joy.* Basingstoke: Palgrave MacMillan.

Wingfield, Nancy. 2003. *Creating the Other; Ethnic Conflict and Nationalism in Habsburg Central Europe.* New York and Oxford: Berghahn.

CHAPTER 14

Sport for Development and Peace (SDP): The Shadow from Within

Cora Burnett

INTRODUCTION

In the first instance, the SDP sector represents a humanitarian oriented social movement described by Bruce Kidd (2008, 370) as "a mushrooming phenomenon, [in] the use of sport and physical activity to advance and broaden social development in disadvantaged communities". The nature of such a movement lies in the wide variety of sport-related interventions designed, managed and implemented by a wide spectrum of agencies, partnerships and networks. Secondly, the SDP sector features multiple stakeholder configurations and institutional frameworks, from the private or commercial and private sectors within and outside the direct sphere of the sport fraternity. Thirdly, it is associated with sport mega event legacy programmes and fourthly, it features policy frameworks from global agencies, such as the United Nations and sport powerhouses (Giulianotti 2011). It also proclaims a high level of civic society involvement through non-governmental or community-based organizations as implementing partners (Kidd 2013; Schulenkorf and Adair 2014).

"Mapping the field" publications show extreme levels of diversity in thematic areas, methodological approaches, knowledge production mechanisms, disciplinary fields and programmes within two different overarching domains, namely relating to sport delivery on wider social issues (sport plus models) and sport as social construct with inherent competitive characteristics and value propositions (plus sport models) (Cronin 2011; Schulenkorf, Sherry, and Rowe 2016). Such comprehensive material seldom penetrates the deeper levels of critical analysis to reveal challenges within the sector.

The dark side for the Sport for Development and Peace field is complex, multi-faceted, layered and multi-levelled. It does not present itself in clear recognizable forms of deviance or transgressions, although such incidences may exist at operational levels of programme implementation. At the core of SDP work, lies unequal power relations, Western domination reminiscent of neocolonial and imperialist notions of superiority and biased knowledge production that questions the very legitimacy of 'development' as a highly ambiguous concept and phenomenon (Coalter 2013a and b; Darnell 2018).

The "darkness" is within the deep structures of SDP as movement (Kidd 2008), the configuration and positionality of stakeholders with the United Nation agencies spearheading the Sustainable Development Goals in partnership with global sport agencies, such as the International Olympic Committee (IOC) and International Federation of Association Football (FIFA). Multiple global and local stakeholders have since 2003 entered into partnerships and continue to dominate SDP interventions in developing contexts (Guilianotti 2011; Burnett 2017 and 2018b). The ingrained fault lines hide uncomfortable truths that reveal crosscutting discourses and critical issues for future policy development, structures and practices.

SDP SECTOR

Profiling the SDP Sector

There is a significant Western ideological bias of programmes implemented by the developed economies or Global North holding ownership and power over projects implemented in the Global South, also known as the two-thirds world (Cronin 2011; Lindsey and Grattan 2012; Darnell et al. 2018). An integrated literature review shows that 92% of the total 383 researchers were from Europe (37%), North America (36%) and Oceania (Australia and New Zealand) (19%) undertaking research in their own regions, as well as in 9% of research conducted in Africa (Schulenkorf, Sherry and Rowe 2016). A different trend emerged for Africa-based sport for development projects and research production.

Findings from a systemic mapping of sport for development in Africa support the assumption held by the Sport for Development and Peace International Working Group that sport-related interventions mainly boast international ownership of sport, play and physical activity programmes in low- and middle-income countries and impoverished communities (Langer 2015). Within a global context, the latter figuration displays geopolitical dynamics associated with development work where international agencies (mostly being from the Global North) engage in cross-border and inter-continental development work. However, this is unique to developing economic contexts as the global systematic mapping of the field demonstrates increasing multi-directional and diverse engagement arrangements (Schulenkorf, Sherry and Rowe 2016). Another special feature of Africa-based sport for development initiatives relates to the fact that most evidence stems from impact assessments driven and funded by international agencies (61%) of which 88% of the programmes delivered involved soccer (Langer 2015).

Global-local Articulation

Global trends, associated with sport and the "developing world", relate to global phenomena, such as the rising states offering sport mega-events and the growth of the SDP movement (Black and Northam 2017 and 2018). The (capitalist) market economy within increased globalization mainly drives sport for development initiatives in impoverished communities and focus on at-risk disenfranchised populations, prioritizing as many as 13 target populations (Hayhurst 2009; United Nations 2018). The latter constitutes an "aid market" with recognizable top-down implementation and tangible "aid effects" to be considered as a (profitable) return on investment (Hayhurst and Giles 2013).

Even in national and local contexts, neoliberal conditions create a market or niche for various agencies to uplift or develop indigenous populations. Such programmes in Canada "pursue Aboriginal peoples as viable targets for SDP interventions" (Hayhurst and Giles 2013, 506). In the Canadian context, critical scholars question the "moral authority" that justifies non-state actors to transmit European values that the local Aboriginal communities want to resist (Hayhurst and Giles 2013).

Guest (2009), who reports a similar case, critically reflects on the notion of universal humanism and Olympism as homogenizing ideology. In this case, local Angolan community members opposed the virtues of individualism and programme outcomes leading to improved perceptions of self-worth. The focus on enhancing the self-esteem of participants rings hollow in a culture that celebrates and supports collective consciousness and value social relationships and networking as survival strategies in the context of extreme poverty.

Circumstances, threatening the survival of a nation or community, breed different value propositions and require well-designed programmes that should address real needs in coherence with other peacekeeping or educational initiatives. Programmes based on neoliberal values that focus on individual behavioral changes and self-regulation, have minimal relevancy or lasting effects (Darnell 2010; Darnell and Hayhurst 2011; Hartmann and Kwauk 2011; Burnett 2018b). Sport for development work may make modest inroads under special conditions in war-torn countries and deeply divided societies as described in the study of Cardenas (2016) that focused on Colombia (guerrilla and paramilitary resistance) and Northern Ireland (Protestant and Catholic divisions). In such settings, overarching political, religious and/or cultural issues and identity formation, shape and temper individual and social change and agency.

SDP programmes are highly dependent on the socio-political will and climate to build personal relationships and break down the stereotypical and divisionary barriers between the reference population and the "othering". The *Football for Peace* programme bears witness to the slow and challenging process of bridging between Jewish and Palestinian youth across socio-political fault lines in different communities (Sugden 2010 and 2014). Influential agencies largely suppress such learnings from local contexts, while spearheading a global policy discourse evident in unequal power relations and changing political landscapes.

Global Policy Frameworks and Configurations

United Nations Leadership

Various UN declarations paved the way for numerous inter-governmental processes and policy mandates. These include the 1959 UN Declaration of the Rights of the Child to play and recreation; the 1978's International Charter of Physical Education and Sport; the 1989 Convention on the Rights of the Child; and the 1999 Declaration of Punta Del Este (United Nations 1959, 1989, 2002, 2003 and 2005).

Since the 1990s, the United Nation agencies propagated the use of sport as a cost-effective tool for contributing to the achievement of the Millennium Development Goals (up to 2015) and more recently, the Sustainable Development Goals (Beutler 2008, Black and Northam 2018). The United Nations provided institutional leadership for mobilizing stakeholders from various sectors by appointing a Special Advisor to the United Nations Secretary-General on Sport for Development and Peace in 2001, and establishing the UN Inter-Agency Task Force on Sport for Development and Peace in 2003. Since then, the UN Assembly passed a series of resolutions focusing on sport as a means to promote education, health, development and peace. At the height of driving this agenda of SDP, the United Nations declared 2005 as the International Year for Sport and Physical Education (IYSPE) (Beutler 2008). By doing that, many agencies within diverse sectors engaged with the SDP sector or negotiated space to advance their own agendas (Levermore 2008; Giulianotti 2011; Kidd 2011; Schulenkorf, Sherry and Rowe 2016; Darnell 2018).

The transfer of the SDP portfolio from the United Nations Office of Sport for Development and Peace (UNOSDP), on its closure in 2017, to the Department of Economic and Social Affairs, accelerated the process of mainstreaming SDP initiatives. This happened through synthesizing information, policy development and focused on the implementation of sport-based initiatives across a broad range of stakeholders (United Nations 2018). This strategic move directed the mainstreaming SDP policies and practices in commitment to delivering on the United Nations 2030 Agenda with meaningful consequences for policy coherence and resource allocation. At the General Conference of UNESCO held in Paris from 30 October to 14 November 2017, all representatives from sport and physical education ministries (MINEPS VI) accepted the Kazan Action Plan drafted under the Chairpersonship of the UN International Working Group for SDP (IWG SDP). This plan serves as:

> ...a voluntary, overarching reference for fostering international convergence amongst policy-makers in the fields of physical education, physical activity and sport, as well as a tool for aligning international and national policy in these fields with the United Nations 2030 Agenda. (UNESCO 2017 as referenced in United Nations 2018, Resolution 71/160—A.4).

By passing UN resolution 71/160 at the UN General Assembly, a new United Nations Action Plan on SDP, coordinated between UN agencies, became a reality as they committed to a common agenda. This agenda focused on "improved coherence and collaboration in placing sport at the service of humanity, as an enabler of sustainable development" (United Nations 2018, Resolution 71/160—Summary). At the core of this resolution and based on the input of members states, the UN system identified 10 of the 17 Sustainable Development Goals and 36 associated targets to be addressed through sport, physical activity and physical education. This resolution contributed to internal changes of UN agencies for a more coherent and aligned approach towards SDP.

The convergence of UN agencies and their traditional stakeholders represent an integrated approach and collective steering of crosscutting agendas. It brought institutionalized sport and physical education practices within its programmatic and policy offerings. For instance, in 2016 and 2017, UNESCO and its partners piloted Quality Physical Education in Fiji, Mexico, South Africa and Zambia for revising national physical education policies and school sport practices, ensuring human rights (child-centered and value-based education) and social transformation agendas (United Nations 2018). Related to the pilot in South Africa, 27 researchers from nine public universities collaborated in a national study on the state and status of physical education in South African public schools. Findings revealed nation-wide engagement of the NGO sector within the Life Skills/Life Orientation school curriculum where physical education is located by offering "life skills" premised on a fusion of SDP work in articulation with prescribed curricula content (Burnett 2018a).

It seems that SDP work and agencies have found their way into formal school curricula as a trend of national-level mainstreaming and service-provision by NGO actors in the field. The value proposition of SDP programmes within schools (physical education and school sport) has been promoted by stakeholders from health and sport sectors in search of finding institutional legitimacy and an expanded reach (Sanders, Phillips and Vanreusel 2012; Shehu 2014). At the local levels, engaging SDP agencies for upskilling teachers is not widely accepted as sound educational practice, despite the offering of additional resources and filling the gap in the absence of government response to the plight of resource-poor schools and communities (Njelesani 2011).

Such development dynamics do not occur in isolation and the UN-IOC partnership inevitably would have implications for traditional SDP agencies and actors in search of new opportunities to expand their influence and presence within SDP spheres.

UN-IOC Partnership and Leadership from the Sport Sector

In a bold strategic move, the President of the International Olympic Committee (IOC), Thomas Bach, and the UN Secretary-General, António Guterras, agreed on the establishment of a direct UN-IOC partnership (*The Sport Digest* 2017). This decision contributed to a more streamlined approach and afforded UN agencies, involved in various SDP initiatives, access to the Olympic Movement as partners. The latter entailed 206 National Olympic Committees and a vast network of stakeholders, from the global to local levels. This partnership thus set the scene for a meaningful symbiosis regarding policy, structure and practice, whilst recognizing the autonomy of both entities. This agreement caught the SDP sector by surprise, but had a long history of engagement with a shared vision and benefits.

Since 2015, the IOC selected six priority Sustainable Development Goals to be a directive for their "development work" in alignment with their strategic objectives and Olympic Solidarity funded projects. These goals include health (Goal 3), quality education (Goal 4), gender equality (Goal 5), sustainable cities and communities (Goal 11), peace, justice and strong institutions (Goal 16) and partnership (Goal 17) (United Nations 2018). In pursuit of these goals, key changes took place regarding ensuring gender equality and humanitarian assistance associated with mega events and legacy programmes. In the new "direct partnership" between the UN and IOC, institutional change is prominent on the agenda for development.

Policy coherence and convergence of SDP work across the UN system led to the adoption in August 2018 of resolution 37/18 entitled, "Promoting human rights through sport and the Olympic ideal", driven by the Social Forum of the Human Rights Council and thematic panel discussion around the Olympic Games, commencing at Tokyo 2020 (United Nations 2018). This set the scene for recent developments and holds specific consequences for the SDP sector in chartering a way on how "development work" may take shape within the elite sport fraternity at all levels of engagement.

For the IOC, this strategic alliance provides a significant avenue for delivering on the Olympic Agenda 2020 mandate with the focus on credibility, sustainability and youth augmented by the *Olympism in Action* strategy (United Nations 2018). The IOC has made great strides since having UN observer status from 2009. The recognition of 6 April as International Day of Sport for Development and Peace, carries special symbolism as date reminiscent of the beginning of the first modern Olympic Games in 1986 (Darnell 2018, 429).

At regional and national level, similar dynamics were at play. The Olympic Movement maintained a high level of independence and focused mainly on delivering competitive sport and athlete development with dealing in SDP types of initiatives through their own commissions (e.g. offering Olympic and Olympism education) or as part of Olympic legacy programmes. There is no clear mandate for national Olympic committees and sport federations at national level to drive SDP initiatives or engage with the NGO-sector as possible implementing or strategic partners (Burnett 2017). *Ad hoc* development work within the sport fraternity delivered examples of good practice and boast a longstanding legacy of exemplary humanitarian actions.

SDP activism gained public recognition when Olympic speed skating champion, Johann Koss, mobilized other stakeholders to donate funds for war victims in Sarajevo and Afghanistan in the early nineties. Such demonstrative acts led to the establishment of Olympic Aid that became the *Right to Play* programme where Commonwealth Games Canada played a key role. A plethora of initiatives and stakeholders came on board to drive a human rights agenda with United Nation agencies providing leadership and strategic (policy) direction (Kidd 2011).

Mega-sport event legacy programmes featured outreach development work with the London 2012 Olympic Games host pledging access to educational sport for 12 million children in 20 countries (Kidd 2011). Prior to, and following the 2012 London Summer Olympic Games, other legacy programmes mostly delivered sport development and sport for development (including Olympic Education) to schools and institutions within the host country (Kay 2012).

Olympic Movement outreach programmes, such as the Olympic Values Educational Programme (OVEP), became part of community-based offerings of National Olympic Committees (NOCs) funded by Olympic Solidarity (Burnett 2017, Naul et al. 2017). In 1988, the then IOC President, Juan Antonio Samaranch, expanded Olympism in Africa through a network of 20 Olympafrica centers (Guest

2009). The UN-IOC alliance affords the Olympic Movement the opportunity to expand on the implementation of the Olympic Values Education Programme (OVEP) for inclusion in physical education curricula in host and non-host countries (Burnett 2017; Naul et al. 2017).

Other global sport organizations declared a similar commitment. For instance, the Commonwealth Secretariat under the leadership of the Head of Sport for Development and Peace, added Goal 8 (economic growth and decent work), whilst the Commonwealth Games Federations (CGF) established a foundation to channel SDP initiatives (Commonwealth Secretariat 2015 and 2017). A key challenge for these two entities relates to the isolated way in which they address similar issues on SDP across Commonwealth countries. Whereas the Commonwealth Secretariat mainly provides the policy directions for the government sector, the CGF has yet to engage with the SDP sector, as its main focus is to ensure that Commonwealth Games associations are well prepared in terms of sport and athlete development to compete in the Commonwealth Games.

FIFA is another key player in the field of sport and development. Although legacy programmes deliver questionable impact associated with sustainable development, it contributed to high levels of liminality and national identity formation for FIFA World Cup host and competing countries (Cornellisen 2011; Black and Northam 2018). The "Sport for Good" agenda of FIFA has made meaningful inroads since the 2010 FIFA World Cup by mobilizing resources and advocating a social agenda for societal change. Since 2010, 20 Football for Hope Centers were established across the African continent and in most cases, these are managed by NGOs delivering sport for development programmes to local communities (Cornelissen 2011). In 2016, FIFA 2.0 was launched as their strategic road map to promote football and harness its "social power …a catalyst for leading and shaping societal change" regarding international development, sustainability and driving an impactful human rights agenda (United Nations 2018). Such initiatives represent a more human face to elite and exclusionary elite sport practices that represent an influential block to the existing SDP sector.

As development and humanitarian work mostly take place in challenging contexts, it seldom follows a linear or smooth pathway or deliver on all intended outcomes. In a sense, it assimilates the messiness of everyday life and, in some circumstances, accomplish little within contexts where systemic and ideological issues dictate "development". Not all challenges lie outside the influence sphere of agencies in the field. Often it is at the very core of well-intended actions or part of the hidden agendas of influential actors. The next section addresses the current discourses of concern related to SDP work as a field of scientific inquiry.

CHALLENGES FACED BY SDP SECTOR

Unequal Power Relations of SDP Partnerships

Hierarchical power arrangements

International and the foreign flow of funding and ownership of SDP projects are rooted in the politics of "development" and construction of neocolonial spaces (Kay 2012). Such spaces, processes and mechanisms are reminiscent of earlier forms of paleo colonialism, described by Chakrabarty (2012, 142) as "European domination" being justified by the notion of developing the under-developed is a "civilizing mission". The one-directional flow of financial resources, socio-political ownership and dominance are evident in dispensing of neocolonial worldviews and products in the form of sport for development initiatives from a northern core to a southern periphery (Colilli 2013). It comes in nuanced and masked forms of subtle persuasion. Envisaged change is premised on the expectations and needs of the donor or dominant partner, who determines what type of change should be engineered and valued (Coalter 2013a).

Sport for development narratives from donors often convey 'bask in the glory effects' of doing good to the less privileged and inform the subtext of the Sustainable Development Goals in tackling global inequalities. Cost-benefit trade-off scenarios suggest a business model where economic capital demonstrates multiplier effects on diverse recipient constituencies (Darnell 2018). Particularly the corporate and private funders reduce complex realities to manageable components. They pursue rigorous management and marketing principles and favor the reporting of "most significant changes" packaged as success stories, regardless of convincing or clear causality between the intervention and outcomes. Not only are outcomes mediated and filtered in pre-determined categories of programme effects without academic rigor or critical scrutiny, but only the most positive achievements feature. This practice of reporting and building a case for a programme and organization is done with evangelical zeal (Tiessen 2011). Positioned at the bottom of a socio-political hierarchy, implementing partners are compelled to demonstrate success or face the prospect of losing a project or continued funding (Coalter 2013a and b).

Issue of Sustainability

Guilianotti (2011) identified key clusters of stakeholders within the Sport for Development and Peace (SDP) sector, namely non-governmental, non-profit organizations (e.g. *streetfootballworld*), intergovernmental and governmental organizations (e.g. UNICEF), corporates (e.g. Corporate Social Responsibility/ Investments, such as the Nike Foundation) and radical NGOs. Social networks boast multiple types of partnership arrangements that varies in degree of formal versus non-formal stakeholder configurations. The funding sources and type of partnerships inevitably reflect the centrality of powerful and resource-rich partners positioned in an asymmetrical power arrangement with relative dependent agencies at the periphery of decision-making (Guilianotti 2011).

Without challenging the seat of power, masked in notions of equal but different partnership arrangements, neocolonial philosophies and dominance continue to govern development work (Bray 2003). Sustainable service delivery has become the key to safeguard donor investment and a way to ensure that an exit strategy is possible within multiple stakeholder arrangements. Top-down planning do not only silence local voices, but override possible multi-directional and complex community level stakeholder collaboration and reciprocal benefits (Schulenkorf and Sugden 2011; Schulenkorf, Sugden and Burdsey 2014).

Stakeholders do not always fit into clear-cut categories and may transcend expected operational arrangements. For instance, the fusion of boundaries account for categorization of competitive sport as sport-for-development practices as in the case of the Pacific Netball Partnership (PNP), where the national Australian Netball Federation and partners assisted with implementing netball in five Pacific Island Nations (Sherry et al. 2017). The latter study identified multi-levelled implementation barriers ranging from culture, patriarchal ideology, infrastructure, health awareness, development priorities and the lack of local stakeholder collaboration in addition to competing sport codes. However, the layers of marginalization based on the national profile, status of netball and accessibility of opportunities for girls and women do not articulate the exclusion of most girls and women, who do not take part in netball within the local contexts mitigating against the assumption of 'shared sisterhood' or the homogeneity of females. It seems to be an emerging trend that donor agencies prefer well-structured and institutionalised sport agencies to become the channels of implementation. Such an arrangement ensures stable governance, optimal reach and sustainable channels for programme management and delivery.

Volunteerism and Youth Empowerment

Volunteerism in Perspective

Peer education forms the cornerstone of many community-driven and community-based, sport for development projects implemented by local NGOs. In many developing contexts, unemployed youth find themselves in a compromising situation of volunteering as sport coaches or facilitators with the expectation of increased opportunities for employment (Burnett 2012). This lays a trap for youth to remain in exploitative circumstances, as an improved employability status does not necessarily lead to formal employment or even steady income-generation (Coalter 2013a). An implementing NGO may recruit unemployed youth, contract and train them as implementers for which they are remunerated. In the African context, it is well known that such youth coaches are paid a minimum wage or stipend based on the level of funding and to the discretion of the employer (Van der Klashorst 2018).

Common practice is to acknowledge peer-educators for their dedication and roll modeling without having the means or access for decent wages or employment (Burnett 2012). This creates a double-edge sword by upskilling youth workers without offering them career pathways, but at the same time facing the challenge of losing them should they be successful in securing other employment. A hybrid model of volunteer-work captures this reality as "youth leaders" (often over the age of thirty and being parents) cannot survive on "pure volunteering". The over-simplification of fixing lives through life skill education for youth, who "volunteered" as coaches in an Olympic grassroots outreach programme, led to high levels of frustration and resistance as the latter expected to be paid for their effort (Guest 2009). This sentiment finds expression in the following narrative:

> The message from the programme coordinators—'this is not for profit it's for the life skills'—did not resonate with Pena residents. The Pena residents felt that they needed jobs more than what seemed to them an arbitrary list of 'life skills'. (Guest 2009, 1345)

Youth Empowerment

In *Stories from the Field,* several case studies attest to the reality that almost all peer-educators or youth coaches struggled to survive on their earnings from their NGO employer (Burnett 2012). These case studies convey a picture of exploitation, helplessness and desperation rather than reported outcomes of "youth empowerment" and positive youth development (PYD). Positive youth development is a contentious concept for they follow a unique trajectory of development within different peer group clustering (Darnell 2010). Neoliberal ideology underpins the notion of youth empowerment guided by societal norms and standards evident in good pro-social behavior. In interlinks with the discourse of individual development and empowerment, which is grounded in the assumption that individuals can make moral and economic choices that would lift them out of circumstances of poverty (Coakley 2011).

In the conceptualization of empowerment, Lawson (2005, 149) exposes false and narrow forms that are not substantiated in real life situations, but mostly found in Sport for development jargon as an assumed result of a one-way process. Similarly, Forde (2014) discusses how empowerment activities and life skill education fail to have meaningful results for individuals and collectives facing systemic and ideological challenges. This is well illustrated by a HIV/AIDS prevention programme that

> …demonstrates that discourses of risk, individualism, and deficiency constructed life skills in a way that aligned with neoliberal approaches to health promotion and development, emphasizing risk management and individual responsibility, while glossing over the broader social and political factors influencing HIV transmission. (Forde 2014, 287)

Contracting HIV is a complex issue and prevention of this disease does not rely on individual will power to abstain from sexual relationships or with an isolated educational response in terms of self-improvement. Programming and utilizing young people as agents of change necessitate that real change in their life circumstances should be on the agenda of sport for development initiatives. Successful agencies, such as *Kick for Life* (located in Maseru, Lesotho) and MYSA (located in a slum area on the outskirts of Nairobi, Kenya), provide scholarships and income-generating opportunities as a pathway toward youth empowerment and employment. Peer educators or youth leaders are part of the vulnerable populations they serve and donors should consider them as first order recipients of development. Burnett (2014, 17) reflects critically on proclaimed youth empowerment by stating:

> It is an issue of perpetuated inequality and partial inclusion masked as notions of empowerment, because training for programme implementation rarely facilitates independence and agency. Making a living out of coaching sport is not a reality, while transferring experience from the sport context to the world of work is equally challenging.

Should a programme not deliver on the perceived (positive) outcomes and development philosophy, the blame for failing to deliver is put squarely on the shoulders of the implementing agency, whose leadership in turn shifts blame to youth offering programmes. Just as a losing team's coach carries the blame for poor performance, if sport for development programmes fail, youth implementers bear the brunt for they are easily replaceable in contexts of high youth unemployment.

Deficit Discourse

The manifestations of poverty are multi-faceted and interwoven in real life circumstances of individuals and collectives. Risk-taking and anti-social behavior do not rest with poor or uninformed decision-making only. It is a wider social issue entrenched in socialization practices, ideology, culture and survival strategies with a reach far beyond bio-power and individual choice (Darnell and Hayhurst 2011). It is also questionable if sport-related interventions alone can address such societal issues on the premise that it is anti-social behaviors that stand to be corrected.

Coalter (2013a) spoke out against the deficit approach and argued that impoverished populations are not inherently "deviant", but shaped by multiple influences in their respective social worlds. Inherent in this critique, is the reality that Eurocentric views prioritize foreign insights of "othering", framed by (Western) ways of knowing and doing, rather than having contextual relevance and transfer agency to people earmarked for development (Tiessen 2011). This reflects a reproductive vision of development and assigning sport for development programmes unsubstantiated outcomes of minimal real relevance for target populations.

Larger societal issues are entrenched in systemic inequalities as voiced by Hartmann and Kwauk (2011, 291):

> …it is not really about structural transformation and change. Rather, it is primarily about sport's ability to resocialize and recalibrate individual youth and young people that, in turn, serves to maintain power and hierarchy, cultural hegemony, and the institutionalization of poverty and privilege. It is, in other words, a fundamentally reproductive vision of development.

Sport for development discourses emanate from various research paradigms and philosophical orientations. One of the main challenges relates to knowledge production, research approaches and researchers' positionality.

Knowledge Production

Neocolonial Domination and Donor Biases

Many researchers schooled in Western research traditions without conducting extensive fieldwork, often reproduce neoliberal understandings of complex social issues (Kay 2012). Although there are researchers questioning the neo-liberal ideas and practices, alternative frameworks as analytical tools are lacking in addition to in-depth comprehension of the social world realities of research participants (Darnell and Hayhurst 2011). This is not an easy code to break as New World black thinkers like C.L.R. James and W.E.B. DuBois argued that Western Marxists remained unconsciously bound by Eurocentric perspectives (Pithouse 2013).

Neocolonial ideology underpins rationalistic models and linear frames of development that reproduces and validates prominent discourses rather than generate new perspectives (Kay 2012). In addition to this bias, reliance on monitoring and evaluation work for generating knowledge, adds another layer to neoliberal beliefs regarding development. Impact assessments of sport for development programmes contribute to a critical mass of knowledge despite apparent biases stemming from donor expectations that in turn is often informed by global policy frameworks and agendas in search of proof of significant social change (Levermore 2011; Schulenkorf, Sherry and Rowe 2016).

Following this reasoning, the outcomes aligned with the expectations of donors may take priority, but should be understood in a broader sphere of influence and acknowledgment of variables that may impact on outcomes. People live their lives in a messy, multi-directional and integrated way with streams of influence and sense-making inclusive of a multitude of experiences. For instance, reporting a positive educational outcome linked an interventionist strategy or it should be positioned and understood in terms of the relationship with broader educational efforts within households, schools and communities (Svensson, Hancock and Hums 2016).

The preference for qualitative research paradigms and explorative or descriptive approaches seek explanations of deep structures embedded in context. Such research provides key insights, but results are not scalable or extrapolated to meaningfully contribute to discourse development. On the other side, positivist quantitative methodology delivered on the scientific rigor, but lack contextually informed explanations and explorative depth (Darnell et al. 2018).

Alternative Approaches and Contextual Realities

The lack of evidence as a prominent discourse in SDP research stems from a need for more rigorous research. It relates to the need of more complex research designs and methodology that would overcome positivistic evaluations inherent in quantitative approaches, whilst addressing the limitations of qualitative localized case studies (Levermore 2011).

The neo-liberal individualistic determination (and, by implication, global consensus) contrasts with non-Western-ness and different non-Western epistemologies (Levermore 2011). There is a dire need for discourse development and theory-building to understand how SDP work carries meaning and motivates actions in intersecting the social worlds of people, collectives and agencies. Postcolonial theory in synthesis with actor-oriented sociology may provide a strategic framework for a critical analysis of and reflection on SDP policies and policy models. The challenge here is about questioning rather than endorsing the assumed cascading of growth effects encapsulated by the grant narratives of developmentalism (Hayhurst 2009).

SDP research favors specific theoretical frameworks like Positive Youth Development and Social Capital, but lack critical sociological inquiry embedded in praxis (Darnell et al. 2018). For this reason, critical work by Coalter (2013a) and Sugden (2014) are highly acclaimed. Sugden draws on the critically grounded sociological work of C. Wright Mills and "the sociological imagination" that centralizes context and historical positioning of phenomena. His choice of left realism incorporates local agency "enabling practitioners to ask pertinent, challenging questions and grow strategies for intervention that are appropriate for the local context within which they find themselves working" (Sugden 2014, 84).

The challenge of producing meaningful and authentic knowledge lies at the ontological and epistemological levels with southern theory and postmodern and postcolonial research paradigms holding most promise. For instance, the Interpretative Phenomenological Approach (IPA) provides an alternative to traditional Western thought systems by producing an understanding of context and process. Such approaches, inclusive of grounded theoretical frameworks, are not used widely (Haudenhuyse, Theeboom and Coalter 2012).

Co-construction of Knowledge

The lack of evidence discourse in SDP research speaks to inadequate scientific rigor, as well as limitations of small-scale projects for extrapolated learnings. In the quest to counter dominant neocolonial and Western paradigms, researchers increasingly utilize Participatory Action Research (PAR) methodology (Darnell and Hayhurst 2011). PAR entails a participatory process and reciprocal agency between researcher and research participant, whilst focusing on capturing indigenous ways of knowing and local understanding of how social phenomena affect them (Nicholls, Giles and Sethna 2011).

A radical understanding of development is required where all parties critically reflect how sport reproduces or challenges inequalities in real-life contexts and report nuanced shifts towards meaningful change with proof of causality and acknowledgment of limitations. Equality in partnership arrangements and shared ownership would not only include the "voices" of the indigenous or target populations, but also elicit meaningful engagement for mutual sense-making and praxis.

The Shadow from Within

The high level of diversity of interventions and developmentalist rhetoric premised on neocolonial insights, morality and entitlement, championed the "power of sport" with idolized politicians (such as Nelson Mandela and Kofi Annan) professing to sport as inherently "good". Critical voices are often seen as overly pessimistic indicating that it is the experience of "sport" or "site of engagement" that may have some effect on some people in specific circumstances.

Not only should critical work question the ontological and epistemology of sport-related phenomena, but further investigate the "deep structures" of knowledge production centralizing context and how real people construct and make sense of their social worlds in which SDP work is located. Addressing neocolonial underpinnings of theory, structures and practices may open a pathway towards a new vision, innovative and meaningful practices and accountability of all engaged in humanitarian work. Bridging the Global-North and South divides does not lie in paternalistic notions of some scholars to "build capacity", which is in itself a "savior mentality", nor does it lie in proclaiming indigenous validity or building a "southern theory" reflective of multiple and subaltern realities.

Critical multi-disciplinary research and knowledge production is in the first instance the obligation of public sociologists and, secondly, the task of scholars who need to conduct meaningful, scientific and strategic research in support of theory building and praxis. In a thought-provoking piece, entitled *Working with the grain to change the grain: Moving beyond the Millennium Development Goals* (Vernon and Baksh 2010), the authors examine processes underlying the transformation in society in search of a different development paradigm for stakeholders at all levels of engagement. This reaches beyond current discourses in the field of SDP. It displays a shadow from within that requires a radical re-invention and reflection of all working in, for and against the "grain".

References

Beutler, Ingrid. 2008. "Sport Serving Development and Peace: Achieving the Goals of the United Nations through Sport." *Sport in Society* 11 (4): 359–69.

Black, David, and Katelynn Northam. 2017. "Mega-events and 'Bottom-up' Development: Beyond Window Dressing?" *South African Journal for Research in Sport, Physical Education and Recreation* 39 (Special Edition 1/2): 1–17.

———. 2018. "Mega-Events and "Bottom-up" Development." In *The Handbook of Sport for Development and Peace*, edited by Holly Collison, Simon Darnell, Richard Giulianotti, and David Howe, 436–55. London: Routledge.

Bray, Mark. 2003. "Editorial." *Policy Futures in Education* 1 (2): 201–8.

Burnett, Cora. 2012. *Stories from the Field: GIZ/YDF Footprint in Africa*. Pretoria: GIZ GmbH Youth Development Project.

———. 2014. "A Critical Reflection on Sport-For-Development Discourses: A Review." *South African Journal for Research in Sport, Physical Education and Recreation* 36 (3): 11–24.

———. 2017. "The Olympic Movement as Stakeholder in the UN–IOC Partnership: Configurations in Southern Africa." *Diagoras: International Academic Journal on Olympic Studies* 1 (October): 35–54.

———. 2018a. *National Research: State and Status of Physical Education in Public Schools of South Africa*. Pretoria: UNICEF SA.

———. 2018b. "South Africa: Trends and Scholarship." In *The Handbook of Sport for Development and Peace*, edited by Holly Collison, Simon Darnell, Richard Giulianotti and David Howe, 495–505. London: Routledge.

Cardenas, Alonso. 2016. "Sport and Peace-Building in Divided Societies: A Case Study on Colombia and Northern Ireland." *Peace and Conflict Studies* 23 (2): Article 4 (21pp.).

Chakrabarty, Dipesh. 2012. "From Civilization to Globalization: The 'West' as a Shifting Signifier in Indian Modernity." *Inter-Asia Cultural Studies* 13 (1): 138–52.

Coakley, Jay. 2011. "Youth Sports: What Counts as 'Positive Development'?" *Journal of Sport and Social Issues* 35 (3): 306–24.

Coalter, Fred. 2013a. *Sport for Development: What Game are We Playing?* London: Routledge.

———. 2013b. "'There is Loads of Relationships Here': Developing a Programme Theory for Sport-For-Change Programmes." *International Review for the Sociology of Sport* 48 (5): 594–612.

Colilli, Paul. 2013. "Late Patrology: The example of Giorgio Agamben." *Toronto Journal of Theology* 29 (1): 3–18.

Commonwealth Secretariat. 2015. *Sport for Development and Peace and the 2030 Agenda for Sustainable Development*. London: Commonwealth Secretariat.

———. 2017. *Enhancing the Contribution of Sport to the Sustainable Development Goals*. London: Commonwealth Secretariat.

Cornelissen, Scarlett. 2011. "More than a Sporting Chance? Appraising the Sport for Development Legacy of the 2010 FIFA World Cup." *Third World Quarterly* 32 (3): 503–29.

Cronin, Órla. 2011. *Comic Relief Review. Mapping Research on the Impact of Sport and Development Interventions*. Manchester: Orla Cronin Research.

Darnell, Simon C. 2010. "Power, politics and 'Sport for Development and Peace': Investigating the Utility of Sport for International Development." *Sociology of Sport Journal* 27 (1): 54–75.

———. 2018. "Sport, International Development and Peace." In *The Handbook of Sport for Development and Peace* (1st Edition), edited by Holly Collison, Simon C. Darnell, Richard Giulianotti and P. David Howe, 429–39. London: Routledge.

Darnell, Simon C. and Lyndsay M.C. Hayhurst. 2011. "Sport for Decolonization: Exploring a New Praxis of Sport for Development." *Progress in Development Studies* 11 (3): 183–96.

Darnell, Simon C., Megan Chawansky, David Marchesseault, Matthew Holmes, and Lyndsay M.C. Hayhurst. 2018. "The State of Play: Critical Sociological Insights into Recent 'Sport for Development and Peace' Research." *International Review for the Sociology of Sport* 53 (2): 133–51.

Forde, Shawn D. 2014. "Look after Yourself, or Look after One Another? An Analysis of Life Skills in Sport for Development and Peace HIV Prevention Curriculum." *Sociology of Sport Journal* 31 (3): 287–303.

Giulianotti, Richard. 2011. "Sport, Peacemaking and Conflict Resolution: A Contextual Analysis and Modelling of the Sport, Development and Peace Sector." *Ethnic and Racial Studies* 34 (2): 207–28.

Guest, Andrew M. 2009. "The Diffusion of Development-Through-Sport: Analysing the History and Practice of the Olympic Movement's Grassroots Outreach to Africa." *Sport in Society* 12 (10): 1336–52.

Hartmann, Douglas, and Christina Kwauk 2011. "Sport and Development: An Overview, Critique, and Reconstruction." *Journal of Sport and Social Issues* 35 (3): 284–305.

Haudenhuyse, Reinhard Paul, Marc Theeboom, and Fred Coalter. 2012. "The Potential of Sports-Based Social Interventions for Vulnerable Youth: Implications for Sport Coaches and Youth Workers." *Journal of Youth Studies* 15 (4): 437–54.

Hayhurst, Lyndsay M.C. 2009. "The Power to Shape Policy: Chartering Sport for Development and Peace Policy Discourses." *International Journal of Sport Policy* 1 (2): 203–27.

Hayhurst, Lyndsay M.C., and Audrey R. Giles. 2013. "Private and Moral Authority, Self-Determination, and the Domestic Transfer Objective: Foundations for Understanding Sport for Development and Peace in Aboriginal Communities in Canada." *Sociology of Sport Journal* 30 (4): 504–19.

Kay, Tess. 2012. "Accounting for Legacy: Monitoring and Evaluation in Sport in Development Relationships." *Sport in Society* 15 (6): 888–904.

Kidd, Bruce. 2008. "A New Social Movement: Sport for Development and Peace." *Sport in Society: Cultures, Commerce, Media, Politics* 11 (4): 370–80.

———. "Cautions, Questions and Opportunities in Sport for Development and Peace." *Third World Quarterly* 32 (3): 603–9.

———. "A New Social Movement: Sport for Development and Peace." In *Sport and Foreign Policy in a Globalizing World*, edited by Steve J. Jackson and S. Haigh, 36–46. London: Routledge.

Langer, Laurenz. 2015. "Sport for Development: A Systemic Map of Evidence from Africa." *South Africa Review of Sociology* 46 (1): 66–86.

Lawson, Hal A. 2005. "Empowering People, Facilitating Community Development, and Contributing to Sustainable Development: The Social Work of Sport, Exercise, and Physical Education Programs." *Sport, Education and Society* 10 (1): 135–60.

Levermore, Roger. 2008. "Sport in International Development: Time to Treat it Seriously?" *The Brown Journal of World Affairs* 14 (2): 55–66.

———. 2011. "Evaluating Sport-For-Development: Approaches and Critical Issues." *Progress in Development Studies* 11 (4): 339–53.

Lindsey, Iain, and Alan Grattan. 2012. "An 'International Movement'? Decentring Sport-For-Development within Zambian Communities." *International Journal of Sport Policy and Politics* 4 (1): 91–110.

Naul, Roland, Deanna Binder, Antonin Rychtecky, and Ian Culpan, eds. 2017. *Olympic Education: An International Review*. London: Taylor & Francis.

Nicholls, Sara, Audrey R. Giles, and Christabelle Sethna. 2011. "Perpetuating the 'Lack of Evidence' Discourse in Sport for Development: Privileged Voices, Unheard Stories and Subjugated Knowledge." *International Review for the Sociology of Sport* 46 (3): 249–64.

Njelesani, Donald. 2011. "Preventive HIV/AIDS Education through Physical Education: Reflections from Zambia." *Third World Quarterly* 32 (3): 435-52.

Pithouse, Richard. 2013. "The Open Door of Every Consciousness." *South Atlantic Quarterly* 112 (1): 91–8.

Sanders, Ben, Julie Phillips, and Bart Vanreusel. 2012. "Opportunities and challenges facing NGOs using sport as a vehicle for development in post-apartheid South Africa." *Sport, Education and Society* 19 (6): 789–805.

Schulenkorf, Nico and John Sugden. 2011. "Sport for Development and Peace in Divided Societies: Cooperating for Inter-Community Empowerment in Israel." *European Journal for Sport and Society* 8 (4): 235–56.

Schulenkorf, Nico and Daryl Adair, eds. 2014. *Global Sport-For-Development. Critical Perspectives*. London: Palgrave Macmillan.

Schulenkorf, Nico, John Sugden, and Daniel Burdsey. 2014. "Sport for Development and Peace as Contested Terrain: Place, Community, Ownership." *International Journal of Sport Policy and Politics* 6 (3): 371–87.

Schulenkorf, Nico, Emma Sherry, and Katie Rowe. 2016. "Sport for Development: An Integrated Literature Review." *Journal of Sport Management* 30 (1): 22–39.

Shehu, Jimoh. 2014. "Post-2015 Development Agenda: Value Proposition for Physical Education in Africa: Physical Education." *African Journal for Physical Health Education, Recreation and Dance* 20 (21): 593–605.

Sherry, Emma, Nico Schulenkorf, Emma Seal, Matthew Nicholson, and Russell Hoye. 2017. "Sport-for-Development in the South Pacific Region: Macro-, Meso-, and Micro-Perspectives." *Sociology of Sport Journal* 34 (4): 303-16.

Sugden, John. 2010. "Critical Left-Realism and Sport Interventions in Divided Societies." *International Review for the Sociology of Sport* 45 (3): 258–72.

———. 2014. "The Ripple Effect: Critical Pragmatism, Conflict Resolution and Peace Building through Sport in Deeply Divided Societies." In *Global Sport-for-Development: Critical Perspectives*, edited by Nico Schulenkorf and Daryl Adair, 79–98. London: Palgrave Macmillan.

Svensson, Per G., Meg G. Hancock, and Mary A. Hums. 2016. "Examining the Educative Aims and Practices of Decision-makers in Sport for Development and Peace Organizations." *Sport, Education and Society* 21 (4): 495–512.

The Sport Digest. 2017. "IOC, UN Partnership closes Office on Sport for Development and Peace." Accessed December 11, 2018. http://thesportdigest.com/2017/05/ioc-un-partnership-closes-office-on-sport-for-development-and-peace/.

Tiessen, Rebecca. 2011. "Global Subjects or Objects of Globalisation? The Promotion of Global Citizenship in Organisations Offering Sport for Development and/or Peace Programmes." *Third World Quarterly* 32 (3): 571–87.

United Nations. 1959. "Declaration on the Rights of the Child, 20 November 1959. 1386/XIV." Accessed November 11, 2017. http://www.unhchr.ch/html/menu3/b/25.htm.

United Nations. 1989. "Convention on the Rights of the Child, Adopted by UNGA on 20 November 1989, A/Res/44/25, entered into force on 2 November 1990." Accessed December 1, 2017. http://www.unhchr.ch/html/menu2/6/crc/treaties/crc/hto=m—Convention on the Rights of the Child.

———. 1999. MINEPS (Ministers and Senior Officials Responsible for Physical Education and Sport). 1999. "Declaration of Punta Del Este, from the Third International Conference of Ministers and Senior Officials Responsible for Physical Education and Sport (December 1999)." Accessed December 1, 2017. http://www.unesco.org/education/educprog/eps/EPSanglais,/MINEPS_ANG/declaration_of_punta_del_estea_ang.htm.

———. 2002. "A World Fit for Children, 10 May 2002, A/Res/S27/2." Accessed December 1, 2017. http://www.unicef.org/specialsession/docs_new/documents/A-RES-S27-SE-pdf.

———. 2003. "Sport as a Means to Promote Education, Health, Development and Peace, 17 November 2003, A/Res/58/5, 8 December 2004, A/Res/59/10 and 17 February." Accessed December 1, 2017. http://repository.un.org/handle/11176/245854.

———. 2005. "International Year for Physical Education and Sport. IYSPE." Accessed December 11, 2018. http://ww.un.org/sport2005/.

———. 2018. United Nations General Assembly, Seventy-third Session—14 August 2018. Sport for Development and Peace, Resolution 71/160.

Van der Klashorst, Engela. 2018. "Exploring the Economic, Social and Cultural Rights of Youth Leaders Working in Sport for Development Initiatives at Grassroots Level in South Africa." *Leisure Studies* 37 (1): 109–16.

Vernon, Phil, and Deborrah Baksh. 2010. *Working with the Grain to Change the Grain: Moving Beyond the Millennium Development Goals*. London: Report, *International Alert,* 1–48.

Dark Sides of Sport

www.ingramcontent.com/pod-product-compliance
Lightning Source LLC
Chambersburg PA
CBHW062026290426
44108CB00025B/2793